FINDING A PATH WITH A HEART

BY DR. BEVERLY POTTER

RONIN PUBLISHING
POST OFFICE BOX 1035
BERKELEY, CALIFORNIA 94701

FINDING A PATH WITH A HEART
ISBN: 0-914171-74-7
Copyright ©1995 by Beverly A. Potter, Ph.D.

Published and Distributed by:
RONIN PUBLISHING, INC.
Post Office Box 1035
Berkeley, California 94701

Project Editor:	*Sebastian Orfali*
Manuscript Editors:	*Aidan Kelly, Ginger Ashworth*
Spot Wordsmithing:	*Charles Darren Richardson*
Cover Design:	*Brian Groppe*
Cartoons:	*Phil Frank, Creative Media Services*
Book Design:	*Judy July*
Page Composition:	*Generic Type*

9   8   7   6   5   4   3   2   1

First printing

Printed in the United States of America by Delta Litho

U.S. Library of Congress Cataloging-in-Publication Data

Potter, Beverly A.
    Finding a path with a heart: how to go from burnout to bliss / by Beverly Potter.
       p.   cm.
    Includes bibliographical references and index.
    ISBN 0-914171-74-7
    1. Vocational guidance.   2. Adjustment (Psychology)   3. Career development.   4. Employee motivation.   5. Career changes.
I. Title.
HF5381.P6736   1994   94-29240
158.7--dc20   CIP

ACKNOWLEDGMENTS

Thanks to my many colleagues and friends who encouraged me along, through the many transformations this book went from *Becoming Intrapreneurial* to *Matching Personal Goals with Corporate Mission* to *Pathfinding Tools for Self-Leadership* to, finally, *Finding a Path with a Heart.* A special thanks to Sebastian Orfali, my partner and best friend, who, as midwife, held my hand, brainstormed ideas with me, assisted in my workshops, and pulled this magnum opus out of my imagination. And appreciation is expressed for Publishers Group West, whose developmental feedback and support was invaluable. I especially appreciate my clients and those attending my workshops who so generously shared their pathfinding experiences.

Finally and importantly, thank you, dear reader. You are especially important in this age of information overload. I appreciate your investing time and energy into this book, for without you there would be no book at all. May this work help you to find your way to bliss in the confusing chaos that we all face in the frontier of the new workplace.

TABLE OF CONTENTS

FOREWORD BY MICHAEL TOMS ix

ACCELERATED-LEARNING PRINCIPLES
IN FINDING A PATH WITH A HEART xiii

1 THE PATH FROM BURNOUT TO BLISS 1

2 THE CRAFT OF PATHFINDING 21

3 COMPASS: GETTING YOUR BEARINGS 35

4 HEART: FINDING YOUR PATH 51

5 MISSION: DEFINING YOUR PURPOSE 73

6 VISION: SEEING YOUR DESTINATION 97

7 SURVEY: SCANNING YOUR TERRITORY 123

8 TARGET: SETTING YOUR GOALS 157

9 MAP: CHARTING YOUR COURSE 179

10 YARDSTICK: MEASURING THE DISTANCE
YOU'VE TRAVELED 199

11 TEAM: ELICITING COOPERATION 221

12 HAT: CHANGING YOUR ATTITUDE 249

13 WAND: TRANSFORMING OBSTACLES IN YOUR PATH 269

14 EYE: PILOTING YOUR JOURNEY 307

BIBLIOGRAPHY 341

INDEX 345

BIOGRAPHIES 357

BOOKS & TAPES BY BEVERLY POTTER 361

FOREWORD

BY MICHAEL TOMS

A recent poll suggested that 80 percent of American workers were unhappy in their jobs. Stress and tension pervade the workplace. Many of us find ourselves spending at least one third or more of our life in our cars driving to work only to arrive at a depressing and ugly workplace filled with people who are stressed and angry. A century ago 90 percent of the labor force worked outside in the sunlight inhaling clean and healthy air. Today 90 percent of the labor force is inside surrounded by concrete and steel, breathing unhealthy filtered air. Advances in technology and material progress have come with the promise of increased job happiness and greater "leisure" time but the reality has not matched the vision and the result has been a high cost in overall health, job satisfaction and less "leisure" time.

Many who have looked forward to security and a better future within their company find themselves victims of downsizing. Computers and technology are replacing thousands of jobs and the United States is no longer alone as a major global economic force. The game board is different. The rules have changed and will continue to change. The bad news, however, is really the good news. We are living at a time when the need for individual creativity has never been more important and the opportunities have never been greater.

If you're going to create satisfying work for yourself the first step is to realize that the old rules don't apply any more and you can make your own rules. No longer do you have to be at the effect of external forces. It is possible for you to create your life and your work exactly the way you want it to be. It may not easy. It may involve facing difficult situations, but always constant will be the knowledge that this is your path and you are following your bliss. How will you know this? The result in your life will tell you.

This may be new and unknown territory for you. The famed dolphin researcher, John Lilly, M. D.., once said, "If you want to be an expert, create the territory." So even if it is new, it is yours and no one else in all the universe brings to it what you bring.

In *Finding a Path with a Heart* Dr. Beverly Potter has written a guidebook to help you create your territory; what it takes to locate your path and how to traverse it once you've found it. This is a valuable book. I wish such wisdom had been so readily available a quarter century ago, when I jumped over the edge into the unknown. At the time I left a promising corporate career, because in the late, famed mythologist, Joseph Campbell's terms, I realized that my ladder was against the wrong wall. Through trial and much error, I fortunately found a way to bring my actions together with my ideals and values, and thus New Dimensions Radio was born in 1973. I might have avoided some of the potholes and deep chasms had I had access to Dr. Potter's words of wisdom and practical suggestions.

This is not a panacea "how to" book. However, if you are in a state of readiness, which means you are ready to do whatever it takes, then this book can be an invaluable guide. Dr. Potter has brought together the ideas and insights of many social pioneers at the forefront of fostering creativity and transforming the workplace. She's combined them with her own considerable knowledge and expertise to produce a step-by-step guide for sourcing your own innate effectiveness, recognizing your unique purpose and becoming a creative force in the world.

If you want to follow your bliss and live your life doing what your soul calls you to do, then I strongly recommend that you take the words within these pages to heart. As the Zen Master says, the three secrets of life are pay attention, pay attention, and pay attention.

MICHAEL TOMS

Michael Toms is the co-founder of New Dimensions Radio and host and executive producer of the widely acclaimed "New Dimensions" national public-radio series. His books include the best-selling An Open Life: Joseph Campbell in Conversation with Michael Toms *and* At the Leading Edge. *He also serves as a senior acquisitions editor for Harper San Francisco and is board chairman emeritus of the California Institute of Integral Studies.*

PERMISSIONS

"Two Monks Who Smoked," inspired by Edward Espe Brown, *The Tassajara Recipe Book*, reprinted by permission of Shambhala Publications, Inc., 314 Dartmouth St., Boston, MA. 02116.

"Either Millwright or Poet," from *Leadership is an Art*, by Max DePree, copyright 1989, reprinted by permission from Doubleday/Currency, 666 Fifth Ave., New York City, NY 10103

"Italian Math" from "The Hottest Entrepreneur in America," by Bruce Posner and Bo Burlingham, reprinted with permission, *INC.* magazine, January, 1988. Copyright 1988 by Goldhirsh Group, Inc., 38 Commercial Wharf, Boston, MA 02110.

"Problems and Solutions," from *Metaphors We Live By*, by George Lakoff and Mark Johnson, copyright 1980, reprinted by permission from The University of Chicago Press, 5801 South Ellis Ave., Chicago, IL. 60637.

"A Good Business Has Interesting Problems," from *Growing a Business*, by Paul Hawken, Copyright 1987 by Paul Hawken. Reprinted by permission of Simon & Schuster, Inc., 1230 Avenue of the Americas, New York City, NY 10020.

Photograph of the statue depicting Genentech's founding taken by Frederic Larson, as appeared in October 24, 1992 *San Francisco Chronicle*, reprinted by permission of the *San Francisco Chronicle*, 901 Mission Street, San Francisco, CA 94103.

THE SECRET OF HAPPINESS

A Seeker traveled through the desert for forty days looking for a Shaman Woman because legend had it that she knew the secret of happiness. Finally he came to the Shaman's beautiful palace. Inside he was surprised to see a hive of bustling activity with tradesmen coming and going. Lovely music filled the air. The Shaman, who did not look at all saintly, was preparing a salad at the head of a grand table filled with guests who watched with anticipation while talking excitedly. She beckoned the Seeker to enter and join them for lunch.

The Seeker told the Shaman, who had just measured out a spoonful of oil, that he wished to learn the secret of happiness. "Ah," the Shaman nodded, as she handed him the spoon with the oil. "Carry this spoon and explore my palace without spilling the oil. Return in two hours and I will tell you the secret of happiness."

The Seeker climbed and descended stairways in the palace, always keeping his eyes fixed on the spoon. After two hours, he returned to the main hall as the Shaman had instructed. "Well," asked the Shaman, "what marvels did you see?"

Embarrassed, the Seeker confessed that he had observed nothing because his only concern had been not to spill the oil. "Well then, go look again," the Shaman insisted.

The Seeker took the spoon and returned to exploring the palace, this time looking closely at the works of art on the ceilings and the walls. He saw gardens filled with sweet smelling flowers and herbs, sampled delicious food, and enjoyed heavenly music. When he returned and described the beauty of what he had seen, the Shaman asked, "But where are the drops of oil?"

Again embarrassed, he admitted that he had forgotten and spilled the oil. The Shaman laughed. "You will discover the secret of happiness when you can enjoy all the marvels of the world, while always remembering the drops of oil in the spoon."

Inspired by Paulo Coelho
The Alchemist
A Fable About Following Your Dreams

ACCELERATED-LEARNING PRINCIPLES IN FINDING A PATH WITH A HEART

*I*n the following pages you'll discover twelve tools for finding a path with a heart. Thinking in terms of *tools* is useful because, like the tools used to craft pots or weave cloth or make leather goods, they are used to act on things in order to create certain effects. Each tool has a chapter devoted to it. But presenting the tools one-by-one is artificial and sometimes frustrating because they are rarely used in isolation. Imagine a book that told you how to drive a stick shift car by devoting one chapter to the gear shift, one to the clutch, and one to the gas pedal. Ultimately to drive, you must use the tools together in a balance that is difficult to describe, and mastery of them requires a "feel." Similarly, pathfinding tools are used together in ways that are subtle and difficult to describe within the linear confines of the printed page.

ACCELERATED LEARNING

To help break through this limitation, accelerated-learning techniques taught by Dr. Charles Schmid at The LIND (Learning in New Dimensions) Institute in San Francisco are used. One accelerated-learning principle is that we don't think in words only. We think with images and sensory impressions, as well as concepts and words. Hence the first thing you'll discover about the pathfinding tools is that each is represented by a stylized picture or icon. (Some people think the use of icons is a gimmick. If the icons make you uncomfortable or seem silly to you, ignore them.) Eventually each icon takes on many associations with a particular tool. Seeing the picture, triggers associations about the tool. It has been said a picture is worth a thousand words; so, instead of repeating many words to remind you of the particular qualities of a tool, we use the icon.

We think with images and sensory impressions, as well as concepts and words.

LEARNING THROUGH ASSOCIATIONS

Another principle is that we think in associations and not linear progressions. An idea triggers another idea. How and why is not always clear. According to accelerated-learning principles, the more that new information is tied to associations, the faster we absorb it and the more we retain. This principle is incorporated into *Finding a Path with a Heart.* The text is highlighted with icons and phrases in "windows," with the latter representing useful tangents or associations intended to shed light on a point being made in the primary text. The appearance of an icon for one of the other tools marks a place where two pathfinding processes overlap or interact with each other. Let us again use the analogy of learning to drive a car with standard transmission: an icon in the text would indicate the use of two skills, such as pushing in the clutch while letting up on the gas. When an icon appears in the text, you might want to turn to the chapter on the tool that the icon represents to take a closer look at that tool, for example. On other occasions the windows summarize the essence of the point made in the main text.

An icon is worth a thousand words.

You'll also see quotes from other people's work interspersed through the text. Like the icons and windows, these quotes highlight or amplify aspects of the subject under discussion in the text, or suggest useful tangents. If you find the quote intriguing, you might take a look at that book. Pathfinding has been shaped by other people's work and the quotes are used to cite sources or influences, something like footnotes.

HOLISTIC PRESENTATION

Another insight from accelerated-learning is that we don't learn in cut-and-dried sequential steps, the way information is presented in school and books. Take learning a language, for example. A child comes into the world of people who talk in full sentences with compli- cated structures and sophisticated vocabulary. Language is not parceled out to the baby in small logical sequences—first verbs, now

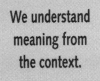

Our learning in the real world is different from the way we were taught in school.

nouns, now adjectives, etc. Words are not usually defined before being used, instead they whiz by at rapid pace. The child is immersed and becomes accustomed to the language. As it becomes familiar, the child develops a predisposition to learn that language and begins to assimilate it.

In *Finding a Path with a Heart* everything is not always defined the first time it is mentioned. A tool may be referred to without first being defined, letting the context act as a frame of reference in- stead. Sometimes the definition is implied in the

We understand meaning from the context.

text. Later, when you get to the chapter dedicated to that tool, it will be familiar and you will already know a lot about it. The material in the chapter will be easier to learn because you'll already have associative hooks, some of them provided by the windows and icons. Return to the image of a child learning a language: the child can communicate effectively with- out mastering syntax and vocabulary. In *Finding a Path with a Heart* you don't have to fully understand a tool in order to use it or to move to another tool. Instead, the meaning of the tool comes

together in a synergistic way. If you're confused, turn to the chapter that focuses on the tool.

NONLINEAR LEARNING

Finding a Path with a Heart is not meant to be read from beginning to end. You can read it that way, but you don't have to. You might turn

> **You don't have to read this book from the beginning. You can start at the end or in the middle.**

right away to the tool you want to know about the most. If there's a reference to another tool, understand it as best you can and go on, or turn to the chapter that focuses on that tool. Skim through it or read until your question is answered, then return to the original tool. Another approach is to begin by reading the windows and stories. When something catches your interest, delve deeper by reading the text. When your curiosity is satisfied return to reading the quotes. Alternatively you might read the Index first.

Repetition is another learning principle that you'll find. It goes hand in hand with the nonlinear presentation. You'll discover that certain concepts are discussed more than once. This is necessary since you may not be reading from beginning to end. So, in some cases, where certain foundation material is necessary to understand a particular concept, that material may be presented a second time as a prelude to introducing the concept. If this bothers you, simply skip those repetitive paragraphs or pages and jump right into the new concept.

ENGAGING YOUR SENSES

Another principle of accelerated-learning is that the more senses we engage, the faster we learn and the more we remember. For example,

> **Learning is fastest when all our senses are engaged.**

in the traditional approach to teaching Italian, the instructor has the students repeat the names of various fruits in Italian over and over. With accelerated-learning the students hold oranges, sniff, and taste them while saying "orange" in Italian. It's much the way the child learns. The mother says, "Orange!" as the child sucks on a section of the orange. This sensory approach connects the image, smell, taste, and concept of orange to the word for orange, making remembering easier and learning more fun.

In *Finding a Path with a Heart* many different modalities are used to convey ideas: sometimes ordinary prose, sometimes stories, sometimes dialogs. Frequently you will be encouraged to picture things in your imagination, a practice that I call going to your "Mental Theater." When you imagine performing in the Mental Theater, engage as many senses—vision, smell, sound, touch, taste—as you can into your performance. When you connect sensory images to the behavior being rehearsed, you learn faster and remember more while having fun.

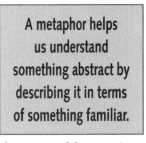

METAPHORS AND STORIES

Using metaphors to convey ideas is another accelerated-learning technique. Metaphors provide a way of tying complicated, abstract concepts to something familiar and known. In *The Way of the Ronin: Riding the Waves of Change at Work,* for example, the Japanese word ronin, or unindentured samurai, is used as a metaphor for a person struggling heroically with self direction within a rigid, mindless system that seeks to squelch one's spirit. We've all had experience with repressive bureaucracies that

> A metaphor helps us understand something abstract by describing it in terms of something familiar.

thwart your every move. So we can image ourselves as noble warriors fighting the righteous fight against the organization's mindless stupidity.

Pathfinding is a metaphor for personal leadership—finding your personal path. Pathfinding is something of an American heritage and beckons to us. Our forefathers forged paths into the frontier, the Wild West. We're now pioneers in outer space and "cyberspace". It is difficult to talk about leading without using pathfinding metaphors: find a direction, blaze a path, chart a course, push forward.

We all know a lot about the idea of pathfinding, partly from the stories in history books and movies, partly from our own personal experiences. You are encouraged to add from your experience to the pathfinding tools. Play with the tools. Use them when they work for you, expand upon them when you know more, ignore them when they don't fit your experience.

Finding a Path with a Heart is about how to find a direction, how to get where you want to go, and how to enjoy optimal experience in your work and leisure. The path you seek to find may be making a career choice, planning how to proceed with a project at work, establishing direction in a hobby or putting together a volunteer activity.

The pathfinding tools are presented primarily within the context of a job where you carry out complex projects that take many steps with little or no supervision. If you work for yourself or if the path you seek is in an avocational, volunteer or community arena, you'll find that the tools work equally well with these activities.

CHAPTER 1

THE PATH FROM BURNOUT TO BLISS

If you follow your bliss, you put yourself on a kind of track
that has been there all the while, waiting for you,
and the life that you ought to be living is the one you are living.
Wherever you are—if you are following your bliss,
you are enjoying that refreshment,
that life within you, all the time.

Joseph Campbell
The Power of Myth

*C*hances are you are not satisfied with one or more aspects of your life.
Perhaps you're relatively content overall, but feel like you're in a holding
pattern that is taking a toll on your creativity and enthusiasm. Perhaps
you feel unfulfilled in your present job and dream of making career
changes. Maybe you feel trapped in a counterproductive relationship
and are looking for a way out. Maybe you feel
drained of energy, or perhaps, you're just com-
placent about life generally. In any case, burnout is something you can relate to, whether or

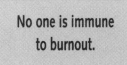

not you're actually suffering from it right now. The idea of overcoming
your present difficulties and finding a path with a heart to bring more
bliss into your life is something you deem worthy of pursuit.

   You are not alone. Like a disease spreading rampantly through an
unsuspecting population, burnout is a very real threat in today's fast-

paced, high-tech world. Burnout can infect anyone, from minimum-wage fry cooks to six-figure executives. No one is immune. Until you get your bearings and realize that you can halt and eventually reverse the circumstances zapping your creativity and destroying your zest for life, the burnout experience can be a very rough ride indeed.

In popular jargon, burnout has been defined as everything from a bottomed-out drug user to a temporary feeling of discouragement and weariness. But for you to break free of the burnout pattern and begin to live in a more blissful fashion, you need to think of burnout not primarily as a state of being, but as a cumulative process that get worse the longer you allow it to go unchallenged through your life. You may experience a very hectic ten-hour day at the office, for example, and tell your friends that you feel "burned out." Yet after a good night's sleep and a nourishing breakfast, you're ready to tackle another day at work. This sort of burnout can be an isolated incident or part of a pattern. If you find yourself experiencing some degree of malaise on a regular basis, it may be time to re-examine your life and initiate a new direction. It is important to remember this is not a perfect world, because every job or career, no

matter how much you may enjoy it, will have its ups and downs. But when you actively set out to find a path with a heart, the ups and downs are experienced in the context of moving in a new direction that will lead to more satisfying work and peak performance.

The sort of chronic burnout that all too often tragically undermines ambition, energy and performance can be avoided. If it is already consuming at your spirit, it can be combated and defeated, allowing you to become a stronger person in the process. The ultimate triumph is moving toward a positive, not just eliminating a negative. Once you understand that seeking a path with a heart is essential to moving beyond a burnout situation, you take a major step toward finding the path that is right for you—and toward finding your bliss.

WHAT IS BURNOUT?

In his great wartime novel *A Farewell to Arms*, Ernest Hemingway wrote that the world breaks everyone and afterward many are strong in the broken places. If you are suffering from burnout, you may feel that the world is against you, the deck stacked, the odds too long for any chance of success. Not only is burnout a painful process in which motivation progressively diminishes, it also tends to affect your worldview and cause you to see things as hopeless when in fact there is much room for hope. Burnout is a loss of enthusiasm, a surrendering of ambition, a sense of resignation that consumes the spirit 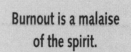 and can even lead to physical ailments. Burnout is a stressful process accompanied by declining performance, people problems, feelings of meaninglessness, negative emotions, frequent illness, and a propensity to engage in substance abuse. A person who is suffering from extreme burnout cannot function at all. Burnout is most apparent in people who were once enthusiastic go-getters, before something happened and they developed a "why bother" attitude.

Burnout is caused by feelings of powerlessness. When people (or animals, for that matter), are put into situations where they perceive little opportunity to control what happens to them, their motivation to try diminishes. If there is nothing you can do, then why bother trying? The worst thing about burnout is that when conditions change for the better, the burnout victim has difficulty bouncing back; so burnout tends to become a self-perpetuating process that feeds on negativity—a trap. It becomes a trap

Burnout is a malaise of the spirit.

Powerlessness destroys motivation and kills the spirit.

because burnout feels bad and is demoralizing. Situations that consistently
put us into such states make us
feel powerless, so we resign
ourselves to expecting the
worst possible scenarios:
"It's bad. It will always be
bad, and there's nothing I can
do to change it."

PERSONAL POWER

Developing personal power, which is a feeling of potency and an I-Can-Do attitude, is the key to beating burnout. A feeling of control is the critical factor in beating burnout, not how much you like or dislike the situation. When you feel that there is something you can do, a negative

> Personal power is a feeling of potency.

situation becomes manageable. Think of a time when you faced an unfavorable work environ-ment. Maybe your boss is one of those people who never expresses gratitude for your work, or who criticizes you after he or she says something nice. Once you realize that you need not take such behavior personally, your options expand. If the behavior continues to bother you, you may want to approach the person in charge and share your feelings. Or, depending on the em-ployee-employer relationship, you may choose to pointedly ignore the unwarranted criticisms, so that the boss can't help but notice that you're not reacting as you once did. And if things are so bad that you feel oppressed in a particular work environment, it may be time to look for work elsewhere.

You can also develop personal power away from the workplace. A person faced with a neglectful roommate who doesn't clean up, for example, may feel trapped because he or she signed a fixed-term lease. Yet by carefully sorting through one's options, people in such situations can empower themselves and decide on the proper course of action so that a bad situation becomes a challenging situation. When you meet a challenge with ability rather than helplessness, your feelings of personal power increase. Success builds confidence, and confidence lays the groundwork for more success.

Conversely, a pleasant situation can be destructive when you have little feeling of control. The poor little rich boy who has everything but who can do nothing on his own is an example. In this syndrome, the parent takes care of everything. If the boy breaks a window throwing a ball, Daddy takes care of it. If the boy gets so-so grades, a donation from Daddy gets him into the best school anyway. The poor little rich boy can become helpless in a plush situation, and personal power is as elusive to him as it is to a downtrodden employee whose spirit has been broken by years of powerlessness.

PATHS TO PERSONAL POWER

Regardless of your station in life, personal power is attainable. In *Beating Job Burnout* I describe nine paths to personal power. Following each path to personal power improves your capabilities. As a result, your sense of control and feeling that you can handle difficult situations increase. Rather than feeling overwhelmed, people with personal power feel that their actions make a difference. The situation may be unpleasant, but there's a sense that "I can do something."

> **There are nine paths to personal power and beating job burnout.**

For example, when following the first path, self-management, you gain mastery over yourself. Your personal power grows because you can get motivated and stay motivated even in situations with few incentives. When you can manage your stress, the second path, you can function at your best when conditions are less than desirable. Building a strong social support system is the third path. Social support buffers us from stress, and cooperative relationships help us get things done. The next path, skill-building, is vital because when you know how to acquire the skills you need to perform well you feel more confident. When you tailor the job to fit you, the fifth path, you feel equipped and eager to give 100 percent. Changing jobs is a path for those who don't have the opportunity to tailor their jobs. Managing your thinking, the seventh path, is crucial because it prevents you from overreacting to a bad situation.

Detached concern is a path that enables you to adequately deal with a situation without feeling it is all that matters in your life. The ninth path is pathfinding itself. When you know how to find the right path for you—the path with a heart—you can venture forth into uncharted territories without getting lost or losing sight of your objectives. *Finding a Path with a Heart* focuses on the art and craft of pathfinding, on leading yourself into the unknown, on blazing trails to your bliss.

THE BURNOUT TRAP

Escape burnout—try heart work.
Dennis Jaffe & Cynthia Scott
Take This Job and Love It

If everything in the world always stayed the same, Earth would be a very boring, predictable place. The unexpected surprises of life, both pleasant and unpleasant, would not be possible. Human beings would plod through their days like zombies, no better than robots programmed never to deviate from one prearranged course of action. But the world is not static, and the ever-changing circumstances of our lives present us with an ironic paradox that can be summed up in the old adage "sink or swim." The same dynamics that keep life on Earth from stagnating into dull routines also present us with an ongoing challenge: swim like champions in the liberating waters of change, or drown like shackled victims wearing self-imposed chains as the water level inches ever higher.

There is no avoiding change. You can try to insulate yourself from the outside world, choosing to deal only with situations you welcome, but as everyone knows, the many roads of life can take unexpected turns. So to successfully navigate your path from burnout to bliss, it is imperative to accept that there will always be changes along the way.

Change can be exciting and stretch your abilities, but it can also be intimidating. You are not alone if you view change with some apprehension. There is always some degree of fear associated with change, because we fear the unknown. With change comes doubt. Maybe you won't be able to handle what comes up. Maybe you're making the wrong decision. Change inevitably triggers feelings of fear, uncertainty, and doubt.

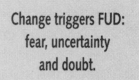

Change triggers FUD: fear, uncertainty and doubt.

Most people tend to resist change because it means letting go of what's known. Even negative situations have a certain comfort when they are predictable. When things are predictable, you know what to expect, and so you can plan. There's a sense of being in control. The situation may be suboptimal or boring, but it's safe because it is known. Attempting to avoid the inevitable consequences that accompany change, some people try to avoid change itself and become trapped. Nellie, for example, had worked part-time at a major supermarket since she was sixteen. When her high-school class graduated and many of her close friends went away to college, she stayed behind, because the store manager promised her a full-time clerking position. But by the time she was in her early twenties, Nellie dreaded going to work at the grocery store and dreamed of going to college to study biochemistry. Still, she felt she couldn't act on her dream, because she had to earn a paycheck in order to meet various responsibilities, and she had no idea how she would earn enough money from a part-time job to meet those needs while attending college. Nellie felt both dissatisfied and stuck with her station in life. This feeling of being stuck can generate more feelings of powerlessness to create a vicious cycle—the burnout trap.

Nellie didn't succumb to her fears and remain trapped. She fashioned her dream into a Vision—a picture of what she wanted to achieve. It enabled her to move beyond the narrow confines of the burnout situation that had left her so exasperated. Nellie made a conscious choice to find a new path—a path with a heart. In so doing, she entered the unknown and became a pioneer on the frontier of change, growing stronger in places where she once felt broken.

Søren Kierkegaard, the 19th-century Danish theologian and philosopher, once made an observation as relevant at the beginning of the 21st century as it was in the 1800s. He noted that people celebrate achievements and call the achievers heroic, but the truly heroic act does not lie in the outcome. Kierkegaard believed that heroism lay in beginnings, in starting out with no guarantee of end results. If we could know

Heroism lies in making a beginning.

that our efforts would lead to success, then the faint of heart would readily transform themselves into robust adventurers and heroes. But success, like recognition, is never assured. The timid recoil from dreams and ambitions. They work on developing excuses instead of skills necessary to excel, and, perhaps most unfortunate of all, their negativism often becomes infectious.

With faith in her abilities and confidence that her hard work would not go unrewarded, Nellie set out to achieve her dream rather than ignore it. Her example is no small matter. Nellie's decision to pursue a path with a heart made a life-changing difference for the better. The commitment to action, although results can never be known beforehand, can make a similar difference for millions of people struggling with burnout.

LEAP INTO THE DANCE OF EXPERIENCE

All a person can do in this life is to gather about him his integrity, his imagination, and his individuality—and with these ever with him, out in front, leap into the dance of experience.

Be your own master!

Be your own Jesus!

Be your own flying saucer! Rescue yourself!

Be your own valentine! Free the Heart!

Tom Robbins
Even Cowgirls Get The Blues

You'll never find bliss if you remain fearful and don't make that leap into the unknown. You can not know the outcome at the moment you leap. Leaping anyway is what makes you a hero—or heroine. But what is the alternative—to continue along a path that thus far has not had a heart? As Robbins says, you must gather around you faith in yourself and the confidence to know that you will find your way if you follow your bliss—because bliss is your beacon. Follow it, and you will find a path with a heart and have a joyful journey.

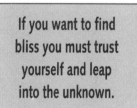

If you want to find bliss you must trust yourself and leap into the unknown.

The founding fathers of the United States recognized the importance of pursuing a path with a heart when they said, "We find these truths to be self-evident: that man is endowed by the Creator with certain inalienable rights, among these are life, liberty, and the *pursuit of happiness*." Thomas Jefferson and the others didn't say that you have a right to be guaranteed achieving happiness, but the right to pursue a path with a heart for you, to seek your bliss. But before you can begin your pursuit, you must know what bliss is.

WHAT IS BLISS?

*There is no separation between action and awareness, thinking and
doing. You are in total harmony with yourself and your surroundings
and all else—time, space, past and future —
pales before the present moment.*
Tim Gallwey and Bob Kriegel
Inner Skiing

Bliss is the enjoyable feeling of well-being experienced when you're
fully involved with what you are doing. There is a sensation of being in
harmony with your surroundings. Loss of self, where you feel "one" with
the activity and the moment, is among its most notable characteristics.
There is no sense of separation between you and what you're doing.

Bliss can be likened to what psychologists call the "flow state." Many
people experience flow while playing sports or dancing. When you are
playing your best tennis, the racket may seem to become an extension of
your arm. Without having to think about it, you

Go with your flow!

connect easily with the ball when you swing,
serving aces and placing the ball exactly where
you want it to go. When dancing, for example, you may feel "one" with
the beat of the music. You're in harmony. Your movements are graceful
and flow without self-consciousness.

The flow state isn't restricted to just sports or other recreational activities. In fact, it is most often experienced at work. As you become absorbed in what you are doing, concentrating is easy and things seem to come together effortlessly. Creative juices flow. Time flies. You're confident you will succeed. Stamina increases. You feel energetic, maybe even joyful. You experience a sense of well-being. Optimal performance comes almost effortlessly. Flow feels good. Being in the flow state is bliss.

> **FOLLOW YOUR BLISS**
> Nearly everyone knows what it is to follow one's bliss. It is, for example, the state of being that we experience when we are totally immersed in our work or in a favorite recreational activity. Often we experience it when we're deeply attracted to another person, or even when we're anticipating the purchase of a wonderful object such as a new car or something for our home. It may also be experienced when we follow a "hunch" about contacting a friend, who, it turns out, was only that moment wanting to talk with us. Maybe we experience it when we honor a "gut feeling" we had about a business associate, who later turned out to be untrustworthy. Or maybe we have seen its expression in our "instinct" for choosing exactly the right gift for a loved one.
>
> **Hal Zina Bennett and Susan J. Sparrow**
> *Follow Your Bliss*

WHAT IS YOUR BLISS POTENTIAL?

We all know that some people seem to be happier than others, independent of their wealth or race or level of education. For some people happiness seems to come naturally, even when the situation is problematic, whereas there are others who seems to have it all but are miserable nonetheless. The Bliss Potential Inventory will help you estimate your current capacity for experiencing bliss.

Flow is most often experienced at work.

THE BLISS POTENTIAL INVENTORY

INSTRUCTIONS: Read over each of the following items and, using a scale from 1 to 9, rate how characteristic it is of how you approach activities in your daily life—both at work and away from work. When you're done add up your score.

RATING SCALE: 1 = Rarely   3 = Occasionally   5 = About half the time
7 = Frequently   9 = Almost always

GETTING CENTERED

_____ 1. I check my feelings.
_____ 2. I clarify what is important to me.
_____ 3. I get in touch with my personal power.

DEFINING PURPOSE

_____ 4. I look for problems to solve.
_____ 5. I articulate a mission.
_____ 6. I appoint myself to act.

DETERMINING DIRECTION

_____ 7. I gather information.
_____ 8. I brainstorm what is possible.
_____ 9. I create a mental picture of my mission accomplished.

SETTING GOALS

_____ 10. I match challenges to my ability.
_____ 11. I align my personal goals with my work.
_____ 12. I set specific targets.

ESTABLISHING MILESTONES

_____ 13. I map out action steps.
_____ 14. I establish standards of achievement.
_____ 15. I evaluate progress quantitatively.

FLEXIBLE THINKING

_____ 16. I look at things from several viewpoints.
_____ 17. I adapt my approach to the situation.
_____ 18. I accept ambiguity.

COURSE CORRECTING

_____ 19. I survey my resources.
_____ 20. I make contingency plans.
_____ 21. I learn from my mistakes.

BY-PASSING OBSTACLES
_____ 22. I view problems as opportunities.
_____ 23. I question assumptions.
_____ 24. I do something different.

GETTING COOPERATION
_____ 25. I create a network of allies.
_____ 26. I build team spirit.
_____ 27. I set up win-win scenarios.

MOTIVATING MYSELF
_____ 28. I engage my values.
_____ 29. I seek excellence, not perfection.
_____ 30. I reward my progress.

ENJOYING THE MOMENT
_____ 31. I accentuate the positive.
_____ 32. I find pleasure in small things.
_____ 33. I get absorbed in my activities.

PILOTING
_____ 34. I find meaning in what I do.
_____ 35. I focus my attention.
_____ 36. I go with my flow.

SCORING: YOUR POTENTIAL FOR BLISS

36–64 **Very Low:** Your potential for experiencing bliss is unusually low. You don't have to settle for a life of quiet desperation. Take immediate corrective action to bring more happiness into your life.

65–130 **Low:** Your potential for experiencing bliss is low. You can have more moments of bliss by changing the way you approach your daily activities.

131–228 **Moderate:** You have potential for many moments of bliss, and if you work at it, you can increase your potential to experience bliss even more often.

229–294 **High:** You have a high potential for experiencing bliss often. You are well on your way to finding a path with a heart.

295–324 **Very High:** Your potential for having frequent blissful moments is exceptional. You are on a path with a heart, a path to your bliss.

Whatever your score on the Bliss Potential Inventory is today it is not fixed. You can change it. Your capacity for happiness and potential for bliss is not genetic and set at birth. Nor is it a chance event. Instead it is something that you can make happen—if you know how. Recent research into the psychology of optimal experience has revealed that when certain conditions exist we are more likely to experience bliss.

CONDITIONS THAT PROMOTE BLISS

Happiness is full use of your powers along the lines of excellence.
President John F. Kennedy

Certain conditions facilitate bliss—flow—and others block it. When we know the conditions and factors that help us move toward bliss, we can increase them to promote more bliss in our lives. As you read on, you'll learn about specific conditions that, when actively cultivated, encourage bliss. In subsequent

> **You can increase your potential for bliss.**

chapters, you'll discover tools for creating these bliss-promoting situations, tools for finding your path to bliss.

Challenge: The Flow Channel

University of Chicago psychologist Mihaly Csikszentmihalyi discovered that certain conditions maximize the possibility of entering into the flow state. Over a 25-year period he and his colleagues interviewed thousands of individuals from around the world, from all walks of life, about their experiences. As part of the study some of these people wore electronic pagers which signaled randomly during the day. When hearing the signal they stopped what they were doing and answered written questions about their experience at that moment. What Csikszentmihalyi found was that the flow experience was described in the same way by men and women, by young people and old, regardless of cultural, economic or educational differences.

> Enjoyment appears at the boundary between boredom and anxiety, when the challenges are just balanced with the person's capacity to act. . . . When all a person's relevant skills are needed to cope with the challenges of a situation, that person's attention is completely absorbed by the activity. . . . One of the most universal and distinctive feature of optimal experience takes place: people become so involved in what they are doing that the activity becomes spontaneous, almost automatic; they stop being aware of themselves as separate from the actions they are performing.
>
> Mihaly Csikszentmihalyi
> *Flow: The Psychology of Optimal Experience*

Csikszentmihalyi's research uncovered an important finding for pathfinders. You are most likely to experience flow when the difficulties of your activities match your ability level. This relationship between difficulty and ability is illustrated on the graph. The vertical axis represents "difficulty," from low to high and the horizontal axis represents "ability," from low to high.

From the graph you can see that when your ability and the difficulty of the situation are both low but in balance, flow potential exists. The same is true when both difficulty and your ability are moderate or when both are high. In other words,

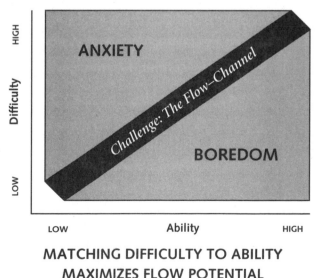

**MATCHING DIFFICULTY TO ABILITY
MAXIMIZES FLOW POTENTIAL**

when there is a balance between the difficulty of the situation confronting you and your ability to deal with it, there is a potential for experiencing flow. We usually think of such situations as "challenging." Challenge is the flow channel, and being in the flow channel is usually a prerequisite for experiencing bliss.

There isn't always a balance between situation difficulty and your

ability, however. Sometimes your ability will exceed the difficulty of the situation. When this happens there's no challenge and you'll probably become bored and restless. Boredom tends to be unpleasant and pushes us toward burnout. When we become trapped in a boring situation, the unpleasant becomes painful, and burnout becomes a real possibility.

Challenge is the flow channel.

At other times, when the difficulty of the situation exceeds your ability—when you're in over your head—you probably experience anxiety. If the stakes are high, your anxiety will probably turn to fear. If the difficulty is very high, fear may give way to panic. Once again experiencing burnout is a possibility, especially when the situation involves job security or something equally important. In situations like this, it is important to consult your Compass, a pathfinding tool that will be explained in detail in Chapter Three. The Compass helps you get your bearings, so that you can make an informed, intelligent decision on how to proceed.

Meaning: Having a Good Heart

Feelings of meaningfulness promote flow, even when the situation is unpleasant. When we're engaged in activities that call upon our values,

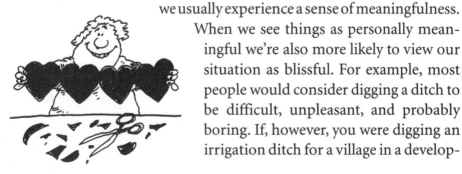

we usually experience a sense of meaningfulness. When we see things as personally meaningful we're also more likely to view our situation as blissful. For example, most people would consider digging a ditch to be difficult, unpleasant, and probably boring. If, however, you were digging an irrigation ditch for a village in a developing country, you might find the experience to be meaningful, especially if helping others is something you value. In this situation it might well happen that you would slip into flow while digging and actually experience a blissful state.

Heart work promotes flow.

This example also makes it obvious that it's not the activity by itself that determines its meaningfulness, but your personal interpretation of the importance of the activity. Clarifying the importance of our activities is the function of the Heart, a pathfinding tool that will be discussed in Chapter Four.

Personal Power: Feelings of Potency

Personal power is the ability to influence what happens and the confidence that comes from feelings of potency. A sense of control promotes flow whereas the fear, uncertainty and doubt that accompany feelings of helplessness make experiencing flow nearly impossible. Personal power is not endowed upon you. It is an ambiance, a sense of confidence, an I-Can-Do attitude that you must create

Transform problems into challenges.

for yourself. When you use the Wand tool to reframe a negative situation as a "challenge," you gain a sense of control and increase personal power. This holds true even in the most dire situations. For example, hostages who regard handling their captors as a challenge suffer less psychological damage than those who give in to feelings of helplessness.

FROM BURNOUT TO BLISS

Going from burnout to bliss requires an understanding of each, as well as your own motives for wanting to leave burnout behind. It should be clear by now that burnout can be experienced in degrees, from having a bad day at the office to feeling so lethargic that you don't even want to get out of bed. Bliss, too, can be experienced in varying degrees. In the chapters to come, we will discuss specific tools that can help you enhance your blissful feelings, tools for finding the path from burnout to your bliss.

ONE PERSON'S BLISS IS ANOTHER'S BURNOUT

I used to know an old man in one of the decrepit suburbs of Naples who made a precarious living out of a ramshackle antique store his family had owned for generations. One morning a prosperous-looking American lady walked into the store, and after looking around for a while, asked the price of a pair of baroque wooden putti, those chubby little cherubs so dear to Neapolitan craftsmen of a few centuries ago, and to their contemporary imitators. Signor Orsini, the owner, quoted an exorbitant price. The woman took out her folder of traveler's checks, ready to pay for the dubious artifacts. I held my breath, glad for the unexpected windfall about to reach my friend. But I didn't know Signor Orsini well enough. He turned purple and with barely contained agitation escorted the customer out of the store: "No, no, signora, I am sorry but I cannot sell you those angels." To the flabbergasted woman he kept repeating, "I cannot make business with you. You understand?" After the tourist finally left, he calmed down and explained: "If I were starving, I would have taken her money. But since I am not, why should I make a deal that isn't any fun? I enjoy the clash of wits involved in bargaining, when two persons try to outdo each other with ruses and with eloquence. She didn't even flinch. She didn't know any better. She didn't pay me the respect of assuming that I was going to try to take advantage of her. If I sold those pieces to that woman at that ridiculous price, I would have felt cheated." Few people in southern Italy, or elsewhere, have this strange attitude toward business transactions. But then I suspect that they don't enjoy their work as much as Signor Orsini did, either. . . . To gain personal control over the quality of experience . . . one needs to learn how to build enjoyment into what happens day in, day out.

Mihaly Csikszentmihalyi
Flow: The Psychology of Optimal Experience

One person's bliss can be another's burnout. Getting easy money may be a "high" for many people, but it was a burnout situation for the

Italian antique seller. He knew what brought him bliss and was willing to forgo a quick buck for it. The specifics of bliss are unique to each person, therefore finding the path to bliss will also be unique for each person. There are general qualities associated with bliss, regardless of your profession, gender, race, age or hobbies. But the mathematician's experience of bliss is quite likely to be different from the house painter's. That's the way it should be. Although humans share a multitude of common qualities, no two people—not even identical twins—are exactly alike.

Still, whether you're an entrepreneur or a factory worker, life is not always going to be lived in situations normally associated with bliss. Yet there are concrete actions you can take, beginning today, to build bliss into what happens in your daily life. First, you must know what is blissful for you. Rather than falling prey to burnout when situations are difficult, you can find opportunities to rise above the negatives and meet the challenges at hand. A challenge allows you to test your ability against a difficulty. By its very nature you expect it to be difficult. Small signs of progress are meaningful because they signal improvement. Success, even when it's small in the face of difficulty, builds confidence and I-Can-Do feelings. And after succeeding in tossing off the cumbersome constraints of burnout, you will feel stronger than ever in places that once seemed irrevocably broken.

PATHFINDING IS LEADING YOURSELF

In *Beating Job Burnout,* the major issue was self-motivation—how to get moving, stay moving, and develop personal power to keep motivation high. In *Finding a Path with a Heart,*

> Beating burnout is a self-management challenge; finding a path to your bliss is a self-leadership challenge.

the focus is on how to use that motivation to propel you toward where you want to go. We will focus on blazing your own trail in an ever-changing wilderness that we view as a challenging adventure instead of an obstacle and trap. We will focus on twelve specific pathfinding or self-leadership tools that help you recognize whether or not your path has a heart. And, like any intelligent explorer venturing forth into new territory, we must bring along that most basic of all navigating tools, the Compass.

CHAPTER 2

THE CRAFT OF PATHFINDING

Happiness is not something that happens.
It is not the result of good fortune or random chance.
It is not something that money can buy or power command.
It does not depend on outside events, but, rather,
on how we interpret them.
Happiness, in fact, is a condition that must be prepared for,
cultivated, and defended privately by each person.
Mihaly Csikszentmihalyi
Flow: The Psychology of Optimal Experience

$\mathcal{E}$ach person is a unique individual. The path to your personal fulfillment is also unique. You cannot depend on another person to lead you to your bliss. To find your path with a heart you must lead yourself.

Bliss is what you experience when you are fully absorbed in an activity. What occurs is something psychologists call "the flow state," a consciousness in which you forget yourself and feel at one with what you're doing. This is when creative juices flow. You feel energized and perform at your peak. Psychologist Mihaly Csikszentmihalyi's

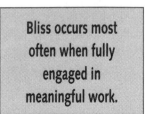

Bliss occurs most often when fully engaged in meaningful work.

research of more than 20 years indicates that these moments of bliss occur more often at work than during leisure times. This should be no surprise, really, because you know that you feel good when you're involved in work and things are going well. That stimulating experience of being "plugged in" and producing is your bliss.

But not all work is good. In fact, some work is downright awful. You've probably had experience with work that squelched your spirit, robbed you of your enthusiasm and left you feeling drained at the end of the day. This kind of demoralizing work engenders an experience that is opposite of bliss—job burnout. You've probably experienced burnout at least to some degree. Most people have. It usually occurs when you feel trapped and helpless in a situation. Burnout is painful and destroys motivation. You probably want less burnout and more bliss in your life.

CHANGING WORK WORLD

You're most likely to experience blissful moments while at work or while working on something important, such as a serious hobby, volunteer activity, artistic endeavor or community project. The work world is undergoing dramatic changes with the speed of change increasing at an ever-rapid rate. Although this change is creating chaos and stress, all indicators are that new work conditions are more conducive to experiencing bliss. Repetitive work, where you are told what to do and do what people before you have done with a supervisor looking over your shoulder, is giving way to a new kind of work, in which, you are given broad guidelines and expected to accomplish something that no one else in your job has done before. In today's work environment, you need to figure out the hows and whats of your work, to manage yourself, and to get it all done in a timely fashion.

> Emerging conditions in the workplace provide opportunities for bliss.

In a sense, you are a pioneer, forging new processes and procedures in your work. It is not smart to wait for someone "above" to set a direction and initiate changes for your specific work. Besides, chances are that you know more about your work and its problems and inefficiencies than anyone else. The people at the top have not been on this frontier either. They're winging it just like the rest of us. The fact is that you are the person uniquely positioned to take the lead in your work—and in your life. Not only that, your company is relying on you to do so. What all this boils down to is that if you are to succeed at work, and if you are going to have frequent moments of bliss, you must become a pathfinder, charting a course into unknown territory, which means leading yourself and sometimes leading others.

INHABIT YOUR JOB

Few jobs are given to you "whole." Usually you are given an outline of expectations, rules, and guidelines. Then you contribute yourself. The way you "inhabit" your job is up to your own personal style and creativity. . . .

Think of your job as an empty house. You move in and look at its form and structure. Then your own creativity takes root. You design your space, decorate, and make the house into your home. You personalize it by putting your stamp on it. Just doing what is expected at work is like living in a bare house—there is no "you" there. It becomes fertile ground for job burnout.

Dennis Jaffe and Cynthia Scott
Take This Job and Love It

PERSONAL LEADERSHIP

If you are going to find a path with a heart—a path to your bliss— you must take the lead. No one else is going to find the path that leads to bliss for you. You must lead yourself to find a way to your bliss. Personal leadership is not something that most of us have had training in. What we know we've learned the hard way, by going down a path only to find that it is a deadend. As you read on you will discover twelve tools for finding your way from burnout to bliss. But before getting into the specifics, let's take a look at how people have led or directed themselves in the past.

In *The Way of the Ronin*, I drew on the work of David Riesman in *The Lonely Crowd*, where he described how people in different stages of social evolution found personal direction. For example, the Middle Ages was characterized by a rigid feudal social order. Life went on for generations with little change, and people rarely encountered anything that conflicted with their culture. Belonging was paramount. Individual choice of lifestyle and goals was virtually nonexistent because occupation was an inseparable part of the station of one's birth. People in this sort of social climate usually look to tradition for direction. Riesman called these people *tradition-directed.*

> **Only you can find a path to your bliss.**

When the Middle Ages gave way to the Renaissance the social environment changed. People were much more worldly. They were more mobile and came into contact with different, often conflicting traditions. The old tradition-directed mechanism didn't work so well anymore. Which tradition should be followed? To keep from floundering around, a new personal-leading mechanism emerged that Riesman called *inner-directed.* Here people lead themselves by following an inner sense of duty and striving for achievement. The word "inner" can be misleading, however. Although the sense of duty was internalized, it wasn't actually chosen by the individual. Instead, a set of rigid beliefs was inculcated early on by the training children received from elders and schools. Being directed by an inner standard, a person can retain a coherent sense of self while surrounded by different cultural traditions. As a result, the inner-directed are able to stay on course in unsupportive, even hostile situations. When faced with rapid change, however, an inner-directed person tends to be inflexible, and to resist the changes needed to adapt and evolve.

> **Self-direction is a modern day phenomenon.**

The postwar era, the time during which most of us were shaped, imposed still different requirements. Our world was an industrial society filled with gigantic bureaucracies and centralized institutions populated by millions of baby-boomers. Rugged individualism was out, conformity was in. To survive in the giant organizations, we learned to be hypersensitive to the actions and wishes of others. Enter the *other-directed* person who looks to peers rather than ancestors or duty for direction. Approval replaced belonging and achievement as primary goals. "I'm okay, you're okay" and "Keeping up with the Jones" are examples of the emphasis on seeking approval.

> **Pathfinders lead themselves.**

Many have lamented that the other-directed person is devoid of a center—a sense of self. We are nothing but shallow conformists. Other direction has a benefit, however. We have become superb adapters. Our fine-tuned social skills enable us to read a situation and adjust by doing what's expected, what's hip, what's with it, what's bad, man! Whatever the prevailing norm, the other-directed change like chameleons. These are the '60s hippies who dropped back in to become the '80s yuppies. These are gang members who wear prescribed colors and commit crimes to gain membership.

In *The Way of the Ronin* I argue that the other-directed are ready to develop a self-directing mechanism which Reisman only alluded to—the *autonomous-directed*. The autonomous have the self-directing capabilities of the other three types, but go beyond them. They follow tradition when they choose to. They are achievement-oriented but, unlike inner-directed, they are not bound by the obligations of imposed duty. They have useful social skills and are sensitive to others but are not enslaved by needing approval like the other-directed. The autonomous lead themselves, sometimes drawing on others, sometimes following duty, sometimes tradition, sometimes inspiration. They find a direction that provides personal meaning while accomplishing the

group's purpose and forging a path. The autonomous seek a path with a heart, a path to personal fulfillment. Interestingly, Csikszentmihalyi says

> **Change is a time of opportunity.**

that his research indicates that people who experience flow easily, even in seemingly adverse situations, are *autotelic,* which he defines as an individual whose goals originate predominantly from within the self, rather than as a response to external demands like biological needs and social conventions. Csikszentmihalyi's observations suggest that the autonomous, the pathfinders, experience more bliss in their lives, even though the paths they travel may be long and hard.

Appropriately, the emergence of the autonomous-directed coincides with a time of incredible change. Conglomerates are breaking up, industrialization is waning. Cultural diversity is commonplace. Rapid scientific and technological breakthroughs are revolutionizing our lifestyles and work.

TIME OF THE PARENTHESIS

We are living in the *time of the parenthesis,* the time between eras.

Those who are willing to handle the ambiguity of this in-between period and to anticipate the new era will be a quantum leap ahead of those who hold on to the past. The time of the parenthesis is a time of change and questioning.

Although the time between eras is uncertain, it is a great and yeasty time, filled with opportunity. If we can learn to make uncertainty our friend, we can achieve much more than in stable eras.

In stable eras, everything has a name, and everything knows its place and we can leverage very little.

But in the time of the parenthesis we have extraordinary leverage and influence—individually, professionally, and institutionally—if we can only get a clear sense, a clear conception, a clear vision, of the road ahead.

My God, what a fantastic time to be alive!

John Naisbitt
Megatrends: Ten New Directions Transforming Our Lives

The pathfinder is the person who sees the road ahead and the craft of pathfinding is the art and skill of personal leadership.

BECOMING A PERSONAL LEADER

I use *ronin*, the lordless or unindentured samurai as a metaphor for the autonomous-directed. Ronin translates "wave man" from Japanese. "Ro" means wave and "nin," like *ninja*, means man or person. We all know that samurai were excellent and formidable warriors. But samurai were property—important and expensive property, but property nonetheless. They were chattel who did as their masters ordered, even to the point of *seppuku* or committing ritual disembowelment. For various reasons some samurai became masterless. Their lords may have died, but they refused to commit seppuku which was expected by tradition when a samurai's lord died. Perhaps they voluntarily separated themselves in order to carry out revenge. Without an identified clan, their enemies had no one to strike back at. A few were actually born as ronin.

However they became free, the feudal society whence they came did not prepare them to be lordless—without a master to lead them. Being a ronin was considered a difficult path. They had to struggle with personal direction in a society that revered tradition and the group above all else. Often the bushi master would order a samurai to "do ronin," which was considered a spiritual trial of personal development.

In feudal Japan, where life was prescribed down to the finest detail, ronin were the freest of all people, and some ronin got to liking it. Musashi, the most famous ronin, wrote in the 1640s *The Book of Five Rings*, which was revered as an innovative business manifesto on the U.S.A. best-seller list in 1980. When feudalism collapsed in 1867 it was the ronin, the change masters, who stepped forth to lead Japan's incredible transition from a backward feudal society to an economic and technological world leader.

Ronin as it is used here is not meant to accurately reflect history. Ronin is a metaphor for an archetypical character who emerges in times of rapid paradigm shifts, when rules change in confusing ways and worlds turn upside down. Ronin, the wave man, rides the waves of change.

The process of struggling toward autonomy is what I call *The Way of the Ronin,* a path one follows through the twists and turns of life. Personal development and personal fulfillment are the primary concerns of ronin as they strive to achieve excellence in all areas, personal as well as vocational. Doing this is easy to talk about but actually finding one's path usually proves difficult. How to set the course, stay on course and traverse the course—while making necessary changes in direction along the way—was not taught in school, where we learned only to follow instructions and memorize procedures. We have to discover how to lead ourselves and others. The cliche about the blind leading the blind characterizes the challenge we face. That is, we must find our paths at the same time that we learn to be pathfinders.

We are on the frontier. This is an exciting time, filled with opportunity. Are you prepared for your pioneer role? Schools and jobs taught most of us to fear rocking the boat and to look to authority for direction. Today success takes vision and stepping forward into the wilderness, the unknown, to become a pathfinder leading yourself and others through change.

PATHFINDING AS A CRAFT

Self-leadership is the pathfinder's craft, and the twelve tools that follow are used to practice the craft. The use of the word *craft* is meant to emphasize that personal leadership is both an art and a science. Just as

> Pathfinding is both an art and a science.

each potter's pottery demonstrates skill executed in an individual style, each person crafts his or her leadership in a uniquely individual way. Potters and other craftsmen use tools skillfully and artfully. Similarly, leadership processes are referred to as tools, which are used with skill and art, to carry out your leadership goals.

Aristotle said that happiness and finding fulfillment is an activity and not a state. That is, we experience bliss when engaged in an activity. Csikszentmihalyi's research shows that some activities are more conducive than others to experi-

encing bliss and that some people seem to enter the flow state and experience bliss, regardless of the situation, more easily than other people do.

THE FLOW PERSONALITY

Some people have an uncanny ability to match their skills to the opportunities around them. They set manageable goals for themselves even when there does not seem to be anything for them to do. They are good at reading feedback that others fail to notice. They can concentrate easily and do not get distracted. They are not afraid of losing their self so their ego can slip easily out of awareness. They do not need to play in order to be in flow, they can be happy even as they work on an assembly line or are languishing in solitary confinement.

Mihaly Csikszentmihalyi
The Evolving Self

Csikszentmihalyi says that a person who is never bored, seldom anxious, involved with what goes on, and in flow much of the time has an autotelic self. From his observations of these self-directed people, he found that they could transform potentially negative situations into bliss opportunities. He gleaned the following guidelines from his observations. First, to experience flow, you must have clear goals to strive for, and in selecting goals, you must be able to identify challenges proportionate to your ability and to use feedback. Second, he found that people who experience flow routinely find it easy to become immersed in an activity at hand. Doing this takes an ability to concentrate. Third, people with flow personalities were able to sustain involvement in what they were doing. Finally, Csikszentmihalyi found that flow personalities know how to enjoy immediate experience even when the circumstances appear unpleasant. Csikszentmihalyi's autotelic self is a pathfinder. Using path-finding tools such as the Target to set compelling goals, the Yardstick to get feedback on distance traveled, and the Wand to transform obstacles into opportunities increase your potential for experiencing flow and having more moments of bliss in your life and work.

THE PATHFINDING TOOLS

With knowledge and practice you can increase your potential for experiencing frequent moments of bliss. Pathfinding is a handbook for personal leadership and finding a path to your bliss in your daily life. Following is a brief description of the twelve pathfinding tools accompanied by the icon or symbol used to represent the tool throughout the book.

Compass: Getting Your Bearings

The Compass is an intuitive sensor of your fear and confidence levels in a situation. It is used to get your bearings by pointing toward bliss, which is an experience of being energized and functioning optimally with little apparent effort, or by pointing to burnout, which is an experience of feeling drained and demoralized.

Heart: Finding Your Path

Yaqui Indian sorcerer Don Juan advised Carlos Castaneda that the secret of a joyful journey is to find a path with a heart. It's the process of working, the journey, that's important. With the Heart tool you uncover and clarify values. When work resonates with your values, so that you're getting meaning and satisfaction from work, you are in tune and your heart sings.

Mission: Defining Your Purpose

You are hired to solve a problem, not to do a job. The solution you were hired to implement is the purpose your company is relying on you to fulfill. You discover your pathfinding Mission when you match your personal goals with this purpose.

Vision: Seeing Your Destination

Pathfinders use Vision to see the road ahead. Vision is the picture of where you're going and what you seek to achieve. To be effective your Vision must be compelling, so that it draws you toward it like a magnet.

Survey: Scanning Your Territory

Before a Map can be drawn, the terrain must be surveyed to reveal the lay of the land. Where are the mountains and passes? Pathfinders use a similar process to Survey available resources, potential projects, allies who can be called upon, as well as obstacles and potential problems along the path.

Target: Setting Your Goals

Targets are goals that act as markers along your path to help you move from where you are to accomplishing your Mission. Without a Target it's hard to know what to shoot for. The Target tool helps you aim and focus your efforts.

Map: Charting Your Course

Mapping is deciding on the specific route you will take, and defines the specific action steps to reach the Target in the order that they are needed. Mapping also involves identifying how and where you might get off-course and preparing a contingency plan for course-correcting.

Yardstick: Measuring Distance Traveled

With the Yardstick you can measure the distance you've come and see how close you are to reaching the Target. This feedback is vital for identifying when you've strayed from the path and when your course needs to be corrected.

Team: Eliciting Cooperation

Very little can be accomplished alone. You need a team and the cooperation of others to reach your destination and accomplish your Mission.

Hat: Changing Your Attitude

Like "putting on your thinking hat," different situations call for different mindsets or points of view. Pathfinders have flexible thinking styles and change Hats to find the most effective approach to the challenges at hand.

Wand: Transforming Your Obstacles

The Wand is the transformational tool used to change obstacles in your path. The key is to figure out a way to transform the barrier into an opportunity vehicle that will move you closer to accomplishing your Mission.

Eye: Piloting Your Journey

You are the pilot at the helm of your journey. With the Eye you oversee and choose which tool to use when. And with the Eye you watch to discover how to motivate yourself and others to move toward your Vision so that you can accomplish your Mission.

THE PROMISE OF PATHFINDING

Like reading personal leadership is an essential skill for functioning in our modern world. You'll use it every day in countless situations. Without personal leadership ability, you'll be at a disadvantage in ways you may not have anticipated. Those lacking skill in pathfinding must depend on others for direction, which may not be fulfilling, or they may launch out, only to get side-tracked and lose their way.

Becoming skilled in pathfinding will provide you with immunity to job burnout, which has reached epidemic proportions. In *Beating Job Burnout* I show how burnout is a process in which motivation is eroded, possibility destroyed. The

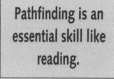

> Pathfinding is an essential skill like reading.

process is very stressful. People get sick more often. On-the-job performance drops, and off the job the burnout victims tend to withdraw from friends and social activities. Substance abuse is common. Burnout victims tend to be depressed and report a sense of meaninglessness.

Burnout is caused by feelings of powerlessness or helplessness. For example, you might be bored with your work, but because of a stagnant economy, feel trapped and unable to leave. Or you might have a critical boss who ignores your achievements and who won't clarify her expectations, leaving you feeling helpless in your efforts to get good performance ratings. Or you might face unending demands to innovate, but be given little direction

> Having control over one's work helps prevent job burnout.

and few resources, so that you feel doomed to fail. Situations that can engender feelings of powerlessness are unlimited. In fact, the World Labor Report of the United Nation's International Labor Organizations released in the early 1990s concluded that stress has become one of the most serious health issues of the 20th century. Burnout is so prevalent in Japan that they coined the word *karoshi* for death by overwork. One of the discoveries of the UN study is the relationship between having little control over one's job or life and high levels of stress. To combat stress in the workplace, they recommend that employers give people more control over their jobs.

Since we can't wait around for employers to improve working conditions, we as individuals must act to improve our lives. On the individual level, burnout can be prevented by developing personal power. Personal power is an "I Can Do" attitude. It is believing that there is always something you can do. You may not be happy with the situation, and you may not like the choices before you, but there is something you can do. You are not helpless. You have choices. This is the essence of personal power. There are nine paths to personal power: managing yourself, handling stress, building a strong social support system, building skills, modifying the job, getting a new job, managing your mood, and developing detached concern. The ninth, and most important, path to personal power is pathfinding itself. It takes personal leadership to identify the problems in your situation and to determine the best path for beating burnout.

Of course, we don't know what obstacles and opportunities we'll face in the future. Skilled pathfinders have the confidence that they can find a way out of life's deadends to get back on track with their personal goals. This confidence is empowering. Pathfinders feel in control of their destinies rather than victimized by change. Pathfinders know how to get their bearings, and carve out an important purpose to set a direction that satisfies personal values while achieving meaningful goals. In times of change pathfinders rise to the challenge of leadership and succeed.

In the following pages you will learn how to sense burnout situations, uncover your core values, define a purpose that is both personally satisfying and important to the company, and conceive of a compelling vision. You'll learn how to survey your assets and liabilities and the challenges before you how to set effective goals, decide on the steps for reaching it, and devise ways to evaluate progress. You'll learn how to get others on-board with your project, how to assume the most beneficial mindset for the tasks at hand, how to transform obstacles into opportunities. And you will learn how to manage yourself more effectively as you lead yourself to your bliss.

CHAPTER 3

COMPASS
GETTING YOUR BEARINGS

There is no freeway to the future.
No paved highway from here to tomorrow.
There is only wilderness. Only uncertain terrain.
There are no roadmaps. No signposts.
So pioneering leaders rely upon a compass and a dream.
James Kouzes and Barry Posner
The Leadership Challenge

$\mathcal{A}$ctions you take today will impact on how your future will unfold and where you will be tomorrow. You are in the wilderness, on the frontier, poised to meet new challenges on the verge of a new millennium. There are no highways or roadmaps. Change is the one constant that can be counted on. In this landscape of uncertainty and flux, you must find a path from where you are to the completion of your goals, the fulfillment of your responsibilities, and the

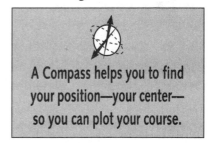

A Compass helps you to find your position—your center— so you can plot your course.

actualization of your potential. To meet these challenges and forge a path, you must break new ground. The challenges can take many forms, from changing careers to undertaking a home improvement project to giving up a habit such as smoking. Having a compass is a necessity; otherwise you could get hopelessly lost, going in circles without knowing where you are. Without a Compass you may find yourself on a bad path, a path toward burnout, whereas bliss is found by seeking a path that feels right, a path with a heart.

In a very real sense, you're a pioneer. Pioneers of old got their bearings by using a compass and looking at the stars to find North. You too need a compass. With a compass you can find your position and get your bearings. A compass helps you stay on course and to correct your course when sidetracked.

THE PATHFINDER'S COMPASS

A compass is a navigational tool that always points North. By lining up the North marker on its face, with the arrow pointing North, you can

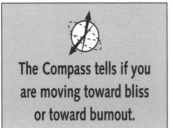

The Compass tells if you are moving toward bliss or toward burnout.

get your bearings. A Pathfinder's Compass is similar. But instead of a single needle pointing North, a Pathfinding Compass has two arrows. One points to bliss, a state of optimal well-being where you perform at your peak. The other points to a negative state of burnout, characterized by fear and loss of control.

The Pathfinder's Compass enables you to read your inner responses in any situation in order to get your bearings. By becoming skilled in reading your Compass, you will be able to tell when you are moving toward burnout—an indication that you are possibly off-course and need to make changes—or toward bliss, which is a sign that you are on a path with a heart.

DEVELOPING YOUR COMPASS

As bad as burnout can be, a surprising number of people actually voluntarily take on work that sets them on a path to burnout. Sean, for example, doesn't like being nagged and doesn't like paperwork, especially if it involves a lot of record-keeping, yet he repeatedly takes on projects that involve just this kind of work. "I hate detail. I'm a concept man, and here I am stuck, logging infernal details!" Because he hates detail, Sean procrastinates until other people begin nagging him, which he says makes him feel brow-beaten and trapped. Why does Sean needlessly put himself in a position to have to do detailed paperwork and get nagged? Part of the problem is that Sean has not developed his Pathfinding Compass.

THE HOMING DEVICE

The Homing Device ... reads messages from virtually every part of the body and sends signals to the brain in the form of thoughts and emotions. Although the mechanisms for doing all this are in place, most of us have never learned exactly how to make full use of them. Either we don't know how to read the messages our Homing Devices send out or, far more likely, we have been conditioned against paying any attention to these messages. For most of us, it is a little of each.

When we pay attention to our Homing Devices and follow their guidance, we invariably feel great about ourselves and in perfect harmony with the people or activities we're involved with at that moment. Decisions are never difficult because we know where we're heading and why.

Hal Zina Bennett and Susan J. Sparrow
Follow Your Bliss

You'd think that we would be alert to situations that are pleasant or unpleasant, so that we could take appropriate action. But not so. It's easy to get trapped, like Sean, in situations characterized by fear, uncertainty and doubt.

By developing a sensitivity to how burnout and bliss feel, you can get your bearings. When you don't see the early warning signs that you are on the wrong path you are likely to keep following that path until you're in too deep. The Compass is a sensing mechanism, much like the "Homing Device" Bennett and Sparrow describe in *Follow Your Bliss.* It can help you sort out your feelings about a given situation. Don't be surprised if those feelings are not always completely clear or easily put into words, because Compass reading is intuitive. As you become skilled at reading your Compass, you'll gain confidence in your instincts about a situation. You'll be able to say, "I know what I know," even though you may not be able to verbalize that knowing.

When you have misgivings or apprehensions about entering certain situations, check your Compass. When the Compass indicates potential burnout, you'll want to take this as a warning that you're heading down a heartless path. When it indicates bliss, you will probably feel confident in staying the course.

ESTABLISH A BASELINE FIRST

Measuring is a powerful source of feedback.

The first thing you must do to develop your Compass is establish a marker that you can use as a reference point. The marker is how you feel now, at this moment, before experimenting with negative and positive feelings. Scientists call this marker a *baseline*.

To establish your baseline, observe how you feel at the moment. This can be difficult because we have a tendency to judge ourselves and to edit what we do and feel to be more socially acceptable. The kind of observation needed to establish a baseline must be objective. This is difficult because our observations, especially of ourselves, tend to be subjective. The trick is to step back from yourself—to watch what you're doing and feeling as if you were another person.

Try this now. Stop reading for a few moments and tune into how you feel right now. Use your Eye tool to observe yourself. Notice how you feel. Notice where you feel it. Don't judge the feelings, simply notice them. Take off your judging Hat and assume an objective fact gathering mindset. Observe what you feel and where

Study yourself as if you were another person.

in your body you feel it. Remember to be like a scientist when objectively collecting data on yourself.

Stop and rate how you feel on the well-being scale from 1 to 10, with 1 being "very negative," "very low," "very bad," "very unpleasant," or "very unhappy" and with 10 representing "very positive," "very high," "very good," "very pleasant," and "very happy." This first rating is your baseline. Write your baseline rating down on the corner of this page, in a notebook, or in another place so that you can refer to it later.

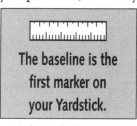

The baseline is the first marker on your Yardstick.

The baseline is a reading of how you feel right now. It will serve as a reference as you experiment with burnout and blissful feelings. You may feel good or you may be depressed when you establish your baseline. However you feel, the baseline serves as a point for comparison to help gauge how you feel later.

STUDY HOW BURNOUT FEELS

In order to calibrate your Compass to read burnout, you must first become objectively familiar with how and where burnout affects you, so that you can recognize it in its initial stages. This is accomplished by studying how you feel when in a burnout situation. To study burnout effectively, place yourself in a situation characterized by fear and loss of control. Then, as a scientist would, observe how you feel when in this burnout situation. The easiest way to do this is to recall burnout situations, relive them one by one in your imagination, and study what you see.

Identify a Burnout Situation

Begin by identifying a burnout situation to use in practice. Don't choose a heavily charged situation. Instead, the situation should be characterized by a relatively mild to moderate degree of fear, anxiety and doubt. It may have been at work, in recreation, or in your home life. It may have been earlier today or yesterday, a month ago, or years ago. Examples might be making a sales presentation to a resistant client, waiting for your spouse who is late and hasn't called, or not being selected for the company debating team and wondering why. The objective is to briefly relive feelings of disappointment and doubt and to study how it feels and where it hurts. Don't overwhelm yourself. Stay away from extremely painful situations like being fired, filing bankruptcy, or going through a divorce.

Recall the Burnout Situation

Once you've identified a burnout situation to study, recall being there, making it as real as you can in your imagination. Actually feel the agitation, disappointment, helplessness and other feelings you experienced in the real situation. Once the emotions are vivid, switch Hats to an objective mindset, and collect data on what you experience. Doing this is a little tricky, because you must be two people: you experiencing burnout, and you watching yourself experience burnout. To do this, use your Eye, the tool of self-management which is vital for pathfinding. How to use the Eye to pilot yourself along your path is explained in Chapter Fourteen. For now, use your Eye to watch in a detached way what you experience while recalling the burnout situation. Notice emotions, like sadness or anxiety. Notice physical sensations, like

> Assume an objective mindset, like that of a scientist.

a stiff neck or itching skin. Pay particular attention to thoughts that come to mind. You might hear yourself thinking, "This always happens to me" or "Why bother, there's nothing I can do." Don't try to change the thoughts or judge them. Simply notice the thoughts as they form. After studying your experiences for a minute or so,

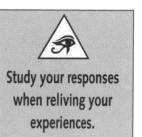

Study your responses when reliving your experiences.

try to identify the critical factor in the situation that made it a burnout. What event or circumstance triggered the burnout feelings and thoughts? What were you responding to? Resist the temptation to judge or change your reactions in any way. Study them for a few minutes, then let the memory go.

Compare the Burnout Rating with the Baseline

The third step is to rate how you feel after reliving the burnout situation in your imagination. Once again, use the well-being scale from 1 to 10. Remember, 1 represents very negative feelings and 10 represents very positive feelings. Write your rating in your notebook or on the corner of this page. How does this rating compare to your baseline rating? Is the rating higher than, lower than, or the same as the baseline?

Measure and compare.

If you're like most people, you probably noticed that after recalling the burnout experience, your well-being rating went down. In my seminars, people report uncomfortable physical sensations when recalling burnout, like headaches and back pain. Sometimes the physical maladies are accompanied by depression, nervousness, hopelessness, and fearful or angry thoughts. Sometimes there's acute anxiety and restlessness that can translate into manic hyperactivity. Optimal performance is rare, if not impossible. Everything is a struggle. People

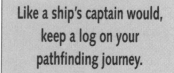

Like a ship's captain would, keep a log on your pathfinding journey.

report feeling off-key, out of tune, lost and stuck. There are feelings of helplessness and a sense of loss of control along with negative emotions like anger and depression.

Factors most often reported as causing burnout include unpredict-able change, being trapped in a job with nowhere to go, no-win situations where no matter what you do you lose, conflict with co-workers, hyper-critical bosses and having to do things that violate your sense of ethics. When involved with such ordeals, most people feel heavy, trapped, and depressed. Burnout feels bad, and most of us prefer to avoid it whenever possible.

It's a good idea to keep notes on the data you collect, like a pioneer or ship captain using a log book to record where they've been. In this manner, you can establish reference points to consult when certain situations arise repeatedly. In a journal or a notebook, indicate the situation you studied, and describe how you felt and where you felt it. Maybe you were demoralized and felt tired. Write this down. If you noticed any physical sensations, like knots in the stomach or a pounding heart, write this down. If you noticed certain thoughts, write these down. Try to recall and record the words in your thoughts verbatim. Finally, what was it about the situation that made it burnout? Perhaps you felt trapped. Write this in your notes. After you've studied several burnout situations you can review your notes for patterns. This can be helpful in revealing how you respond when faced with such obstacles.

STUDY HOW BLISS FEELS

Study bliss to calibrate the positive pole of the Compass. Use the same procedure followed in studying burnout. First, identify a blissful situation to study. Pick a time when you were fully involved in what you  were doing, where you felt "one" with the moment, and your actions were effective. Examples might include a physical activity such as dancing, playing tennis, or skiing. Or better yet, a work experience when you were so completely absorbed in what you were doing that you forgot about time, perhaps when solving a programming problem, working on the details of a proposal, or giving a lecture to a receptive and attentive audience.

Following the same process as before, bring the blissful situation to mind and relive it, making it as vivid as you can. The first sign of flow is a narrowing of attention on a clearly defined objective while being involved, concentrated and absorbed. Use your Eye to notice what it feels like to flow in the blissful situation. Notice where you feel it. Is the sensation in your muscles? In your stomach? Notice what emotions you experience while remembering it. Do you feel happy or sad? Content or angry? Notice what thoughts come to mind.

Now shift your Eye to the situation and try to discover what made it blissful. Look for the key elements that facilitated your going into the blissful state. Take your time in studying this. Remain detached like a scientist and just watch the situation don't judge or try to alter it. After a minute or so let the memory go.

Measure and compare.

Once again, using a well-being scale from 1 to 10, with 1 representing very negative feelings and 10 representing very positive feelings, rate how you feel after remembering bliss. Write your bliss rating in your log or on the corner of this page.

HOW FLOW FEELS

An enormous variety of enjoyable activities share some common characteristics. If a tennis player is asked how it feels when a game is going well, she will describe a state of mind that is very similar to the description a chess player will give of a good tournament. So will be a description of how it feels to be absorbed in painting, or playing a difficult piece of music. Watching a good play or reading a stimulating book also seems to produce the same mental state. I called it "flow," because this was a metaphor several respondents gave for how it felt when their experience was most enjoyable—it was like being carried away by a current, everything moving smoothly without effort.

Mihaly Csikszentmihalyi
The Evolving Self

If you're like most people, your well-being rating is higher than it was after reliving the burnout situation. Many people report that their ratings were also higher than their baselines. The impact of burnout and bliss is so powerful that simply remembering the feelings for a few minutes can alter your sense of well-being.

People report remarkably similar things when they recall blissful events. They tend to feel relaxed, light, and energetic. Actions seem to come naturally and easily. Emotions tend to be enthusiastic and happy. Thoughts focus on confidence and optimism. Most importantly, people report feeling in control and confident that what they are doing will succeed. They feel in command, without thinking or trying.

RECALIBRATE OFTEN

It is important to recalibrate often. The objective is to develop a sensitivity to the subtle early signs of burnout and bliss. Doing this takes

The Compass helps you to get centered.

practice. The process is much like judging weight by comparing the weight of one stone in your right hand to another stone in your left hand. The more you practice the more sensitive you become to small differences in weight. By collecting data on how you feel in several burnout and blissful situations and by identifying their characteristics, you can develop a sensitive Compass. So far you've concentrated on one burnout and one blissful event. Repeat this process with different positive and negative memories. Always begin by establishing a baseline to mark how you feel before studying burnout and bliss. Use only mildly upsetting events in the beginning. Later, study events that caused you to be more fearful, doubtful and uncertain.

Knowing how you are responding in a situation and how you are likely to respond in similar situations is important for mastery and autonomy—individual freedom. Emotions translate directly into motivation. Negative responses usually tend to motivate people to move away or avoid situations associated with the negativity, whereas feelings of well-being tend to motivate people to move toward situations associated with the positive response.

The Compass enables you to get better control of your motivation so that you can use it to get where you want to go. Without a Compass you can go around and around with no bearings like a ship lost at sea— no center, just responding moment to moment. Read your Compass often. When you sense burnout, stop and reorient toward bliss. Ask yourself, "How can I turn this into a challenge?"

MOTIVATION

Burnout and bliss play a substantial role in determining the direction and intensity of your motivation. Think of motivation as moving. There are two ways to move: moving toward bliss and moving away from burnout. Moving toward bliss or *seeking motivation* occurs when you act in anticipation of a positive outcome. Making a final edit of a report in hopes that the Division Chief will notice the extra effort is an example of seeking or moving toward motivation.

You can move to avoid burnout or move to seek bliss.

Moving away from burnout or *avoidance motivation* is operating when a negative situation exists and you do something to avoid it or to turn it off. For example, suppose you have a headache; so you take an aspirin. You are moved to take the aspirin by the desire to turn off the headache. Similarly, a person who pretends to look busy when the boss walks by in order to avoid additional assignments is engaging in avoidance motivation. Another example is making a final edit of a report because you're afraid that the Division Chief will criticize your spelling again.

TWO KINDS OF MOTIVATION

(Seeking)	*(Avoiding)*
Moving Toward Bliss	Moving Away from Burnout
Striving for something positive	Attempting to avoid or turn off something negative

---

It is easy to fall into a habitual pattern of moving only to avoid negatives. Avoidance motivation is learned early on from parents and in schools. Many of us endured long, boring lectures where we pretended to be interested in order to avoid incurring the wrath of teachers. In the process, we developed a habit of procrastinating when it came to studying, then cramming to avoid a failing grade.

Avoidance motivation requires a threat, which can be real or perceived, to get moving. The inevitable changes of life tend to be viewed as threats, and actions become defensive, aimed at preserving the status quo. By remaining in the avoidance mode, change can feel something like a tidal wave slamming your life broadside when it finally hits.

> Avoidance motivation requires a threat to get moving.

Your Pathfinding Compass can help you to develop seeking motivation, to ride the waves of change rather than being tossed to and fro like a ship without a rudder. The object is to know what bliss feels like and to move toward situations that encourage blissful moments. This is analogous to using the needle that points North on your Compass to establish where you are. When you discover where you are, it becomes much easier to forge a path to where you want to be. The second needle reads the burnout potential of the situation. This alerts you to the necessity to take corrective action and to reorient yourself to a move-toward mode. Doing this calls on other pathfinding tools which we'll get to later.

MAKING DECISIONS

Often people make decisions solely upon "facts," only to discover afterward that they don't like the result. Then they try frantically to undo the decision.

■ Consider Nancy:

When Nancy was offered a promotion from engineering to a middle-management spot, with a sizeable increase in pay, she jumped at it. The new position meant moving from corporate headquarters in San Francisco to a regional office in the Midwest. The decision sounded like a good one. The promotion was good for her career as well as her pocketbook. So off she went to Sioux Falls, South Dakota. The first several weeks were exciting and hectic as she met the new team and got herself settled.

But then depression set in, which took Nancy by surprise. She was rarely down in the dumps. Nancy hadn't anticipated the difficulties she would face in making new friends and integrating into a new community, and she hadn't anticipated her reaction to the long, subzero winter. In less than six weeks she was on the phone with the division manager, begging to go back to her old job. But the job was filled. Out of desperation, she took a subordinate position with a cut in pay. Not surprisingly, her company concluded that Nancy just didn't have management potential.

Had Nancy checked her Compass when deciding what to do she could have discovered that the move was fraught with burnout potential. A check of her Compass would have better prepared Nancy to deal with the inevitable negative aspects of the move, or perhaps she would have decided to refuse the promotion altogether.

USING YOUR COMPASS WHEN MAKING DECISIONS

You can make better decisions by using your Pathfinding Compass. Here's how. Take each alternative you're considering and, one-by-one, imagine that you are in a future time and place where you have selected that alternative. The object is to make this fantasy seem as real as possible,

Use your Compass to make better decisions.

so that you experience now what you would experience later if you chose a certain alternative. For example, if you're considering a job in Sioux Falls, imagine that it's a dark and cold winter day with temperatures at 10° below zero. You must start the car before eating breakfast so that it can run for twenty minutes or so before driving. Imagine driving to work in blizzard conditions. And so forth.

Once you get a vivid picture in your mind, then check your Compass. How does this alternative feel? Does the Compass indicate burnout or bliss? Gathering enough good information for each alternative is critical to making this technique work. Interview people who are in the new job or live in the area. Read about its history and traditions. If possible, try to arrange an advance visit. Above all else, make sure you thoroughly consider the ramifications of your decision. Although it may not be completely true that you can never "go home again," it's practically assured that if you do go home, things won't be the same as before. When you imagine yourself in one of the alternatives under consideration, make sure that you study the impact of your decision on people around you. How will your family feel if you choose this alternative? How will your friends be affected? Imagine that you have selected this alternative. Picture yourself in a future where you have selected this alternative. What are your children experiencing? Your spouse? Your friends? Your pets? Read your Compass often. Again, it is a good idea to keep notes in your log book about your responses to each alternative, so that you can review them later.

BURNOUT INOCULATION

Sometimes trudging through an adverse situation is necessary in order to move forward along your path. Nancy, for example, couldn't

Study and prepare.

have an instant social life in a new city. A period of adjustment and inevitable loneliness was unavoidable. If Nancy wanted to reap the benefits of the change she made she had to go through a period of fear, uncertainty, and doubt, not run from it.

Burnout inoculation could have helped. This procedure is analogous to a vaccination, in which weakened microbes are injected into the body, causing it to develop antibodies and thereby create an immunity. Similarly by experiencing a weakened version of the distress you'll encounter in the future, you can develop a resistance to it. Later when you experience the real distress, you'll have some immunity to its force and be less inclined to run from it.

Had Nancy used inoculation before moving, she would have imagined herself being lonely on weekends with no friends, experiencing and studying the lonely feelings with her Eye. Then she would have imagined several ways of dealing with the loneliness, trying out each possibility, one at a time, in her imagination. For example, Nancy loves hiking and the out-of-doors. She may have imagined herself calling the library and other information sources to locate nature and environmental groups, going on a hike and enjoying herself as she met new people with similar interests. In this way Nancy could have developed a plan for acting when she became lonely. The lonely feelings, while unhappy, would have been familiar and manageable because she had a plan.

BURNOUT INOCULATION STEPS

1. Bring the future burnout situation into your imagination.
2. Experience the negative feelings triggered by the burnout situation.
3. Mentally enact your action plan, and see it work.
4. Notice feelings of relief from burnout.

When you mentally rehearse your plan of action, it is important to *see it work* in your imagination and to *experience a relief* from distress. For example, Nancy could have rehearsed by imagining herself alone on the weekend in Sioux Falls, feeling lonely and homesick. She could have let herself experience the gloom and powerlessness for a few moments, then picture herself enacting her plan of joining a hiking club and meeting new people. She could have imagined the plan working, noticed happy feelings and relief from her loneliness. To get maximum benefit,

"See" your plan working.

repeat the inoculation process several times.

Anytime you contemplate change, take time for burnout inoculation. You'll make better decisions and feel more in command. In the process you'll view the situation as a challenge, which is an important step in going from burnout to bliss.

USE YOUR COMPASS OFTEN

Change is everywhere, casting you into the wilderness to face uncertain terrain. There are no roadmaps or signposts to the future. You must forge ahead and blaze a trail with only the courage of your convictions as a guide. You need a Compass to get your bearings; without it you could get hopelessly lost. With your Pathfinding Compass you can read how you're responding to situations. When you know how you feel, you can focus and get your bearings. But if you lose sight of your feelings, you lose your bearings and respond in a reactionary fashion, tossed about back and forth by forces seemingly beyond your control. When you are out of touch with your feelings, it's very hard to find bliss.

A well-calibrated Compass is essential for developing the Heart, your next Pathfinding Tool. When you use the Compass and Heart together, you can take the first step toward finding a path to your bliss.

CHAPTER 4

HEART

FINDING YOUR PATH

Does the path have a good heart? If it does, the path is good.
If it doesn't, it is of no use. Both paths lead nowhere,
but one has a heart and the other doesn't.
One makes for a joyful journey.
As long as you follow it you are one with it.
The other will make you curse your life.
One makes you strong and the other weakens you.
Carlos Castaneda
The Teachings of Don Juan

*I*t's the process of working, the journey, that's important. If you're
getting meaning and satisfaction from work, if your projects stimulate
and excite you, your path has a good
heart. Meaningfulness is one of the
conditions that promotes going into
the flow state and experiencing bliss. If,
on the other hand, you're simply putting in time or struggling frantically to
the top, you're probably on an unfulfilling track with no heart, headed for
burnout.

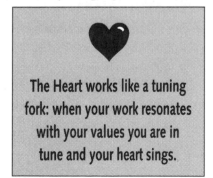

The Heart works like a tuning
fork: when your work resonates
with your values you are in
tune and your heart sings.

    A path with a heart is one that is attuned to your values because
values come from the heart. Values embody how you feel about things

and what's important to you. Values are your ideals and the principles you live by. Work that enables you to play out your values makes for a joyful journey, because you are doing something that has meaning for you. Meaningful work builds confidence, making you strong. In Don Juan's words, when you follow a path attuned to your values you feel "one with it." It is easier to go into the flow state and experience bliss when doing things that engage your values.

A path may have a heart for one person and not for another. Embarking on a course that is socially correct but out of sync with who you are and what you care about is sure to weaken you. Questioning what you're doing and wondering if it matters erodes confidence, and as self-esteem falters, a "why-bother" attitude can take over. Don Juan cautions that following a path that has no heart for you, one that doesn't engage your values, or worse, that is contrary to your values, could make you curse your life.

THE HEART TOOL

> *It is with the heart that one sees rightly;*
> *what is essential is invisible to the eye.*
> Antoine de Saint-Exupèry
> *The Little Prince*

It is easy to talk about values philosophically, but actually discovering your own values can be surprisingly difficult. Values are what really matters to you, what you find important and essential. Identifying values clarifies who you are and what you stand for. When values are unclear it is difficult to define your purpose or mission in life. Values determine priorities, what's important and what isn't, what's right and what's wrong. They may be conscious or unconscious, spoken or unspoken, written or un-written.

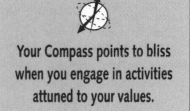

Your Compass points to bliss when you engage in activities attuned to your values.

Most of us learned to look to what others think and do for meaning. David Riesman called us other-directed in his ground-breaking book *The Lonely Crowd* on modes of conformity. Stated in other words, our important life choices are directed by others. This is a mistake because it encourages following a cultural stereotype of what you "should" care about and who you "should" be. If you don't match this picture of shoulds, self-doubt sets in and you tend to question yourself rather than the cultural imperative.

Many people don't know what they value. For example, some people make decisions based on what brings in the most money, even while insisting that money is not important. Remember the old adage: "Actions speak louder than words." The way you act and what you choose are more accurate revela-tions of your values than what you *say* you value.

Reading emotions helps clarify values.

Reading emotions is a reliable way to identify values. Positive emotions like joy, enthusiasm, enjoyment, and satisfaction are usually associated with activities that we value. By contrast, negative emotions like anger, hate, and dissatisfaction tend to be associated with activities that conflict with our values. The heart is a universal symbol of positive emotions, especially love. It is with the Heart tool that we read our emotions. By studying the relationship between your emotions and your actions, you can clarify your values.

Values change. Think of all the 1960s hippies who became 1980s yuppies! Friends, family, and co-workers have a tremendous impact on your values. Owen, for example, prided himself on valuing honesty. Being rather shy, he was thrilled the first time Ray, the star salesman, invited him to have a couple of beers after work. Ray was so smooth; he

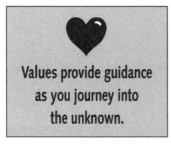

really knew how to play the game. Without realizing it, Owen assumed Ray's values, little by little. Owen became a "slick dresser," bought a "sexy" car—red, of course—and began padding his expense account.

That little lie didn't bother him because, just as Ray said, he was meeting his sales quota. He came to think of it as a perk he'd earned.

Reviewing your values can be a tremendous aid when struggling with a difficult decision. But you must identify your values before you can call on them for guidance. Unclear values make it difficult to know what is most important. When your values are in conflict, choosing is hard, because all your values cannot be satisfied. You may value both making a contribution to society and making money, for example. Some decisions may force you to choose between these two values. Maybe you value attention and personal recognition but also modesty and being low-profile. This apparent conflict is bound to cause problems if you have not prioritized what's important to you.

> **Values provide guidance as you journey into the unknown.**

Could you make a list of your values right now? To find a path with a heart, you must know what you want, what you value. It's a matter of attunement. When you do things that engage your values your Heart resonates like a tuning fork. Stop and notice if your Heart resonates with your path. If it does, the path is good—for you.

Reading your Compass helps you to focus on your center, how you feel. It points toward bliss when you are engaged in activities attuned to your values, and toward burnout when activities conflict with your values.

HOW TO IDENTIFY VALUES

*To transform the entirety of life into a unified flow experience,
it helps to have faith in a system of meanings
that gives purpose to one's being.*
Mihaly Csikszentmihalyi
The Evolving Self

Generally, when you engage in an activity consonant with what is important to you, you find it enjoyable. Use this principle to discover your values. The value-discovery process is an introspective one in which you relive positive or negative experiences, consult your Compass for a bliss or burnout reading, and try to isolate the specific factors that triggered your feelings. What

Check direction.

you discover are clues to your values. After doing this with several experiences, you then look for patterns and themes in the clues. These patterns show your values.

Begin by studying things you really love doing to uncover what specifically you love about them. Try this now. Write down 20 things you really love doing in your journey log or on a piece of paper. You might begin with work-related activities you enjoy, then list avocational, recreational,

Identify what
helps you flow.

social, and family pastimes that bring you great satisfaction. Do this quickly, writing down the first examples that come to mind. Include anything that makes you happy, that is fun, that makes you feel good.

RELIVE THINGS YOU LOVE DOING

Csikszentmihalyi's research and our own experience tells us that it is the journey, following the path, that brings joy not being at the destination. It is in the process—the experience of doing something—that we experience bliss.

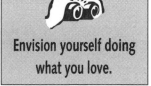
Envision yourself doing
what you love.

> Something emerged from my observations of artists at work. What impressed me was how totally involved the artists became with what was transpiring on canvas. An almost hypnotic trance seemed to seize them as they struggled to give shape to their vision. When a painting was beginning to get interesting they could not tear themselves away from it; they forgot hunger, social obligations, time, and fatigue so that they could keep moving it along. But this fascination lasted only as long as a picture remained unfinished; once it stopped changing and growing, the artist usually leaned it against a wall and turned his or her attention to the next blank canvas. . . . What was so enthralling about painting was not the anticipation of a beautiful picture, but the process of painting itself.
>
> Mihaly Csikszentmihalyi
> *The Evolving Self*

To uncover your values and what is meaningful to you, examine your experiences, the things that you love to do. Take the first item on your list of 20 things you love doing, mentally relive a time when you were doing it, and notice how you feel. Close your eyes and bring the time when you were doing the thing you loved into your mind's eye. It helps to think of your imagination as a "Mental Theater" with a screen where you can watch the movie, just as in a movie theater. When you close your eyes, the "Viewing Screen" is on the inside of your eyelids or the backside of your forehead. Project the memory of you doing what you love to do onto the Viewing Screen and rerun it. Then project yourself *into* the scene you are reviewing. Try to make it as vivid as possible. Some people can actually "see" the memory, as in a dream. If you can, that is good. If you can't, imagine what it would be like if you could. The important thing is to put yourself *into* the memory. Just enjoy reliving the memory of doing what you loved. Stop and let the memory go.

Calibrate bliss reading.

Notice how you feel. Using a rating scale where 1 represents very low bliss and 10 represents very high bliss, rate how you felt when reliving the first activity on your list. Record the bliss rating next to the activity on your list of things you love doing. If the Compass indicates a burnout reading, write "burnout" in the rating column and cross the activity off the list. This is rare since we don't generally like activities that feel like burnout.

Be careful that you don't rate activities as you "should" rate them. Instead, notice how your Heart responds. Does it resonate? Do you flow? Check your Compass. How do you feel while reliving an activity you love doing? Repeat this process with each item on your list of things you love to do. Take your time. Relax by taking several deep breaths between items to clear your mind.

LOOK FOR CLUES TO YOUR VALUES

Values aren't always obvious. Fortunately, activities that you love doing hold clues to your values. For example, Tamara loves working in the community pottery center and goes there every chance she gets. It would be easy to assume that she values creativity or working with her hands. But when she probed what she loved about working at the center she discovered, although she enjoyed creating with her hands, what was most satisfying was the intellectual and political debates she had with the other potters. It takes a bit of detective work and a lot of persistence to root out the values satisfied by an activity you love doing.

Start with activities having the highest bliss rating. Bring the memory back into your mind and relive the activity, making it as vivid as you can. When you feel the bliss, ask your Heart, "What do I love about this?" Rather

Use your inner Eye to "see" your values.

than listening for words, use your inner Eye, to *see* the answer. Look for clues to what contributes to the feeling of flow. As you *see* answers, ask your Heart again, "What do I love about this?" Or "What about this feels good?" "What about this really matters?" "What's working for me here?" The answers are clues that reveal your values. Write the clues down in your journey log or notebook. Repeat this process with other activities on the list of things you love doing that have high bliss ratings. As you zero in on factors associated with your bliss, your Heart tool's sensitivity will increase.

LOOK FOR PATTERNS AND SURPRISES

"See" patterns.

Review the clues. This is where it helps to have written the clues down so that you can read them over, looking for patterns. What common threads do you find? How do the clues fit together? What doesn't fit? What surprises are there? Try to *see* the patterns with your inner Eye. Write your observations down in your journey log or notebook.

ARTICULATE YOUR VALUES

Review the patterns you discovered. What do they reveal about your values? Describe who you are by weaving the patterns and surprises into a brief story. Use phrases like, "I enjoy," "I value," "_____ is important to me," "I derive meaning from _____." Write this story down in your log book, so that you can come back to it whenever you feel like it.

Remember, identifying your values helps you be clear about what matters when making choices. Then setting goals is easier. Pathfinders look to values for guidance when journeying into new territory because following values is the secret to finding a path with a heart.

JOB FIT

Following a path with a heart will greatly facilitate your performance on the job and your career progress in general. The same is true off the job in community, work and leisure pursuits, even in family activities. When you follow a path with a heart, you'll feel better, achieve more of the results that you seek, and experience more moments of bliss. The secret is to get into an organization and a job that "fits" your values and strengths. When there is a good fit, your values and interests are compatible

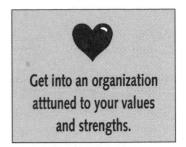

Get into an organization atttuned to your values and strengths.

with those of co-workers, vendors and clients, making it easier to develop cooperative relationships, which is important, because most people rely on the work of others to get their own jobs done.

> People are no longer willing to submerge themselves in a work role which expresses values that differ from or conflict with personal values and lifestyles.
>
> Trudy Heller
> "Authority: Changing Patterns, Changing Times"
> *Transforming Work*

When your work resonates with your values, learning the substance of the job and developing a knowledge base about the industry is easier. When you love what you're doing, you're likely to do well on the job, build credibility with a good track record, develop more and better relationships, and gain access to resources. With such a solid base in place, you can perform even more difficult tasks well.

POOR FIT

Many people get into companies and jobs that do not fit their capabilities and values well, usually because they have not clarified their values, or sometimes because of poor job-hunting strategies. We are encouraged to look for "good" opportunities in terms of income, benefits, and what's acceptable among family and friends. It is easy to overlook the importance of a good fit. Money, glamour, or a clever pitch on the part of a recruiter can seduce you into a poorly fitting job. Other times it is fear that compels us to grab what's available—fear that the alternatives are worse. You can get into a job where the people, products,

Moments of bliss are few in a poorly fitting job.

and services don't really excite you. Working in an industry that is out of sync with your interests makes learning about it a chore and, therefore, more difficult. When you don't share many of the interests and values of the people around you, developing cooperative relationships is harder. These pitfalls can be avoided by identifying the values of the company where you now work, so that you can assess your fit.

The work we do is one of the most obvious areas where our values may be in conflict with our actions, but it is by no means the only one. In Jim's case, something he once loved doing became a chore. As a businessman in his late 30s, Jim spent a lot of his free time volunteering for the local Rotary Club. For nearly a decade, his involvement was rewarding. After his son was born, Jim wanted to spend more time with his family, but he still felt compelled to donate some time to the Rotarians. This went on for a year, until Jim, got in touch with what was important to him today—spending more time with his son. He decided to tell the Rotary Club he no longer wished to be as active within the organization as he once was. Some of his long-time associates and friends took the news a little sadly, but Jim was pleasantly surprised to find they understood the importance of his family and encouraged him to do what he felt was important. His friends encouraged Jim to be true to his values.

Vickie worked as a literacy teacher between her junior and senior years of college, and she felt very good about the work she was doing. When she graduated the Center offered her a permanent position. But Vickie dreamed of being an environmental specialist and accepted the job for the summer only. For a few weeks, she felt as if she were a "bad" and "selfish" person for wanting to quit her literacy work. Then she realized that although helping people to read was still important to her, her future was important, too. She was able to clearly identify her values and act on them, allowing her summer to be far more blissful than it would have been if she had kept working when her heart wasn't in it. Being true to her values helped Vickie avoid burnout and experience moments of bliss instead.

IDENTIFY COMPANY CULTURE

Whether weak or strong, culture has a powerful influence throughout an organization; it affects practically everything— from who gets promoted and what decisions are made, to how employees dress and what sports they play.
Terrence Deal and Allen Kennedy
Corporate Cultures: The Rites and Rituals of Corporate Life

Most people spend most of their waking hours on the job working for a company, so most people will find a path with a heart within the company where they work. For this reason, the discussion of group culture and how it affects individual members will focus on the traditional work environment, the corporation. But these principles are by no means unique to companies. They apply equally to all groups, including social, political, recreational, even familial. If your con-

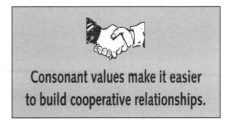

Consonant values make it easier to build cooperative relationships.

cern is with a nonwork situation, then substitute "club," "committee," "union," or "group" for "corporation," "company," and "organization" in the following pages.

Just as you have a heart so does the company. That is, culture reflects corporate values. Conflict and bad fit are more common reasons for being fired or pushed out than poor performance is. Like corporate tribes, each company has its own unique culture. When you choose a company you're choosing a way of life and a clan. If you don't fit in, it's

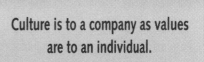

Culture is to a company as values are to an individual.

easy to rub people the wrong way, and after that you'll have trouble getting support, because co-workers will be less inclined to cooperate with you. Some may even sabotage your efforts.

When there is a poor fit between your values and the culture of the company where you work, a vicious negative cycle of declining performance can develop, because when values conflict, it is harder to build cooperative relationships with others in the company. Without coopera-

Check your center.

tion, it is difficult to perform well, which makes it harder to develop a good track record. This, in turn, erodes confidence and self-esteem, which predisposes you to job burnout and declining performance. Both the Compass and the Heart help you tell if your job fit is good or poor. When the fit is good, the Compass will point to bliss, and your Heart will resonate.

You get to the heart of the company by studying its culture, much as an anthropologist would. An anthropologist studies the culture of a primitive tribe by observing what the tribesmen do and say, looking for patterns and generalizations. The culture of a corporation is studied in the same way. Basic concepts and beliefs of an organization reflect values which form the heart of the corporate culture. They reveal what is considered right or wrong in the company and the way in which things get done.

An organization's values can be identified by examining practices and operations through observation and asking questions. Outsiders, such as consultants and vendors, and newcomers often find it easier to see uniqueness and patterns from the outside than do long-time insiders. As one becomes acculturated, it becomes increasingly difficult to observe the culture.

AUDIT THE CORPORATE CULTURE

Survey the way the company does things.

Within a large company, departments usually have their own subcultures. When you are contemplating a move, whether to a new company or to a different department within your company, conducting an audit of its culture as part of your decision process can prevent culture shock. If you're considering a move to a new community, joining a new volunteer association, or enrolling in a club, auditing its culture is equally important. Observe what people do and say, as an anthropologist would. Avoid value judgments. Count and record events and behaviors, then look for patterns and inconsistencies. Look for myths and rituals. Find out about accepted protocol. Pay particular attention to the heroes and

role models. Stories about these people reveal what is valued in this culture. Identify the power structures and communication networks. Look for the buzzwords. The questions listed in the table that follows are those an anthropologist would ask to uncover company values.

The question that always comes up is, "How can I find out all this about a company without first taking the job?" Or about a business association without first joining. The answer is to read catalogs and brochures. Be attentive while in the reception area waiting for your interview appointment. Read bulletin boards. What are the furniture and interior decorating like? Do they make you sign in and wear a badge? How does the receptionist greet people and answer the phone? Talk to friends and acquaintances who have worked for the company. With an association, ask if you can attend one of their events. Watch and listen. Get members' cards and follow up with phone calls to discuss what the association does, they way they do it, and how you might fit in.

QUESTIONS THAT REVEAL CORPORATE CULTURE

MYTHS

- What does the company say about itself in reports and promotional literature?
- What have you heard about the company's history?
- What is the vision of the company's future?
- What stories are told?

RITUALS

- What is the average workday like?
- What are the common activities?
- What happens in meetings?
- What are the main events of the year?
- What are the off-hours activities?

MORES

- What are the official rules? Posted rules?
- What are the unwritten do's and don'ts?
- How are transgressions handled?
- What's considered a successful career?
- What are the company's goals?
- What does an employee have to do to get ahead?
- What is rewarded? How? What is punished? How?
- How do people feel about working here?

CUSTOMS

- How do people dress?
- How are friendships formed? Handled?

- How do things get done?
- What is money spent on?
- What emotions are expressed? How?
- What is the physical setting like?
- What do people gossip about?
- How long do people typically stay in a job?

BUZZWORDS AND STORIES

- What is the common jargon?
- What are the company slogans?
- How are outsiders described?
- What stories are told?

COMMUNICATION NETWORKS

- Who talks to whom?
- Who has the boss's ear?
- What are the communications channels?
- Who hangs out with whom?
- Where do employees get together?

POWER STRUCTURES

- Who makes decisions? How?
- Who decides how money is spent?
- What drives the company? Sales? Service? Profits?
- Who gets things done?
- Who are people willing to follow?
- Who do people go to for information?

ROLE MODELS

- Who are the company heroes?
- Who gets ahead?
- Who's popular?

How to Make a Quick Audit

An easy place to begin auditing a organization's culture is by noticing the buzzwords and metaphors commonly used. For example, Stanford University is nicknamed "The Farm" and is also known as "The Country Club." Hewlett Packard, in its earlier days, was called "The Garage." Revenue officers refer to the IRS as "The Service," but outsiders call it "The Tax Man." What images come to mind when you think of a farm? Of a garage? How are these images the same or different? Labels like "The Garage" or "The Service" reveal something about the ambiance of the culture. "The Service," for example, suggests a place where people serve others, whereas "The Garage" suggests a environment filled with tools, and workbenches with exposed ducts and cement floors.

CORPORATE BUZZWORDS REVEAL ITS CULTURE

Hewlett Packard	Stanford University	Internal Revenue Service
• The garage	• The farm	• The service
• Next bench	• Country club	• Tax man
• Team player	• Consensus	• Meet and deal skills
• Individual contributor	• World class	• Firm but fair
• Bill and Dave	• Leland, Jr.	• Big Brother/Uncle Sam
• Total Quality Control (TQC)	• Quality, Service and Productivity (QSP)	• Quality first
• Shared values	• Shared community	• Shared authority
• Hoshin goals		• Service not enforcement

At the IRS, successful Revenue Officers have "meet and deal skills," whereas in Hewlett Packard the emphasis is on "individual contributors" being good "team players." Stanford, on the other hand, expects its staff to "build consensus" and administrators to use "consensus management." Compare "shared values" at HP, "shared community" at Stanford, and "shared authority" at the IRS. These phrases reveal the cultural values of each institution and the expectations placed on their members.

> **Buzzwords and company nicknames reveal a group's culture.**

An audit, like a snapshot, catches a moment in time. As these organizations evolve, their cultures change. For example, as HP became market-driven, the engineering phrase "next bench" was used less frequently. Similarly, as Stanford moved into an era of "repositioning," emphasis on consensus receded. For this reason, it's important to periodically audit your company's culture to find out if your fit with the company's values has changed. With increasing diversity and international focus, company cultures can evolve quite rapidly. If you've been away, such as on assignment, sabbatical, or maternity leave, conducting a quick audit can help you tune into the company's values.

WHAT'S THE STORY

> *Storytellers preserve institutions and their values*
> *by imparting legends of the company to new employees . . .*
> *Storytellers also reveal much about what it takes to get ahead in the*
> *organization.*
> Terrence Deal and Allen Kennedy
> *Corporate Cultures*

Metaphors, or the "picture words," used by a company's staff, especially those in power, are particularly indicative of the company's culture. For example, Steve Jobs, during the development of the Macintosh computer, moved his team to a separate building, called it a "pirate ship," and hoisted a black skull-and-cross bones flag. There are reports that he threatened that those who didn't "get on board" with the program would have to "walk the plank." This metaphor communicated that the MAC developers were expected to be brash, risk-taking buccaneers who break rules and hijack ideas. During the years under John Scully's lead, Apple shed its pirate persona and went main- stream. Nonetheless, the impact of Apple's early identity penetrated the entire industry and lingers on in the vernacular years later. People who copy software without a license are called "pirates." The pirate metaphor reinforced the message communicated by Apple's logo, which is an apple with a bite out of it reminding us that Adam and Eve ate the forbidden fruit of knowledge.

Or consider this: after a period of astonishing growth, the CEO of a large Silicon Valley firm was often heard saying, "We're pissing with the big dogs now!" when referring to his company entering a market dominated by long-established mega-companies. Unwittingly, the CEO's use of a dog metaphor set a tone and sent a message, both inside the company and to outsiders, that competition is a dogfight

> A story has the capacity to powerfully communicate a central value.

over territory. Successful are the big (male) dogs who mark their territory by urinating on the perimeter. When performance didn't meet expectations, employees feared being "chewed out," after having heard of people "leaving with their tails between their legs."

Whether primitive tribe, modern nation, or high-tech corporation, most groups have stories or myths about how they were founded, how

> **Every group has a story.**

they fared during crisis periods and what's right and wrong. Frequently, newcomers and customers are taken aside and told "The Story." For example, when visiting the Banta printing plant, a West Coast independent publisher who was considering using their services was told the story of how the founder, George Banta, had a vision of providing quality textbooks to frontier schools. So he loaded his printing press into a covered wagon and went west to Menasha, Wisconsin where the plant grew into one of the leading book printers in the nation. The story communicated Banta's dedication to the educational value of books and of helping "frontier" publishers.

Deal and Kennedy, authors of *Corporate Cultures,* relay a popular IBM story. Thomas Watson, Jr., son of the founder, often told about a bird watcher who put feed out at a local pond for the wild ducks heading south. With this feed available, some ducks took to wintering on the

pond. Eventually they grew fat and flew less and less. Watson ended the story by pointing out that you can tame wild ducks but, once they are tamed, you can't make them wild again. This story was told and retold within IBM. Watson's message was that IBM needs its "wild ducks" and should not try to tame them.

Identify Your Company's Stories

Stories and metaphors embody the values of the culture. Stories reveal how the company sees employees and customers as well as what is rewarded or punished. Stories communicate what is important and how we do things around here. Listen for metaphors and the particular ways that people describe the company or group in question. For example, when consulting with GTE Strategic Systems I noticed phrases like "in the trenches people," "he's a Hitler," "the rank and file," "the tank," and "the room was filled with bunk desks." Taken together the phrases suggest a military tone in the culture, which was not too surprising, since many of the managers were retired military personnel.

You don't get the stories and anecdotes by asking directly, "What is the myth?" "What is the story?" If you do, people will surely clam up. Use the indirect approach by asking about the company or group and how it "should" be. Also ask the person you're interviewing how he or she got to be in the group. Remember to listen for the little stories that are told just by way of example. Stories told by many different people are particularly significant. They are the ones that convey important messages about the culture. Specific data and information are of interest only insofar as they establish the context for the story.

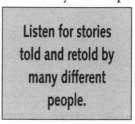

Listen for stories told and retold by many different people.

You can tell when a person begins telling "a story," because it is almost always signaled by a shift in body position. At first the person may be slouching or sitting stiffly in a chair, but when the story begins, the person will usually lean forward as if to engage you, the listener, and will become more emotionally expressive, moving arms about, eyes lighting up, smiling, and speaking in a voice singing with emotion.

ASSESSING YOUR FIT

When your company's values are compatible with your values, the fit tends to be good. When fit is good your Heart tool resonates. Things important to the company are probably important to you, too. Working toward the company's goals is likely to provide a means for working toward your own goals. The way things are done around the company is generally compatible with the way you do things. Flowing is easier, and

**Envision being
in the situation.**

blissful moments come more often. You don't find
yourself in a tug-of-war.

If you've clarified your values and conducted
an audit of your company or group, you are now
able to assess your fit with the Heart tool. Your
imagination or Mental Theater is a good place to
start. Imagine being in a typical situation that exemplifies the way things
are done in the organization. Strive to make the scenario vivid in your

Check your center.

mind. Focus on those aspects of the situation that
reflect what usually occurs. Check your Compass.
Notice how you respond. Are you in bliss or in
burnout? Check your Heart. Is it in tune and resonating? Company values that promote flow experi-
ences are compatible; those associated with burnout experiences are
incompatible. Repeat this exercise with several situations.

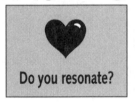

Do you resonate?

The final step in assessing fit is weighing compatible and incompatible values. No situation will
be a perfect fit. If the incompatible value has a
relatively low priority, it probably won't interfere
with your fit in the group. Conversely, there may be
many value compatibilities and still a poor overall fit if one or two of the
incompatibilities touch on central values. For example, Lois loved her
job as an account executive with a major advertising firm, because it
enabled her to interact with many stimulating corporate leaders and to
draw on her creativity. Nonetheless, she found herself in conflict with her
department head. She felt that many of the ad campaigns were demean-
ing to women and often she said so. Regretfully, Lois quickly became
isolated, and things deteriorated from there. Had she collected information about the company from press releases, talked with people knowledgeable about the company and conducted a "Corporate Culture
Audit" before joining the firm, she might have avoided a painful experience that damaged her career.

Based on your understanding of the corporate culture, rate the
importance to the company of each value you identified. A good fit is
indicated when the company's high-ranking values are compatible with

your values and when company values that are incompatible with yours are low-ranking. When incompatible values are high-ranking among the corporate values, the fit is probably poor.

YOUR PATH TO BLISS

It's the journey that counts, because, as Don Juan said, all paths lead nowhere. When the path you follow makes for a joyful journey, it is a good path for you. A path with a heart is one that provides meaning for you and en-ables you to play out your values. Finding and following the path with a heart is an ongoing process because you change. What was good for you ten years ago may not be so good now.

Developing your Heart tool involves clarify-ing your values. The more that you know what is important to you, the easier it is to make satisfying choices and to find your path. Using your Com-pass to read your reactions is vital in developing

Read reactions.

your Heart, and as your Heart grows, you will find that your values fit within a larger context. Your values are inexorably intertwined with the third tool, your Mission.

CHAPTER 5

MISSION

DEFINING YOUR PURPOSE

We can find meaning and reward
by serving some higher purpose
than ourselves—a shining purpose . . .
The problems before us may be different,
but the key to solving them remains the same:
it is the individual, the individual who steps forward.

President George Bush

$\mathcal{E}$ngaging in meaningful activities promotes bliss. Activities that provide meaning do so by engaging your values, what you feel is important. When your activities are important, you're doing something that makes a difference. You are infused with a sense of purpose, which lifts you above the mundane and dreary. Even if activities

A Mission is a driving purpose, a reason for being.

are repetitive or menial, you perceive them in the larger picture of "making a difference." With this mental attitude, bliss comes easily. By the same token, meaningfulness buffers you from burnout. Few people can sustain a "Why bother?" attitude when they believe they are doing something important. Pathfinders use the Mission tool to create meaning. Without meaning in your pursuit, it is unlikely that you will find a path with a heart.

WHAT IS A MISSION?

Purity of heart is to will one thing.
Søren Kierkegaard

Mission is one of those words we all know, yet have a hard time defining. A mission is more than a goal. It's not something that you set aside at five o'clock. A mission is a cause or crusade. When we hear someone mention "his mission in life," we know it refers to a driving purpose, a reason for being, implying passion and a strong commitment.

Generally a mission involves taking action to do something important and difficult. The person taking on a mission is usually authorized by a higher authority, such as a general, the church, or even God. Consider a military mission, for example, in which a general sends a combat team out on a night bomb run. Missionaries who are sent by the church to foreign lands to save the heathen is another example. In both examples a difficult assignment was made by a higher authority to accomplish something risky but important for the greater good. Remember the TV series "Mission: Impossible"? The voice on the tape says, "Your mission, if you choose to accept it, is . . . ." Here a mission is an assignment one can accept or reject. Other times, a mission is a "calling," perhaps by God, to a special task or purpose for which a person is destined in life, such as to serve the poor or to communicate peace through art.

**PATHFINDER'S
MISSION**

Acting
with enthusiasm
and authority
to engage one's values
in accomplishing
an important purpose
of the enterprise.

There is a lot in the definition of the Pathfinder's Mission. "Acting" is the first part; it means taking action, going out, doing something. "With enthusiasm" refers to passion. The Pathfinder's Mission is not simply a goal, but something that you feel strongly about achieving because it "engages one's values." Pursuing a Mission provides meaning, because you're doing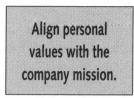

something worthwhile and important. "And authority," as you'll discover later in this chapter, means that *you give yourself authority* to act. The final portion of the Pathfinder's Mission is "accomplishing an important purpose of the enterprise." As you'll discover, *the key is to align your personal values with your company's mission* so that you become a partner with your employer and begin working for yourself to accomplish something important to you and your company.

THE PURPOSE OF THE ENTERPRISE

How the people in an organization define the nature of their business can have a tremendous impact on what they do and how they do it. When the Southland Corporation realized that their 7/11 stores were not really in the "grocery" business, but rather in the "convenience" business, it led them to an entirely different marketing strategy and inventory for their stores.
William Miller
The Creative Edge

Have you ever noticed how birds flying in a flock can suddenly change direction in unison? If you're like me, you've wondered how they do it. I doubt that there is a lead bird with a radio microphone telling the flock which way to turn. A flock of birds is the image that comes to mind when I think of the challenge facing companies. Today companies must change direction quickly, as the birds do. The employees, now called "individual contributors," must fly together while quickly changing direction with little guidance or central coordination. In a sense, compa-

nies are trying to achieve what the birds seem to do naturally: individual birds flying in unison.

An organization's mission can help its staff to fly together. It is the group's statement of purpose and says to its members, "We are going *that way.*" Individuals needing direction can look to the mission to discover which way to fly. All too often, however, when a company member is asked, "What is this group's mission?" the reply is; "Mission?"

If your company (or work group, association, union) hasn't articulated a clear mission, it can be difficult to align your efforts with its goals, and you may not know in which direction to fly. Don't let this stop you. You will have to muddle along like a lot of others. Remember, you are inventing your job and helping to re-invent your company. So if your department hasn't put forth a clear mission, make your best guess.

> **A Mission is a powerful tool for providing direction.**

When a company member is asked, "What is the purpose of the enterprise?" "To make money" is a stereotypic answer. But few companies exist solely to make money. Money comes from the pursuit of a mission to provide a service or to fill a need. In other words, making money is necessary for the company to exist and prosper, but it is rarely the overriding purpose for its existence.

UNCOVERING AN ORGANIZATION'S MISSION

You can uncover an organization's mission by asking its members questions about the reason for the group's existence, what it hopes to accomplish and who it serves. The organization's purpose is evolving and changing; so the question, "What is my company's purpose?" ("What is this project's purpose?" "What is this

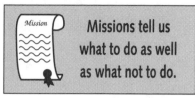

Missions tell us what to do as well as what not to do.

association's purpose?" "What is this team's purpose?") is one you should return to often. The answer will help you to keep on course, despite change.

Identify people who you think understand the organization's purpose and whom you have an opportunity to talk to. When it is your company that is the focus of your inquiry, for example, you might talk to your manager, the division head, your team leader, co-workers, people in other departments, vendors, clients, and customers. When the opportunity arises, ask each the following questions: What is my company's purpose? What is the major reason why my company exists? What is my company expected to accomplish? Who does my company serve? You can ask the same questions about your department or work team within a company, or about a volunteer program, or even about recreational groups like the swim team. Although the words company, corporation and organization are used, the principles can be applied to any group of which you are a member.

QUESTIONS THAT UNCOVER AN
ORGANIZATION'S MISSION

What is the organization's purpose?
What is the major reason why the organization exists?
What is the organization expected to accomplish?
Whom does my organization serve?

Analyze the Organization's Literature

Often the organization's mission is spelled out explicitly in the Annual Report. Sometimes it is called the "Corporate Philosophy" or the "Corporate Objectives." When there is no specific mission statement, you'll have to deduce it. Look over newsletters and promotional material including product ads and program announcements. Listen to speeches by the organization's leaders, such as a CEO, association president, departmental directors, and other executives. What messages do they give about the organization's overriding purpose? Phrases like "quality," "fast service," "improve lifestyle," "highest-quality health care," "latest technology," "better living through chemistry," "support the First Amendment, "aid the downtrodden," and "expect excellence" provide clues to the organization's mission. Look for words used repetitively or with special emphasis.

Review the words you've collected and the opinions you received from the people you polled. Patterns and themes in these words point to the organization's mission. Spend time on identifying the organization's mission. Make it an adventure. In a sense, you are an anthropologist. Keep a log where you can jot down observations and thoughts. Remember, organizations are alive, evolving beings. They keep changing. Hence you'll need to update your conclusions periodically.

> Organizations are alive, evolving beings.

The company mission is a powerful tool for providing direction. For example, Pacific Bell was formed out the divestiture of AT&T in the mid-1980s. Being a new company it issued statements of its purpose. "Our Commitments" were listed in a document called *Blueprint*. One of PacBell's six commitments was: "We are creative, can-do people. We have the freedom to act and innovate to meet our customers' needs as though each of us owned the business. Strategy guides our direction; sound judgment guides our daily execution. We take prudent risk and are each accountable for our actions."

Based upon this and similar formal position statements Elaine, in the special sales department, got an idea. She had read one of my books and attended a couple of my lectures and felt others in her department could benefit from the material. Elaine wanted to bring me in for a training session called "Managing Yourself For Excellence" but she had no budget and getting approval was a complicated process.

Thinking about the commitment that promised each PacBell employee "the freedom to act and innovate as if one owned the business," Elaine wondered what she would do if she really did own the business. Elaine arranged for a special day-long training session in her home. She and about fifteen others "signed out for San Ramon." San Ramon was the site of the new corporate offices, about 35 miles away from the San Francisco facility. The travel back and forth made it difficult to track where someone was at any particular time. Instead of going to San Ramon, everyone met at Elaine's house. Normally, such a session would be costly, but the idea of a staff of people from the phone company playing hooky to get professional training was so intriguing that she convinced me to do it gratis. Elaine had taken seriously statements that PacBell issued and so she acted as if she owned the company.

IDENTIFY YOUR PURPOSE

> *A life without a cause is a life without an effect.*
> *Barbarella*

When asked, "What is your job?" most people give a list of tasks: "I type." "I debug," "I supervise," "I sell." Looking at your work as a "job," or worse, as "just a job," is an old-fashioned way of thinking about work. "Doing a job" implies completing a prescribed list of tasks, with the focus being on details and routine: "It's not in my job description," "I'm just doing my job, Ma'am." The implication is that the "whats" and "hows" of the task have been decided by someone else. This approach made sense and worked well in the industrial workplace, where work projects were broken into repetitive pieces and bosses knew more about the process than the workers did.

Today, however, looking at your work as "doing a job" is problematic. Work today is more holistic and not broken into assembly-line pieces.

> **You are inventing your job.**

Chances are you know more about your work than anyone else, including your boss. Most importantly, you are probably doing things in your work that no one has done in your job before you. When you think about it you'll probably realize that you are inventing your job because *you* are deciding the whats and hows of your work. The worst thing about the "just doing a job" mentality is that it tends to encourage an "I'm just putting in time" approach to work in which you don't feel challenged or fully engaged. It is extremely difficult to achieve bliss with such an attitude, because bliss comes when we feel fully involved and engaged. This "putting in time" sort of work rarely engages values, and rarely presents more of a challenge than not getting too bored on the job. If you feel that you're just putting in time at your job, the potential for burnout is high, and the potential for bliss is low.

YOU WERE NOT HIRED TO DO A JOB

You were not hired to do a job. You were hired to solve a problem. At first thought, there may seem to be little difference between "just doing a job" and "solving a problem." But think deeper. Clearly, an

organization hires a person because there is a problem that needs solving. It may be a seemingly minor problem, such as the wastebaskets overflowing and creating a lot of clutter, or a major problem like cost overruns that cut into profitability. Unfortunately, once a position or "job" is defined, it tends to take on a life of its own. When incumbents leave, jobs tend to be refilled without reevaluation. As a result, outmoded, possibly irrelevant, lists of tasks tend to become fixed jobs.

Virtually any job can be revitalized by reframing it as a problem you're responsible for solving. What you'll discover is that your new prospective is empowering and sets the stage for innovation. This transformation is a critical step toward discovering your purpose in the enterprise. Having a purpose generates a sense of meaningfulness and feelings of satisfaction because the organization is relying on *you* to accomplish something important.

THREE BRICKLAYERS

During construction of the Notre Dame Cathedral a bishop was surveying the progress when he noticed three bricklayers. Curious, he asked the first man, who was scowling, what he was doing. Without raising his eyes, he answered gruffly, "I'm laying bricks." When the bishop asked the second bricklayer the same question, the man looked up briefly to say, "I'm building a wall." When the third man was asked what he was building, he smiled broadly and with obvious pride said, "I'm building a cathedral!"

Finding your purpose encourages looking beyond repetitive tasks and routine details to see the larger picture, one where you play an important role. Take the duties of a receptionist, which is often considered to be a position of little consequence, as an example. When asked, "What is your job?" the receptionist is likely to say, "I answer the phone, schedule appointments, and tell my boss when visitors arrive." Sounds boring, with little room for creativity.

> Look to the larger picture— the meta-level.

Without a receptionist, however, other staff must leave their work to greet, screen, and route people who call or come to the office. Clients wander into private meetings; patients interrupt doctors' examinations. Customers leave in a huff because there is no one to help them. Phones ring endlessly until prospective clients go elsewhere. Receptionists are needed to solve these problems.

The receptionist creates that critical first impression as customers enter the company. A good first impression can lead to a sale; a bad impression could turn a customer away forever.

Consequently, receptionists can set the stage for the sales staff. Clearly, the receptionist's actions are vitally important to the company.

Similarly, accountants, marketing directors, and CEOs all exist in the company to solve particular problems. Unfortunately, many employees as well as many employers have lost touch with this fact. When work was so specialized that a person did nothing but screw on a widget, it was difficult to see the bigger picture. Bureaucratic paper pushing often obscures the real purpose for being hired.

Solving the problem you were hired to solve is the purpose the company is relying on *you* to fulfill. When Queen Isabella sent Columbus

to find the New World, she didn't tell him what route to follow. Columbus was an explorer and she relied on him to discover the way. The same process goes on in pathfinding. You have a mission from the company and it is up to you to chart your route. Question tasks that you routinely complete. You may be spending a lot of time doing busywork that has little to do with solving the problem you were hired to solve.

WHAT IS THE PROBLEM YOU WERE HIRED TO SOLVE?

As basic as this question sounds, the answer is not always obvious, especially if you have been focusing on tasks rather than the big picture. One way to get a picture of the problem you were hired to solve is to imagine what would happen if no one did your job. Try to imagine what would happen if the problem assigned to you went unsolved. Exaggerating can help in calling out the problem. For example, a custodian who attended one of my workshops pictured unemptied wastebaskets overflowing. Papers were knee deep everywhere so that people could not walk around the office. The bathrooms were filthy and repulsive. It suddenly became clear to him that he was fulfilling an important purpose. If nobody dealt with the custodial problems, eventually it would be impossible for anyone to work there.

See the Problem

Close your eyes and relax by breathing in and out slowly and deeply. In your imagination picture a movie screen on the inside of your forehead. Use your Vision tool to project your workspace onto the screen. Like an anthropologist observing a foreign culture, observe *yourself in your workspace.* Ask yourself: "Why does my company employ me? Why am I here? What would happen if no one were doing

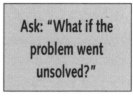

Ask: "What if the problem went unsolved?"

my job? What would happen if no one were solving the problem I was hired to solve? What would happen if the problem that I'm here to solve were left unsolved?" The objective in asking these questions is to get a picture of the black hole, of the problem itself.

"See" the problem occurring on your mental screen. It helps to exaggerate the problem. Study what you see. How does the problem affect others? What secondary problems are caused by your problem going unsolved? Identify those spin-off problems and watch them occurring. Follow these problem-causing chains out to the end. What happens? How does the problem being left unsolved affect the overall organization?

Imagine what would happen by "seeing" the problem occur.

How does your problem being unsolved affect customers? Repeat this exercise several times, until you get a clear picture of the problem you were hired to solve.

Problem versus Solution

Make sure you focus on the problem you were hired to solve, the solution you've been implementing. For example, John, an association librarian, described his problem as "organizing and cataloging reports and other vital documents." Organizing and cataloging are not problems. They are actions or procedures John used to solve problems of disorganization. The problem John needed to solve was that the reports and documents were in chaos; so the librarians could not find them quickly enough. Looking beyond the immediate problem, he could see that because reports were often misplaced, association executives were not adequately briefed and lost credibility; this situation led to lost membership and declining treasury balance. From this vantage point, John's job took on greater meaning, as he began to see that he was playing a significant part in fulfilling an important purpose of the enterprise.

State the Problem You Were Hired to Solve

Try to articulate the problem that is your domain. Describe what would happen if nobody did your job and nobody dealt with the problem

Transform tasks into challenging problems matched to your ability.

assigned to you. Emphasize the major, overall problem. Keep working on this description until you can succinctly complete the statement, "The problem I was hired to solve is to. . . ."

If you're like people who come to my training workshops, in studying the problem you were hired to solve, you will see that your purpose is quite important and affects many others, perhaps the entire organization. You may begin to see your job as an evolving process, not a static set of routine tasks. You may discover that your work holds opportunities for creativity, because your job is not just a series of predetermined tasks, but a problem you are mandated to solve.

Knowing that you are fulfilling an important purpose of the enterprise is motivating for most people. The company is relying on *you* to fulfill the purpose assigned to you. This sense of being significant promotes self-esteem, adding to job satisfaction.

When you think of your work as problems to solve rather than tasks to complete, you dramatically increase your bliss potential. By definition problems pose a challenge. You'll recall from Chapter One that challenge is the flow channel. When the challenge matches your ability the conditions are set for bliss. When the challenges are meaningful and engage your values, bliss potential increases even more. The final bliss promoting condition is personal power. When you define your work in terms of problems that the company is depending upon you to solve, you demonstrate personal power, at the same time that you enhance it. By looking at your work, not as a "job," but as a problem you're being relied upon to solve, you can change a ho-hum job into one with many bliss-filled moments.

ENGAGE YOUR VALUES

> *The exciting thing about work today is that there is a growing compatibility between the needs of people and the needs of the companies in the Information Society.*
> John Naisbitt
> *Megatrends 2000*

Key in developing a Pathfinder's Mission is figuring out a way to engage your values while accomplishing an important purpose of the enterprise. Most people want meaning from their activities, especially their work. We don't want to set aside our personal goals to meet those of the company. Who wants to choose between their personal goals and those of their employer? By using the Heart tool you can match personal goals with the company mis-

Match personal goals with the company's mission.

sion. Remember, the Heart tool works like a tuning fork: when it resonates you are in tune and your heart sings. Remember, we're most likely to experience bliss at work when engaged in meaningful activity that presents a challenge matched to our abilities, and when we feel able to influence it. The trick is to *engage your values in the course of fulfilling your purpose in the organization.* When your goals are aligned with those of the company, you can get personal meaning from working there. Work changes from "a labor" to "a labor of love" when your values are engaged. The likelihood of going into the flow state is increased. You have more moments of bliss. Sustaining enthusiasm is easy, even when the work is difficult or fraught with setbacks.

PATHFINDER'S SLOGAN

Ask not what your company can do for you.
Ask what you and your company
can do together.

The essence of the Mission tool is engaging your values by aligning your personal goals with those of the company, so that your personal and professional lives are congruent, each supporting and promoting the other so that your moments of bliss will be frequent. With the Mission tool you can decide on your direction and generate the passion to begin the journey.

BE A PARTNER

Alignment occurs when organization members act as parts of an integrated whole, each finding the opportunity to express his or her true purpose through the organization's purpose.
Roger Harrison
"Leadership and Strategy for a New Age"
Transforming Work

Stop thinking of yourself as working "for" the company! Instead think of your company as a partner and ask what you can do together. Your company can be a tremendous partner in helping you to accomplish your personal goals and finding a path with a heart. The secret is in aligning your goals with the company's mission.

> **The company's resources are for you to use to solve the problem you were hired to solve.**

Think about your company's resources: equipment, cash flow, talent, special information, technology, staff, expertise, facilities and markets. These resources exist to accomplish its mission. These resources are available to you to accomplish your Mission when your personal goals are aligned with the company mission.

Imagine that you were in business for yourself. To accomplish your business's goals you would have to get certain equipment, staff, and facilities, and you would have to pay for these resources. Because you would need the help of certain experts, like accountants, marketing pros, and designers, you would have to hire consultants. In contrast, when you work with a medium to large company, these resources are available, and you don't have to pay for them. The challenge is getting access to the resources you need to accomplish your Mission. If you need design advice, there is most likely someone on the staff with such advice. You can consult with that person—free of charge. If you need equipment to fulfill your purpose, chances are it is available somewhere in your company and is potentially yours to use. Of course, organizations do tend to put obstacles in your path. They will assign you a purpose and simultaneously prevent you from achieving it. Pathfinders have the Team, Hat, Wand, and other tools for finding ways around obstacles.

■ Cheryl's Story:
Cheryl, a chemist working for a large worldwide medical research and supply firm, complained of burnout and contemplated leaving the field of chemistry. She loved the research but felt that the company was too conservative and structured. She wanted more human interaction and cre-

ativity. Sometimes she fantasized becoming a counselor, at other times of developing a jewelry import business. On the other hand, Cheryl had many good friends in the firm that she hated to leave. And she didn't have any idea how she could match her high salary. Starting over by going back to school seemed like the only way to become a counselor, but realistically, that could take years.

The company's mission emphasized quality: quality products, quality service, and quality work environment. Employees were expected to develop formal "self-improvement goals" and submit them, along with their job-performance goals, to their supervisors. In a step toward her goals, Cheryl signed up for a pathfinding workshop where she developed her Compass and clarified her values (the Heart tool). When Cheryl returned to work, her supervisor noted Cheryl's enthusiasm and asked her to make a presentation to the work team summarizing what she'd learned. Cheryl discovered that sharing the Compass and Heart tools was very stimulating and fulfilling. When a number of co-workers asked for her advice, she began a weekly discussion session about matching personal values with work goals.

Cheryl's discussion sessions helped to achieve the company's mission to enrich the employees' lives and engaged Cheryl's desire to have more creative expression and to help others. Cheryl's frustration changed to enthusiasm. Over time Cheryl's ad hoc role was formalized; she became an internal consultant working with the chemists. She traveled globally from division to division. Cheryl had succeeded in aligning her goals with the company's mission.

■ **Loren's Story:**

Loren is an office manager for a successful, medium-sized accounting firm. Although she drew an impressive salary, Loren constantly dreamed of leaving the firm. She often caught herself daydreaming about a job she had had about ten years earlier when she worked for a video company as a gal friday. Even though she made only minimum wage, she loved the job. The accounting firm was formal and conservative. Loren longed for the intensity, the creativity, and the group brainstorming she had experienced in the video company.

Loren insisted that she would quit in a minute if it were not for her responsibilities. "I have obligations. I have a mortgage, and I have bills," she said over and over. She saw herself as trapped in an either/or dilemma of choosing between security and job satisfaction. The accounting firm's mission included providing quality service to clients. When Loren worked with her Mission tool, she discovered that she could match her personal goals with the accounting firm's mission. Loren proposed that the firm create a video for customers called "How to Get the Best Service from Your CPA." The firm loved the idea. Loren coordinated the project.

AUTHORIZE YOURSELF TO ACT

> *In many big companies it is easy to spend a year asking for permission to begin. Intrapreneurs don't ask permission, they just begin.*
> Gifford Pinchot, III
> *Intrapreneuring*

You are the most important aspect of the Pathfinding Mission. When you know your purpose, you don't wait for your boss or some other higher authority to tell you what to do. Your purpose, the mission the organization has mandated as yours, is the problem you were hired to solve. When you have a clear picture of this problem you don't have to be told to start. You can authorize yourself to act because you know your purpose. *You* can send yourself out to accomplish an important purpose of your department or organization.

Jobs evolve. Maybe the last person in your job didn't have a lot of imagination and expanded the details. You don't have to stick to that. When you get a very clear understanding of the problem you were hired to solve, you can redefine your job into something more vital and exciting. For example, when I worked as a social worker with men in the county jail, I realized that my purpose was, in part, to help with their transition back into society. With this in mind, I began a database of services and freebies helpful for these men. Additionally, I invited service providers from other agencies to meet in my office to share information. The person who had had the job before me did not do these things, and no one assigned them to me. I authorized myself to act and then I acted. Not only did it make my job more interesting for me, I became more effective in helping the men integrate back into society.

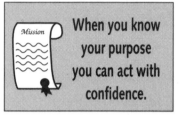

When you know your purpose you can act with confidence.

Your Mission statement is an articulation of your purpose, the problem you were hired to solve. Remember that a mission is authorized. In pathfinding you authorize yourself. Confidence to self-authorize comes from having carefully analyzed the problem you were hired to solve. This knowledge is empowering. You don't have to wait to be told what to do, because you know your purpose. Like the birds, you know which way to fly.

CHANGING CAREERS AND STARTING A BUSINESS

> *Job satisfaction and fulfillment come from the inside out,*
> *not the other way around.*
>   Barbara Braham
>   *Finding Your Purpose*
>   *Learning How to Follow Your Heart*

Perhaps you've decided to make a change to a new career. Maybe you're bored or burned out. Perhaps you've plateaued and feel that you've done everything in your current career and there is nowhere to go. Maybe you've concluded that you've been in the wrong field all along. Or perhaps, you want more adventure. There are many reasons for wanting to change careers.

■ **Alex's Story:**

Alex loved planes. As a boy he would sit for hours on a hill near the airport, watching the planes take off and land. Years later, when he was the general manager of a large metropolitan airport, he couldn't understand why he hated to go to work. Sure there were planes all around, but the excitement was gone. His days were filled with struggles with unions, regulations, threats of terrorism, lawsuits, meetings and reports. When he finally dragged himself out of the office, he had to face over an hour of freeway traffic jams on the way home.

Alex longed for a new life. He began dreaming of being far away from it all. Eventually, he had to force himself to go to the airport. Finally, he resigned, sold his home, and moved to a small town 150 miles away. His wife had to relocate her business. His kids had to transfer to a new school.

For the first several months Alex loved doing simply nothing. But eventually, he felt the necessity to get back to work. But what was a high-powered executive to do in a small rural town? He assessed his skills and concluded that perhaps he could teach. Alex signed on as a substitute for grades 7 to 12 and took courses at night to get his credentials. A year later he was hired to teach math and history.

The money wasn't great, but he enjoyed working with the kids. It didn't take long for the other teachers to discover Alex's administrative abilities. He was drafted for committees. One thing led to another, and Alex found himself the

principal. The school budget was small, the teachers com-
plained that the pay was inadequate, and the PTA com-
plained that the kids were being shortchanged. It all seemed
so similar to the old days at the airport. Alex wondered
where he had gone wrong and why job satisfaction was so
difficult to obtain.

Alex made a mistake that many people desiring to change careers make. His motivation was rooted in avoiding an unfulfilling situation rather than seeking to accomplish a satis-

> **If you don't know where you want to go you probably won't get there.**

fying purpose. Alex's avoidance motivation paid off. He succeeded in getting away from the stresses of a big-city airport and urban life, but because he didn't engage in seeking motivation he didn't establish a direction to move toward. He didn't have a Mission. Consequently he was led by the desire *not* to be on the freeway and *not* to have administrative hassles. Without direction he was pulled along by the needs of the other teachers and the school district.

Alex's experience is a common one. Nurses often get so burned out that, in an effort to get away from a bad hospital situation, they leave nursing, for example. The danger is throwing the proverbial baby out with the bath water.

ASK: WHAT IS THE PROBLEM I WANT TO SOLVE?

The important question to ask when changing careers or going into

> **Check your center.**

business for yourself is: What problem do I *want* to solve? Answering this question can be difficult and takes time. Use your Compass and Heart tools. As often as not, people discover that they are already working on the problem they want to solve. Alex had a life-long love for airplanes. He might have discovered that private airplanes landing at big airports were a serious hazard to airlines and could have embraced a mission to improve airport safety, for example. This might have lead him to become a consultant,

Does your Heart sing?

working with airport managers and the Federal Aviation officials. Alternatively, Alex may have decided that he was seriously concerned about the decline in science competency among secondary-school students and taken on himself the mission of stimulating student interest in science. Having set such a direction for himself, he would not have been so easily seduced back into administration by the needs of the teachers and the school district.

CHOOSING YOUR MISSION

When contemplating a new career or going into business for yourself, you would be wise to first decide on a purpose you can commit to achieving. Begin by identifying important purposes that you've fulfilled in the past. Brainstorm problems you might

See yourself.

work on. Make a list of all the possibilities you can conjure up. Use your imagination to evaluate each possibility. One at a time, bring the purpose or problem to mind and project it onto the movie screen in your imagination. Put yourself into the picture. *See* yourself working on the problem. Check your Compass. How does it feel? Like bliss or like burnout? Does working on the problem engage your values? Check your Heart. Is it in tune and resonating?

Choosing a Mission can be difficult. You are setting a direction for yourself, deciding on the course of your life. Give yourself time to think things through. Follow the exercise described earlier in this chapter, and write down a tentative problem you want to solve. Then set it aside; come back to it later and repeat the analysis. Do you come

Find a need and fill it.

up with the same problem? Perhaps after some time and reflection it feels different. Set it aside again and come back to it later. Repeat the analysis as many times as necessary. Don't let yourself be driven by escapist motivation and desires to get away. Stick with it and set a positive course for your future.

OTHER BENEFITS OF IDENTIFYING YOUR PURPOSE

Most jobs need periodic alteration. Unfortunately, what usually happens is that more tends to be added to a job, but very little is taken away. When we are caught up in daily demands, it can be very difficult to distinguish between aspects of the job that are vital to solving the problem we were hired to solve and aspects that have become mere habitual routines. Consequently, we find ourselves having too much to do and not enough time to do it. Articulating your purpose provides an objective basis for demonstrating to your supervisor that certain aspects of your job should be altered. Some activities may no longer be needed and should be dropped.

Identifying the problem you are hired to solve can help considerably. It provides a standard by which you can measure what is important and what is no longer needed. If you need to get a supervisor's approval for dropping certain aspects of your work so that you can better handle the new things, you will have a solid argument when you can point to the impact a particular activity does or doesn't have on solving the problem you were hired to solve.

Similarly, being able to look to the problem you were hired to solve provides a means for identifying busywork, setting priorities, and allocating your time and other resources. It provides you with a direction, so that you don't run amok. Even when you get little direction from your supervisor, you can proceed with confidence when you have a clear understanding of the problem you were hired to solve. It becomes easier to communicate your role to co-workers when you present it in terms of the problem you were hired to solve. This is especially true when co-workers have a good understanding of their own problem assignments.

YOUR PATHFINDING MISSION

Having a Pathfinding Mission is empowering. When you know your purpose, the problem you were hired to solve, you have the confidence to act, and need not wait to be told what to do. You can shed the demoralizing "I'm just doing my job" mentality to become a self-starter and a self-leader following a path to your bliss.

When you have a Mission, you have a basis for making decisions about what to do. Using sports vernacular, the problem you were hired to solve is "the ball." "Keep your eye on the ball" and you'll always know which way to go. Once you've articulated your Mission, then you're ready to develop a Vision, a picture of where you are going, your destination.

CHAPTER 6

VISION
SEEING YOUR DESTINATION

Some men see things as they are and ask, "Why?"
I dream of things that could be and ask, "Why not?"
Robert Kennedy

I have a dream. I have seen the promised land.
Martin Luther King, Jr.

$\mathcal{V}$ision is a mental picture of a desirable future. For pathfinders a Vision serves as a point on the horizon. With Vision, you can build a bridge between your Mission and the future you want to create—a picture of your bliss. Your Vision is a picture of an outcome you seek, an end product, the results you want to achieve. It is an overriding goal from which more immediate goals and a plan of action can be derived.

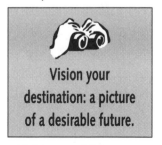

Vision your destination: a picture of a desirable future.

Your Vision is an image of how you want things to be, and provides a basis for deciding how you want to grow or evolve. It can span years, and serves to keep you focused on the future. Having a picture of the end you strive to achieve enables you to translate purpose into doable activities and attainable outcomes.

What matters is not so much what the Vision *is*, but what it *does*. Vision opens your creative potential and allows you to move beyond current limits and constraints. For one thing, the way things are today is not the way things always have to be. You can imagine an ideal future. Your dreams can be the wellspring of hope and enthusiasm. Having a dream fosters pride, boosting self-respect and self-esteem, all of which are antidotes for burnout and promote bliss. When you have a Vision you exude a sense of commitment and come across as someone who has a direction, that you know where you're going.

LEARNING TO ENVISION

Learning to envision is similar to learning to speak. Although the *ability* to speak is an innate capability, speaking itself must be learned. Forming the sounds and learning the meaning and syntax of language does not come naturally. You must work at it. You've probably heard stories of infants lost in the wilds who were raised by wolves or lions. The children learned to bark or growl but not to speak. Although the idea of children being raised by wild animals is unbelievable, it illustrates a parallel to envisioning. We have the ability to envision, but most of us haven't learned how to use this fantastic and uniquely (so far as we know) human tool. And worse, many of our teachers and schools suppressed, often unwittingly, our natural inclination to envision. If this happened to you, don't despair. You can begin now.

RELAXING HELPS

Nobody knows why, but being in a relaxed state facilitates envisioning. There are lots of techniques for relaxing. Deep breathing is one you can use any time in any place. Breathing slowly and deeply relaxes the body and mind. This may sound elementary, but most of us tend to breathe too shallowly, which creates tension. Practice the following exercise, and you'll be able to relax more deeply.

RELAXATION EXERCISE

Make yourself comfortable: Wiggle around a bit to remove any pressure on your back, legs or other areas. Kick off your shoes. Loosen your belt and any tight clothing.

Breathe in slowly: Close your eyes and take a deep breath while slowly counting to three. Let the air go all the way down into the lowest part of your abdomen. Pause, while holding the breath in. Notice the feeling of fullness.

Exhale slowly: Exhale the air while slowly counting to three again. When the air has gone out, exhale a little more until no more air goes out. Pause. Notice the sensation of airlessness.

Focus attention on your breathing: Continue breathing in and out slowly and deeply to the count of three on the inhales and on the exhales for two or three minutes. Notice how you relax a little as you breathe out. Notice how it feels good to breathe in and out slowly and deeply.

Continue to breathe deeply and slowly: Enjoy the pleasure of feeling relaxed as you breathe in and out slowly and deeply. Continue deep breathing for five or ten minutes.

YOUR MENTAL THEATER

We all have an imagination or Mental Theater, but most of us don't use it purposefully. In fact, scientists have not been able to agree on where imagination actually occurs. But it helps to think of the back of your eyes or the inside of your forehead as a Viewing Screen or Stage. Virtually anything can be projected onto the Screen or created on the Stage. You can sit back and observe action or you can project yourself

Your imagination is like a Mental Theater.

into the image, much as in a dream. But unlike dreams, which seem to come and go on their own, you can orchestrate images on the Viewing

Screen. In your Mental Theater you can create pictures of the future, try them on, see how they feel and rework them. The results can be powerful. The first step is creating your Mental Theater.

GO TO YOUR MENTAL THEATER

Enter your Mental Theater: Simply close your eyes and relax by breathing slowly and deeply. Pretend you are in a screening room like those used by movie producers to watch pre-released films. Imagine a large Viewing Screen on the inside of your forehead. Imagine that the screen is covered by a curtain. If you can actually *see* the curtain, that is good. But if you can't actually see the curtain, simply imagine what it would be like if you did see it.
Observe the curtain: What color is the curtain? What kind of material is it made from? Imagine that you have zoom lenses in your eyes. Zoom up to the curtain. What does it look like close up? Imagine touching the curtain. How does it feel? Sniff the curtain. How does it smell? Zoom out. How does the curtain looks from several feet away? Zoom out again. How does the curtain look from the back of the theater?
Open the curtain: While watching the curtain, continue breathing slowly and deeply. Allow the curtain to open a little each time you breathe out. Just breathe in and out slowly until the curtain is completely open and the Viewing Screen behind it is in view. Notice how calm you feel while looking at the Viewing Screen.
Observe the Screen: How does the Screen look? What kind of material is it made from? Zoom up to the Viewing Screen and touch it. How does it feel? Sniff the Viewing Screen. How does it smell? Zoom out. How does the Viewing Screen look from several feet away? What images or colors do you see on the Viewing Screen? How do you feel while watching the images or colors on the Viewing Screen? Let your Viewing Screen go blank and continue to breathe slowly. Whenever anything comes onto the Viewing Screen, just notice it and then let it go. Study the Viewing Screen for a while. Then, whenever you care to, leave your Mental Theater.

Some people will find the Mental Theater exercise easier than others, but do not be discouraged if you experience difficulty the first few times you try these procedures. We all have the capacity to develop a Mental Theater to help us in our quest for a path with a heart, but as with most worthwhile skills, development takes time. Most of us have no problem walking once we reach early childhood, but just watch a toddler struggling to take his or her first steps and you'll be reminded how far you've come. The same holds true with the Mental Theater. If you are faithful to these exercises, in a short time you'll be able to access your Mental Theater at will.

VISION DRILLING

Our brains are made up of two hemispheres, left and right. The left side of the brain controls logic and language skills. The *right brain* uses color, sound, smell and feelings in ways we experience but can have trouble describing. The right brain makes leaps, and illogical connections, and controls imagination. In grade school we developed analytic or *left brain* capabilities through drilling, "One and one are two. Two and two are four." But few of us have exercised our right brain in any systematic fashion, so our abilities to envision have not been developed as much as they could be.

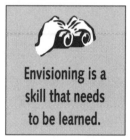

Envisioning is a skill that needs to be learned.

Mentally turning an object around in your imagination and looking at it from this side, and that side, even imagining getting inside it, helps develop envisioning skills. Systematically comparing one mental image with another one is a way of "drilling," as we did with the multiplication tables, to develop the right brain's envisioning capabilities. The exercises that follow will give you practice manipulating and comparing images on your Viewing Screen.

Just as in any drill-type training, there is a great deal of redundancy in the exercises. Although this can help us develop skills, it can be a bit tedious to read each step of the drills; so feel free to skim the next several pages the first time around. Later you can return to sections you want to practice and read them more carefully at that time.

VISION DRILL ONE:
WORKING WITH IMAGES ON YOUR VIEWING SCREEN

Close your eyes and return to your Mental Theater. Notice the curtain again. Open the curtain, just as you did before, by breathing in and out slowly and deeply. After opening the curtain, focus on the blank Viewing Screen as you continue breathing slowly and deeply.

When you feel calm and relaxed, project a pencil onto your Viewing Screen. Don't worry about actually "seeing" the pencil. Just imagine a pencil being on the Viewing Screen. Study the pencil. Like a scientist, be dispassionate as you study it. Don't

 judge the pencil or criticize it. Just observe the pencil. What kind of pencil is it? Wooden, plastic or mechanical? What color is the pencil? Does the pencil have an eraser? Is it new or used? Turn the pencil around as you examine it. Notice any words or designs on the side of the pencil? Is the point sharp or dull or unsharpened? If the pencil is wooden, has it been chewed on? If it is a mechanical pencil, is there lead in it?

VISION DRILL TWO:
COMPARING IMAGES ON YOUR VIEWING SCREEN

Compare the way the pencil looks on different colored Viewing Screens. Change the color of your Viewing Screen to blue. How does the pencil looks on a blue Viewing Screen? Compare the way the pencil look on blue to the way it looked on the normally colored Viewing Screen, which we'll call "clear." Change the color of your Viewing Screen to red. How does the pencil look on a red Viewing Screen? How does the pencil on red compare with the way it looked on the blue Viewing Screen? Change the color of your Viewing Screen to yellow. How does the pencil on yellow

compare to the way it looked on red? On blue? Return the
Viewing Screen to clear, its normal color. How does the way the
pencil looks on clear compare to the way it looked on yellow? On
red? On blue?

Zoom into the pencil. Imagine that
you are *inside* the pencil. What is the
light like inside the pencil? Imagine
sniffing. How does it smell inside the
pencil? Make a fist and knock on the
inside of the pencil. What does the
knock sound like? Look around the
inside of the pencil. What do you see

In your imagination you can
see things from different
perspectives—including
from the inside out.

inside the pencil? How do you feel being inside the pencil? Come
out of the pencil and zoom it back onto your Viewing Screen. See
the pencil on the Viewing Screen again, and notice how it looks
now that you've been inside the pencil. Let the pencil go. Let your
Viewing Screen go blank. Focus on breathing deeply and relaxing.

Although the intricacies of an
imaginary pencil may not seem
exciting to you, this exercise
is very important be-
cause you are beginning
to consciously work on
developing your envi-
sioning skills. Although
you can't physically get
inside a pencil, you can
do so with imagination.
A secondary benefit is that
exercises such as these enable

you to break out of seeing the world from one fixed perspective. This is
helpful in problem solving as well as in resolving conflicts.

INVOLVE YOUR SENSES FOR POWERFUL VISIONS

The most powerful images are those you experience in all five senses.
William Fezler
Creative Imagery: How to Visualize in All Five Senses

Envisioning is focused imagination. The more vivid and real your image, the more effective your visions will be in helping you to *see* your destination. Many people mistakenly equate envisioning with mental pictures. Although mental pictures are important, envisioning involves

Make your images vivid by including all five senses.

more than simply seeing "pictures." Visions become more vivid when you enlist all your senses. When you imagined the curtain over your Viewing Screen, you didn't just picture it; you smelled it and felt it. When you were exploring the pencil, you noticed the light, knocked on it and listened to the sound, smelled it and pictured it on different colors. You imagined in all five senses: sight, hearing, touch, smell, and taste.

AT THE BEACH

Imagine the sound of waves crashing on the beach. Imagine the smell of ocean air. Imagine the feel of sand running through your hands. Imagine the taste of salt water. Now create a vision of a beautiful day at the beach. Notice how the sound of waves, the smell of the ocean, the feel of sand, and the taste of salt water are all part of the vision.

People's abilities to envision vary. Some people can easily "see" vivid pictures in color in their imaginations. Other people can't see anything, but they can "hear" sounds clearly and experience "taste" so strongly that their mouths water. Don't worry if you can't see images. If this happens, just imagine what you would see *if* you could see images. The important thing is to involve as many senses as you can when envisioning.

VISION DRILL THREE:
ENVISIONING IN ALL SENSES

Return to your Mental Theater with deep breathing. Project a paper clip on your Viewing Screen. If you can actually *see* the paper clip, that's good. Otherwise, just *imagine* what you would see if you could see the paper clip on your Viewing Screen.

Turn the paper clip around on your Viewing Screen and study it objectively like a scientist. What does the paper clip look like? What kind of paper clip is it? Metal or plastic? How big is the paper clip? What color is the paper clip?

Compare the way the paper clip looks on different colored Viewing Screens. Change the color of your Viewing Screen to blue. How does the way the paper clip looks on blue compare to the way it looked on a clear Viewing Screen? How does it compare to the way the pencil looked on a blue Viewing

Your imagination is a powerful tool for creating your future.

Screen? Change the color of your Viewing Screen to red. How does the paper clip on red compare to when it was on a blue Viewing Screen.? How does it to compare the pencil on a red Viewing Screen? Change the color of the Viewing Screen to yellow. How does the paper clip on yellow compare to when it was on red? On blue? How does it compare to the way the pencil looked on yellow?

Let the Viewing Screen return to clear, its normal color, and zoom right *into* the paper clip. What does the light inside the paper clip look like? How does the light in the paper clip compare to the light in the pencil? Sniff. How does the inside of the paper clip smell?

How does the paper clip smell as compared to how the pencil smells? Knock on the inside of the paper clip. What does the knock inside the paper clip sound like? How does it compare to the sound of knocking on the pencil?

Study anything that is inside the paper clip with you. Study how it feels inside the paper clip. How do your feelings being inside the paper clip compare to those you had when inside the pencil? Come out of the paper clip and zoom it back up to your Viewing Screen. Study the paper clip again for a moment and then let your Viewing Screen go blank.

Again, it may seem frivolous to imagine being inside a paper clip, but remember that this is a drill to help you expand your imagination. As you become more comfortable with using your Mental Theater, you'll find that many of the exercises that may seem difficult or even impossible now will become second nature.

STUDY PLACES

Study.

Thus far, you've experimented with inanimate objects on the Viewing Screen. But any object and any place can be projected onto your Viewing Screen and studied. Sometimes when you project a well-known place onto your Viewing Screen and study it dispassionately, like a scientist would, you discover perceptions and sensations you hadn't noticed when you were actually in that place. Doing this is good practice for enhancing your abilities to envision, and it may have other benefits in terms of greater awareness. One very interesting place to study on the Viewing Screen is your workspace.

Assume an objective mindset.

VISION DRILL FOUR:
STUDYING YOUR WORKSPACE

Open your curtain with deep breathing, and put the place where you work on your Viewing Screen. Observe yourself in your workspace. What do you look like? What are you doing and saying? Be dispassionate when watching yourself. Don't judge or try to change the picture. Just observe.

Zoom into yourself in your workspace and take a deep breath. What is the air like in your workspace? How does the air in your space compare with the air in the paper clip? How does it compare with the air in the pencil?

Listen to the sounds in your workspace. How does the way your workspace sound compare with the sounds in the pencil? How do the sounds in your workspace compare with those in the paper clip? Notice the light in your workspace. How does the light in your workspace compare with the light in the pencil and in the paper clip?

Notice how you feel in your workspace. How does the way you feel in your workspace compare to the way you felt in the paper clip and in the pencil? Clear your Viewing Screen. Take several deep breaths and notice yourself relaxing.

What did you learn about your workspace that you didn't already know? Does it feel more or less comfortable than exercises with the pencil and the paper clip? Do you feel free or constrained there? How do you think this exercise will make you feel about your workspace the next time you are actually in it?

STUDY PEOPLE

You can learn a lot about other people by studying them on your Viewing Screen. You can imagine being inside people to understand their priorities, how they see things and how they see you. You can try out various approaches to dealing with the person and watch how he or she responds, for example.

VISION DRILL FIVE:
STUDYING A CO-WORKER

Go to your Mental Theater and open your Viewing Screen again with slow deep breathing. Project a co-worker onto the Viewing Screen and study this person. Just image the person as vividly as you can. Don't judge or criticize; instead observe the person objectively as a scientist would.

What is your co-worker doing and saying? How does your co-worker look? What is he or she doing? Zoom into your co-worker and *imagine you are your co-worker* in your workspace. What does your co-worker see when in your workspace? How does what your co-worker sees when in your workspace compare with what you see there?

Project yourself into the person.

Sense how your co-worker feels when in your workspace. What does your co-worker like about you? What does your co-worker want from you? What about you frustrates your co-worker? How does the way your co-worker feels when in your workspace compare with the way you feel there? Zoom out of your co-worker and clear your Viewing Screen.

It can be very illuminating to study your boss on your Viewing Screen. Especially important is the process of getting inside your boss and viewing yourself from his or her perspective. If you're self-employed, your "boss" may be a partner, a spouse, or a lender. Your boss is anyone who bosses you or whom you feel bossed by—including yourself.

VISION DRILL SIX:
STUDYING YOUR BOSS

Return to your Mental Theater and use slow deep breathing to open the curtain. Project your boss or someone you feel bossed by onto your Viewing Screen. Study your boss. Don't judge or criticize him or her. Just observe your boss objectively as a scientist would.

How does your boss look? What is he or she doing? What is your boss saying? Zoom into your boss and *imagine you are your boss* in your workspace. What does your boss see when in your workspace? How does what your boss sees compare with what your co-worker sees when in your workspace? How does what your boss sees compare with what you see when in your workspace?

Sense how your boss feels when in your workspace. How does the way your boss feels when in your workspace compare to the way your co-worker feels when in your workspace? To the way you feel when in your workspace? What does your boss like about you? What does your boss want from you? What it is about you that frustrates your boss?

Zoom out of your boss. For a moment or two observe your boss again now that you've been inside him or her. Notice any changes in your perception of your boss. Let the image of your boss go and clear your Viewing Screen.

A customer is someone who "buys" or uses your services. Some co-workers who rely on certain output from you might be customers, for example. This might include other team members who rely on your

Who is your customer?

output. Clients and customers usually have different priorities than we do. Just as it can be helpful to observe your boss in your Mental Theater, projecting yourself into your clients and customers can give you an entirely new perspective.

VISION DRILL SEVEN:
STUDYING A CLIENT OR CUSTOMER

Go to your Mental Theater, open your curtain and project a customer onto the Viewing Screen. Observe your customer without judging or criticizing. How does your customer look? What is he or she is doing and saying?

Zoom into your customer and imagine *you are your customer* in your workspace. What does your customer see when in your workspace? How does what your customer sees compare to what your boss sees when in your workspace? To what your co-worker sees? To what you see?

Sense how your customer feels when in your workspace. How do your customer's feelings compare with your boss's feelings when in your workspace? With your co-worker's feelings? With your feelings? What does your customer want from you? What is it about you that frustrates your customer? Zoom out of your customer and clear your Viewing Screen.

As you can see, developing your Vision is a process that requires breaking free of your usual patterns of thinking. Not only does this allow you freedom to explore other points of view and perspectives, it also liberates you from ingrained beliefs and behaviors that may be blocking you from achieving the very goals you envision. This process can feel both exhilarating and disheartening, but in the big picture of finding a path with a heart, it is a necessary step toward bliss.

PRACTICE USING YOUR VIEWING SCREEN

The more you practice using your Viewing Screen the more power it will provide you in studying situations and developing creative solutions. Comparing one image to another, as you did with the pencil and paper clip on different colored Viewing Screens, is analogous to comparing the weights of two stones, one in each hand. The more you practice, the easier it becomes to decipher finer and finer gradations of

Practive, practice, practice.

weight. With your Viewing Screen, the comparison process helps you fine tune your imaging ability.

Projecting people onto your Viewing Screen, and actually zooming yourself into them gives you an opportunity to see, hear, and feel things from a different perspective. Not only does this further develop your envisioning skill, but it can enhance your sensitivity to others.

People attending my workshops have all kinds of reactions to these exercises. Marilyn's and Ralph's reactions are illustrative.

■ Marilyn's Experience:

I saw that the things I put up in my workspace tell my colleagues about me. I realized that I have to welcome my boss into my area. He needs to feel that he can come in and sit in my place and tell me if something has to be changed. Right now he doesn't feel he has access to me. He zeros in on the computer and that's all he sees.

■ Ralph's Experience:

I got two different kinds of views from two different customers. One was looking in with wonder and thinking, "There are mysterious things behind that counter. This person holds the key to the information I want. Maybe he can give me what I'm looking for." The second customer looked at me behind the counter and saw a person of little substance or interest. I was just there—a nobody. She thought, "If he were somebody, he wouldn't be stuck in this cramped, stuffy office with fluorescent lights."

CREATING A VISION

Vision— a very practical tool
by which we create the blueprint for our desired future.
Linda Marks
Living with Vision

Whatever the mind can conceive and believe, the mind can achieve.
Napoleon Hill and W. Clement Stone

Your Vision is an important business tool and essential for pathfinding. Most people use envisioning when solving problems even though they may not realize it. Without Vision, problem solving can be difficult and frustrating, even impossible.

Envisioning is a mental process in which you imagine what is possible. It is with Vision that you conceive what is possible. You imagine a desired destination and then journey toward it. This is how you find your direction in pathfinding.

Some people are put off, even intimidated, by the notion of envi-

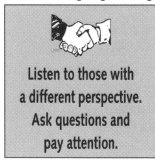

Listen to those with a different perspective. Ask questions and pay attention.

sioning, perhaps because they think envisioning demands an original picture or idea, one that no one else has considered before. Don't impose this demand on yourself. Visions don't have to be original to be effective. In their research, Bennis and Nanus, authors of *Leaders: The Strategies for Taking Charge,* found that leaders usually choose an image that is used frequently by people around them. They articulated it, gave it form and legitimacy and focused attention on it, but they rarely conceived of the Vision in the first place. So you need not feel that you have to be original or a genius.

Being a superb listener, however, is essential. The ideas and perspectives you get from others can help tremendously in conceiving a Vision. Listen especially closely to those who have a different perspective from you and who advocate new ways. Likewise, asking questions and paying attention is important. Put yourself in a position to interact with advisors, consultants, other leaders, scholars, planners, and people with varying opinions. Then listen and ask questions.

START WITH THE PAST

When presented with a problem we draw on past experiences to find a solution. From what has worked and not worked, we select relevant information, make relevant comparisons and integrate experience with the current situation. Scanning the past for relevant information can occur very rapidly and often intuitively. When developing a Vision, reflect on your past experiences with similar situations. Talk to others with experience in similar situations to discover what has and hasn't worked for them. Identify analogies from historical information that might apply to the current problem. Gather as many attempted solutions, good and bad, as you can. These are then projected onto your Viewing Screen for observation.

For example, the founding fathers of the United States did not start from scratch when writing the Constitution. Instead, they looked into the past to Athenian classical culture. Classical architecture with its Greek columns is evident in many of the buildings built at the time in Washington. Although the Constitution's authors drew on classical principles, they also drew upon the English philosophers Locke and Hobbes, and on principles they learned from Native American inter-tribal pacts. The result was a new and original vision of a democratic society.

You don't need to start a new country, however, to apply these principles to your own life. Remember Nellie, the young grocery clerk in a previous chapter who dreamed of studying biochemistry at college but felt bound by her work obligations? Nellie is a prime example of someone who drew upon her past experiences to find a solution to her problem of feeling stuck in the grocery store. She realized that her current dilemma resulted chiefly from her failure to act because of her shyness and lack of confidence. Nellie began by reviewing times in the past when she acted with confidence. She remembered when she went to summer camp. In contrast to her usual meek approach to things, she had been persistent in making an application for the camp. She went to her Mental Theater and projected that time onto her Viewing Screen, where she relived it. What she noticed was that during the days before camp, she kept telling herself "camp will be fun and an adventure." Nellie then took the memory of herself acting with confidence in applying for the camp, and saw herself confidently sending for and filling out applications for college. Whenever doubts and fears began to cloud her Vision, she imagined herself laughing it off with "college will be fun and an adventure." Several times a day Nellie took a moment to project the image of her confident self onto her Viewing Screen. After several days, she noticed a curious thing—she felt more confident. Soon she told Jennifer, her best friend at work, "I'm going to go to college in the Fall. It'll be fun and an adventure." This was Nellie's first big step on a path with a heart and a brighter future.

CREATE A PICTURE OF THE SOLUTION

A pathfinding Vision is a picture of your destination, a mental image of a desirable solution to the problem you are solving. Like a jigsaw puzzle, it's easier to put the puzzle together when you have a picture of the puzzle solved. The difference is that in pathfinding *you* create the picture of the solution, then solve the puzzle of getting there.

You'll recall from the last chapter that there are two kinds of motivation: *avoidance motivation,* or moving away from negative situations, and *seeking motivation* or moving toward something you desire. When you get caught up in the burnout cycle, by necessity you must enlist avoidance motivation in order to beat burnout. But the problem is that you are trying to avoid or move away from a situation where you feel helpless and trapped. You know what it is that you don't want but this doesn't necessarily help you to know what it is that you do want. Seeking motivation requires that you have something positive to move toward. This is where your Vision tool is essential. You need to develop a picture of your bliss.

A Vision is a picture of the solution, not the steps achieving it.

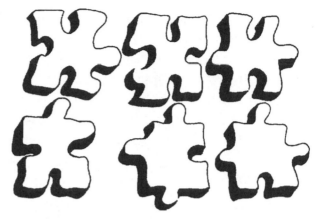

You may wonder what that has to do with solving the problem you were hired to solve. But blissful moments are most likely to be yours when you are working toward something meaningful to you. Many people believe that being free from responsibility and engaging in meditation is necessary to achieve bliss. The opposite is true, however. Csikszentmihalyi's research revealed that people are most likely to experience flow when they are engaged in absorbing work. In fact, most people find that when they have nothing to do, they feel uncomfortable and out of sorts. In short, the path with a heart, the path to your bliss is most likely to be one where you are engaged in solving important, but practical problems.

> ### THE JIGSAW PUZZLE PRINCIPLE
> It is easier to put the puzzle together if you can see what is on the box cover. In any organization, people have different pieces of the organizational puzzle. Members may have detailed descriptions of their roles and responsibilities, but very often they lack information about the "big picture"—about the overall purpose or vision of the organization.
>
> **James Kouzes and Barry Posner**
> *The Leadership Challenge*

When creating the picture, don't be concerned with the steps from the present to the future state or how you will achieve them. Before you can move toward the solution, you have to have a concept or a picture of it. Once you've formulated the image of what you want to achieve, your Vision, then you will work backward from the future to the current situation to establish a Map and figure out what steps are needed to implement the Vision. Remember, the Vision is an image of the solution, not the steps to the solution.

Put on Your Brainstorming Hat

In the beginning, imagine as many different solutions to the problem you're working on as you can conjure up. Go beyond the usual to imagine silly or even absurd solutions. Resist the tendency to evaluate potential solutions at this step, because that will stifle your creativity. Sometimes it helps to imagine putting on a brainstorming Hat, one that enables you to think of new ideas, to see things in different ways. You can always put your analytical Hat back on later when it's time to critically evaluate the merits of your ideas. The Hat is a powerful pathfinding tool which we'll study later. For the time being, your objective is to imagine what might be possible.

Assume a creative mindset.

When weather is stormy, it is wild and unpredictable, as though the forces of nature have been unleashed. A brainstorm is similar, in that your creative and imaginative powers are given permission to run wild in your mind, with no internal censorship. Many of the thoughts you get may seem impractical, but you should not view them in that light. Think of all your ideas, regardless of how silly they may seem, as a process that will finally result in the solution you choose to put into play.

HOW TO BRAINSTORM SOLUTIONS

Envision an excellent solution: Go to your Mental Theater. While breathing slowly and deeply, open the curtain over the

Viewing Screen again. Using your personal standard of excellence, *see* an excellent solution to the problem you were hired to solve.

Don't worry about constraints or being practical. Just imagine what an excellent solution might be. Remember, in your imagination you can add whatever you need to the picture. If money, personnel, equipment are required, just imagine them being

Play with ideas in your Mental Theater.

available. Study the excellent solution. Then clear your Viewing Screen and breathe slowly and deeply to relax.

Envision a second excellent solution: Imagine a second and different excellent solution. Put on your brainstorming Hat again. Let your imagination run. Play with ideas on your Viewing Screen. *See* a second excellent solution. Don't worry about how to achieve the solution or how to get from point A to Z. Just see the excellent solution and study it. Watch it working. Then clear your screen.

Envision a third excellent solution: Use deep breathing to enter your Mental Theater again and open your Viewing Screen. This time picture a third and different excellent solution. Imagine putting on a brainstorming Hat that enables you to think of all kinds of possible solutions. Don't worry about being practical or realistic. Try an

See silly—even absurd solutions.

absurd or silly solution. Turn things upside down and inside out. Operate from a new premise. View the problem from someone else's eyes. Picture it on your Viewing Screen and study it. Clear your Viewing Screen.

Push yourself to imagine several solutions, even after you think you can imagine nothing more. You can discover new ways of dealing with the problem that can lead to exciting results. Do this often and you will develop the ability to break out. Here's what Margie and Joseph saw.

■ **What Margie Saw:**
I counsel job seekers. A lot of my work consists of finding ways for them to use guerilla tactics in the job market. But

*the job market is diffuse and for me to have these kinds of
contacts is tough. When I imagined excellent solutions, I
started looking at it as marketing my clients to the public
sector. I began wondering how I would go to the "market"
and how I would do "marketing." I never thought of marketing as being part of my job before this.*

■ What Joseph Saw:
   *I oversee all of the parking planning—where to build lots
or garages and who should have A, B, and C permits. These
are the kind of responsibilities I have. I imagined a team of
parking consultants going out to interview everyone in every
office. Then I imagined conducting the interviews on-line
through E-Mail. And you know, it's not a half-bad idea!*

From these examples, it should be obvious that Vision brainstorming produces results. Think of instances from your past when Vision
brainstorming might have resulted in a more desirable outcome than
what actually happened. And remember the words of Stone and Hill:
"Whatever the mind can conceive and believe, the mind can achieve."

PUSH TO SEE MANY POSSIBILITIES

Repeat the Vision brainstorming exercise often. To review, *see* the
problem you are to solve solved. Remember, don't be concerned with the

**Imagination is
an attitude.**

steps for getting there. Just study the image of the
solution. Don't be practical; let your imagination go
wild. After you go through your more-standard
solutions, you may discover that new possibilities
come to mind. This is what happens during brainstorming and what you strive to achieve—to break
out of your usual way of thinking. Imagination is an attitude as well as a
style of thinking. It is a readiness to consider more possibilities, to search
more widely, to consider even the alternatives that seem improbable or
outlandish.

   Mentally try out lots of different solutions to the problem that is
yours to solve. Eventually you will formulate a picture of an excellent

solution to the problem you were hired to solve. This picture is your Vision of what's possible.

> ## LOOK FOR THE THIRD ALTERNATIVE
> I had a mentor who taught me to always look for the third alternative. When there is only one option you have a problem, not a choice. Two alternatives creates a dilemma, but still no real choice. It's only when there are three alternatives that you have a choice. We often stop brainstorming at two alternatives, but for a real choice push to find that third alternative.
>
> Ole Anderson
> The LIND Institute

CHOOSING A VISION

Vision does not spring full grown from Adam's rib.
It usually starts in a fumbling groping way,
reaching toward some shadowy dream
that cannot easily be verbalized or defined.
Harold Leavitt
Corporate Pathfinding

The Vision doesn't appear, like a revelation or flipping on TV. It usually starts in a fumbling, groping way. You must strive toward it, little by little. Every problem has many potential solutions. There is no one right way of doing things and no one correct path. If there were, we wouldn't be concerned with pathfinding. The question is which is the best direction to achieve your purpose while you follow the path with a heart. When you've envisioned many possibilities, you need to evaluate them to choose a destination. Review your Mission to decide how well each picture fulfills it. Does it resonate with your Heart? Will others support it? Without support, it could be a difficult path. Lack of team support, for example, does not mean you should abandon a potential path, but it should be weighed in evaluating a solution. As you'll discover later, the Team tool can be helpful in uncovering areas of opposition and building support.

EVALUATING SOLUTIONS

Go to your Mental Theater. Open the curtain with slow deep breathing, and project the solution you're evaluating onto the Viewing Screen like a movie. Study it. If you can't actually *see* the picture, imagine what it would be like if you could see it. Remember to enlist all your senses, seeing, hearing, touching, smelling, and tasting.

As you envision the solution, ask: How well does this solution fulfill my Mission? How closely attuned is this solution to my values? How receptive and supportive will co-workers, family, and other people be of this solution? It helps your evaluation to use a rating scale from 1 to 10, with 1 being very low and 10 being very high. Write the ratings down so that you can compare solutions later.

When you find a solution that helps fulfill your Mission, is attuned to your values, and will be supported by the people around you, review it many times. If you decide upon it, this movie is your Vision. Describe your Vision in words, it helps to write it down. Go back to your Viewing Screen for another look, then add to your written description. Keep this Vision Statement. You'll probably want to review it again in the future.

VISION INSPIRES

> *Every social movement begins with a dream.*
> *The dream or vision is the force that invents the future.*
> James Kouzes and Barry Posner
> *The Leadership Challenge*

The picture you described is your Vision. To be effective it must be inspiring. Picturing it must infuse you with passion and a desire to reach your destination. Inspiration comes from the Vision's attunement with your Heart. When you strive to accomplish something that has meaning for you and fulfills your

Picture your Vision often.

purpose, it fills you with spirit. You become inspired and motivated.

ITALIAN MATH

Italian math is a concept that has little to do with numbers and much to do with people. McCormack learned it from his friend Nick Leone, whom he met when he was selling washing machines.

As McCormack tells the story, Leone was an Italian immigrant who had come over on a freighter and jumped ship in Philadelphia. After working as a janitor and a chef, he had somehow wound up with a small-time catering hall in Long Island, N.Y., where he eked out a living charging $8 a head. "It was a real loser," says McCormack. But Leone had a dream. He planned to build an elegant hall fit for great banquets, and there he would charge more than $20 a head. Trouble was, he couldn't come close to affording it.

So he hired a designer to draw up some plans, which he began showing to potential customers. Impressed, several of them booked dates at the unbuilt facility. With actual bookings in hand, he was then able to persuade some of his suppliers to extend him credit, thereby freeing up cash. The cash served as a down payment on construction of the new hall, which he also managed to get his food suppliers to help finance. The hall was built and—within two years—Leone's annual revenues had grown from $150,000 to $800,000. Soon afterwards he build a second hall.

"The thing about Nick," says McCormack, "is that he wasn't just a chef, and he wasn't just a manager. He was a creator. It was brains and foresight. He showed me that one and one doesn't have to equal two. Sometimes it can equal three, or four, or even seven. It all depends on who the one and one are." Italian math.

Bruce Posner and Bo Burlingham
"The Hottest Entrepreneur in America"
INC Magazine

Return to your Vision often, especially when making decisions and contemplating your direction. Once you've formulated your Vision, it isn't always necessary to open the curtain with slow deep breathing. You can simply "flash on the Vision" and imagine the Vision for just a moment, perhaps even *seeing* it in your mind's eye.

The Vision is not a fixed point. Remember, the purpose of the Vision is to define a destination and set a direction. But ultimately, you are the pilot, and you can change your course if you choose. As you move along your path, continuously shape and reshape this picture of your destination. Your Vision can and should change as you travel, gaining new information and making new choices. Whenever you feel it necessary, you can add to or alter your Vision.

Once you've created your Vision you are ready to move to the next phase of pathfinding: Developing an action plan for getting to your destination. This involves using the Survey tool to scan the territory for the best route to your destination, the Target to set your goal, the Map to identify action steps, and the Yardstick to measure distance traveled.

CHAPTER 7

SURVEY

SCANNING YOUR TERRITORY

*The natural formation of the country is the soldier's best ally;
but a power of estimating the adversary, of controlling the forces
of victory constitutes the test of a great general.*
Sun Tzu
The Art of War

$\mathcal{L}$et's suppose you have a Vision and know where you're going. You've still got to figure out how to best get to your destination before you set off into the wilderness. If you launch off without getting the lay of the land you could easily discover that you are unprepared for the obstacles you will encounter, because rarely will the route be a straight line. There are bound to be mountains and lakes, perhaps hostile natives, wild animals and other hazards that can detour your journey. If you come up against a seemingly insurmountable obstacle, you could feel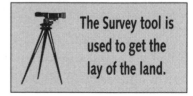

The Survey tool is used to get the lay of the land.

stifled, trapped, and powerless. When we succumb to powerlessness, burnout is not far behind. This hazard can be mitigated if, before you begin your journey, you gather information about the possibilities you'll confront.

Conducting a Survey will reveal the lay of the land and help you decide where to look for passes through the mountains, where obstacles lie, ways around these barriers, and what supplies you'll need. From this

topological view, a general route can be mapped out. Success and speed in reaching your destination are enhanced or impeded by the quality of your survey. Hastily made vague sketches of the territory can lead to false starts, dead ends, and back tracking.

The Survey tool is used to get the lay of the land, giving an overview of the terrain you will move through. The Survey is a comprehensive examination of the situation or arena in which you travel. It measures the size, shape, and positions of boundaries, and reveals what obstacles exist and where they block your path. It also identifies the major players in the territory, their reactions to your Vision, who might be an adversary, resources available to you, your competitive edge, and any vulnerabilities you might have.

Surveying summarizes the main features of the landscape you must be concerned with and gives a picture of the territory. It is very important to survey who is affected by your Vision and how they may respond. Who are your allies? How might they be helpful? Who are the hostiles? What barriers might these hostiles erect across your path? Most often your arena is a corporate setting, small business, or home office, but it can include artist communities, professional or social associations, volunteer or community organizations, political groups, or even a family. Although companies, corporations, and organizations are referred to herein, you should fit the process to your own environment.

WHY SURVEY?

Surveying starts with identifying which aspects of the territory are important. Data are gathered from observations and by polling the opinions of trend setters, customers, bosses, key players, co-workers, and competitors. Writings such as corporate media releases and product literature can be reviewed. Finally, the data you collect must be compiled and evaluated.

Only after you have gotten a comprehensive picture of where your powers and weaknesses lie, what resources you have available, and who might help or hinder your efforts, should you begin to sketch out a route to your destination.

IDENTIFY AVAILABLE VEHICLES

> *When a person receives an order,*
> *he accepts an external goal that is not his own.*
> *But in carrying it out, he can almost always superimpose*
> *on the actions he performs another goal, a goal of his own.*
> *The external goal is a carrier for his personal goal.*
> *And, as long as the two do not conflict,*
> *the total goal is a synergistic one.*
> N. Arthur Coulter
> *Synergistics*

If you work solely to meet company needs, you become a virtual slave, existing to serve others. But when your goals match the corporation's, your work

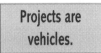

Projects are vehicles.

serves you as well as your company. In terms of meaning and personal goals, you are thus working for yourself.

The projects you work on serve as vehicles that can carry you toward your destination. You can get a lot of mileage from some projects, others can take you down cul-de-sacs to a deadend or get you off-track. The object of the Survey is to decide which projects can carry you toward your Vision. Accomplishing this means identifying a range of potential projects and surveying their degree of alignment with your Mission. Those that move you toward your Mission are the ones that you can elect to take on.

MAKE AN OPPORTUNITY LIST

Moments of bliss come most often when you are absorbed in meaningful activities. Projects aimed at accomplishing an important
purpose provide opportunities both to advance yourself in the organization and to experience bliss. To discover your opportunities, compile a list of possible projects you might undertake. Begin by observing troublesome situations in your work en-

| Complaints often carry opportunity seeds. |

vironment. Make observations while you're at work or by reviewing situations in your Mental Theater. Look for customer or client needs that are not being met. What obstacles and inefficiencies do you notice? During your day be alert for problems that increase costs and slow progress. Listen to what customers, co-workers, competitors, and supervisors say. Complaints often carry opportunity seeds. So pay close attention to complaints—especially customer complaints. Remember the old saying: "Find a need and fill it." Identify needs, and you uncover opportunity vehicles for pursuing your Mission.

List needs, inefficiencies, obstacles, costs and problems you've noticed. Add ideas you have for innovation, being more effective, and increasing quality and excellence. Each item presents an opportunity. Return to this list often when you notice additional problems or have ideas and add them to your Opportunity List.

You can't ride every opportunity on your list; so don't even try. Instead, decide which problem opportunities move you toward accomplishing your Mission. These are your "suitable projects." If a project is suitable, it is part of your job and there's no reason to wait to be told to do it. Instead, you can assign yourself to the project. To Survey which projects and activities hold potential for carrying you toward your Mission, ask: Is this a suitable self-assignment? By conducting a SUIT-Analysis you can align your personal goals with your company's mission. SUIT-Analysis helps you survey opportunities to decide which assignments you can ride to your Vision. Identifying the SUITable assignments is a major step in charting the course from where you are today to accomplishing your Mission. Later you'll discover how to Map out your specific action steps.

Analyze What Is SUITable

The objective of doing a survey of problems is to decide which has potential to be an opportunity vehicle you can ride toward your Vision. To evaluate the suitability of the items on your Opportunity List, subject each opportunity to the following four questions:

S—Can I Solve it?

Will this vehicle carry me to my Vision?

About each obstacle or inefficiency, ask yourself: Is it something that I can solve or accomplish? Is it in my sphere of influence? Can I make an impact on it? For example, I cannot influence the national budget deficit. It is a problem I can observe, and be concerned about, but I do not have the ability to influence it. I can't solve the budget problem. On the other hand, I can influence cost overruns in advertising my workshops.

Consider the item solvable if it is something that you can accomplish or cause to be accomplished, even if you must get the cooperation of others or learn a particular skill first. Put an "S" next to opportunities that lie within your sphere of influence or on which you can make an impact.

U—Is it Unassigned?

People will think you are aggressive and say you're not a team player if you grab concerns that belong to others. They will feel you've invaded

Trouble + Crisis = Opportunity

their territory. Even when you have a good idea, it will probably be resisted. On the other hand, unassigned problems are needs, obstacles, and inefficiencies that haven't been assigned to anyone and aren't part of anyone else's territory. Such free-floating projects are potentially yours for the taking. You can take the assignment and still be a teamplayer, because you're not treading on others' toes.

Organizations undergoing a lot of change are particularly fertile in unassigned projects, even when the change is negative or the company is in a downturn. In Chinese, the word for "opportunity" is written with two characters that mean "trouble" and "gathering crisis."

Review your list of opportunities and write a "U" for unassigned next to those opportunities that don't belong to anybody else or that are already assigned to you. If nobody else is working on the problem and it is not a part of anyone else's responsibility, then it is unassigned and available for you to take.

I—Is it *Interesting* or *In line* with my values?

The fact that an opportunity exists doesn't mean you should grab it. Does it interest you? Use your Heart to check if it is attuned to your

values. Do the activities you'll engage in while working on the opportunity resonate with your values? Read your Compass. Does this opportunity interest you? Will the opportunity be likely to promote bliss experiences? Consider an opportunity interesting if it makes your Heart sing and is in line with your values. Put an "I" next to each opportunity that interests you.

T—Is it on *Target* with my Mission?

Would filling this need, correcting this inefficiency, or removing this obstacle move you closer to achieving your purpose in the company? Will it help you to do an excellent job of accomplishing your Mission—the problem you were hired to solve? Put a "T" next to those opportunities that are on target with your Mission.

One by one review the needs, ideas, obstacles and inefficiencies from your Opportunity List. Subject each opportunity to the SUIT-Analysis questions: Can I solve it? Is it unattached? Is it in line with my values? Is it on target with my Mission? Those opportunities that meet the four SUIT criteria are vehicles that can move you toward your Mission and are suitable self-assignments.

Repeat this process frequently. When you see a need to fill or you come across an obstacle or inefficiency during the routine of your work, jot it down on your Opportunity List. Soon you will have a long list of opportunities—potential assignments that may help you move toward your Mission. Periodically submit the items on your Opportunity List to a SUIT-Analysis. Some people try to grab at every opportunity, so that each derails completing the previous one. Such people come across as unfocused, unable to zero in. SUIT-Analysis helps identify where you can get the most mileage from your efforts while avoiding side-tracks and derailments.

Q & A

Question: What if, in my analysis of the opportunity, I find I'm interested in the problem, it is unassigned, and it is on target with my Mission, but I don't have the ability to solve it. Is it suitable for me?

Answer: Having the ability to solve something doesn't mean that you necessarily know what to do right now. Instead, ask whether or not it's in your sphere of control. Can you do something about the situation?

Suppose the situation is within your sphere of influence, but you don't have the skill needed to deal with it. Then the question becomes: Can you get the skill? If so, acquiring the skill becomes a preliminary assignment before taking on the project.

Few people wake up one morning having every skill needed and feeling competent. More commonly we blunder into things, acquiring the needed skills as we struggle with problems as they arise. In other words, obstacles and inefficiencies become bar-bells upon which you can develop skill muscles. If improving the situation is on target with your Mission, is interesting and is in line with your values, it's a good idea to develop the skills needed to handle it.

Question: I work in customer service and encounter continual dissatisfaction. I identified "making people happy" as an opportunity, but I feel helpless because I can't make every customer

Reframe the question?

happy. What should I do?

Answer: You can increase your ability to affect a situation by narrowing your focus. Instead of asking if you can make *every* customer completely happy, ask if you can *increase* satisfaction and *decrease* dissatisfaction. Or stated in another way, if you can't

make every customer completely happy, can you help more customers be more satisfied as a result of what you do? The new question can be answered "yes" with almost every customer. By reframing your question, you transform an unsolvable situation into a solvable one. More on this when we study the Wand tool.

SURVEY YOUR POWER BASE

Another aspect of the landscape that you need to Survey is your power base. Power conjures up images of bossing people around and steamrolling over others. Naturally, most of us shun such negative

Power is the capacity to cause something to happen.

images. At the other extreme, powerlessness is a negative state that promotes helplessness and leads to burnout.

Power is the capability to influence, to impact, or to cause something to happen. Having power and knowing how to use it productively is essential to

leading yourself. Power is not static. It is a composite of behaviors, attitudes, and results that are built or reduced through day-by-day encounters and activities.

> ### THE MYTH OF INSIGNIFICANCE
> **There is a widespread belief that what you do doesn't matter, that you don't have an impact. Believing the myth, you don't act and, as a consequence, you make no impact, and so you reaffirm the myth.**
>
> **Colin Wilson**

To successfully accomplish things in an organization you must know how to make power dynamics work for you instead of against you. We all know people who seem to have a knack for getting things done. These are powerful people, because the ability to move projects forward and get things done is a measure of one's power. More power translates into greater ability to influence and accomplish. Some people try to avoid "office politics." This is a mistake, because we make things happen through people. Even if you're self-employed, an artist, or a freelancer you must still deal with clients, contracting compa-nies, suppliers, and so forth. No man is an island, and no one operates in isolation—even when it may seem otherwise.

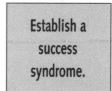

Establish a success syndrome.

People who are successful at developing power establish a "success syndrome," according to John Kotter, author of *Power and Influence.* Year after year, they find ways to increase their personal skills, their coopera-tive relationships with others, the amount of relevant information they process, the resources they command, their track records, and the size of their jobs. Success and power do not come overnight, but result from persistence and ongoing effort to build your power base. Power pro-motes successful results, and success builds power to create your success syndrome.

Many very capable individuals fail to develop a power base or project a success syndrome. Kotter says the mistake these people make is paying attention to the wrong things when measuring career progress and making bad career decisions which get them into jobs over their heads. This is a common phenomenon in high-tech firms, where engi-

neers move into manage-
ment positions because
they believe it is the
route to the "top."
Then they dis-
cover that they
have little liking
or aptitude for managing
people, so their ineffective perfor-
mance leads to lower self-esteem, and damage to their success syndrome.

Your power base is developed by taking risks with your power and investing it, much as entrepreneurs invest money. Kotter's research shows that it is created by accumulating relevant information, developing cooperative relationships, expanding personal skills, gaining control of important resources, establishing a strong track record, and getting progressively more important jobs.

INCOME AND PROMOTIONS

There is a strong tendency among capable young people to focus on income and promotions as the most appropriate measures of career progress, even in the short run. The rule of thumb is simple: the faster income goes up and the more promotions one gets, the better. This guiding principle leads people not to pay enough attention to developing relationships, knowledge, a track record, skills, their reputations, etc. As a result, they often don't systematically build the power base they need, or they unintentionally undermine it.

John Kotter
Power and Influence

A power base is difficult, if not impossible, to transfer from one territory or work arena to another, because it is tied so closely to individual relationships and perceptions within the group. People who make frequent job changes from one company to another operate at a disadvantage, because they must prove themselves anew with each move.

By comparison, people who make lateral moves within one company build and strengthen their power base. They can retain and call on relationships in old jobs, and they understand the company's culture, for example.

SOURCES OF POWER

When we think of power, we think of success, of achieving what we want, of having the ability to get things done. Power is necessary in any success story, whether it be personal power or holding power in a large organization. But power isn't something you automatically get when you graduate from college or spend a certain number of years on the job. Power must be cultivated, and to be successful at understanding and developing a power base, you need to be ready to work with others. Kotter identified the following sources of power in organizations.

Knowledge

> *Information is power.*
> *If you know the facts, you can prevent catastrophes*
> *or encourage time- and money-saving activities.*
> *If you have the right information, you can be in the right place*
> *doing the right thing at the right time.*
> *If you have good contacts, you can help others*
> *who are in positions to help you.*
> Anne Boe and Bettie B. Youngs
> *Is Your "Net" Working?*

Knowing the demographics, markets and major players of your industry is vital. "Think globally, act locally" applies. Consider your Vision, which is your destination, in the microcosm of your local arena and macrocosm of the larger industry—nationally, perhaps internationally. What are the trends? Who are the key players and up-and-comers? It is easier to maneuver within the industry territory when you know how the values of major players are similar or different, who's inside, what they care about, and where they are going.

Relationships

Cooperative relationships with bosses, co-workers, subordinates, subordinates of subordinates, people in other departments and other companies, suppliers, customers, colleagues, and community members increase your ability to get the information you need to get things done.

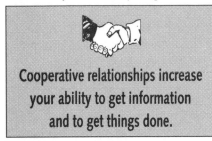

Cooperative relationships increase your ability to get information and to get things done.

It is a truism that we'll do more for people we know and feel good about than for strangers and newcomers. Good relationships with people you depend on to get things done are particularly important. The greater your dependence, the more important the relationship. The more good relationships you have, the greater your power, because you can call on more people to help you accomplish something.

Networking Skills

Networking is an organized method of making links from the people you know to the people they know, gaining and using an ever-expanding base of contacts to exchange information, advice, contacts, and support.
Anne Boe and Bettie B. Youngs
Is Your "Net" Working?

Networking is a process of making acquaintance links with people who might be able to link you to other people who may be able to help you in various ways. A study conducted in the 1970s yielded a fascinating statistic: the average number of acquaintance links between you and any other person in the United

States is 5.5. Besides proving that it's a small world, what does this statistic mean? If you need certain information or are seeking a person with particular abilities, you have a good chance of finding the information you seek with five or six calls—if you have good networking skills.

The wider your base of acquaintances, the easier it is to find the information or person you need. In other words, the ability to network, or link up with others, increases your power. Good networking skills are critical for professionals, the self-employed, sole practitioners, home workers, activists, and political organizers, as well as employees of small companies and others working outside the organizational mainstream.

Fitting In

A "good fit" between the organization and your values provides important leverage for developing your power base. You are poised to perform well and succeed. It is easier to develop the business information you need to succeed because people tend to be more open with people they see as being like themselves. The work is interesting, and it is easier to develop good working relationships, because you like and understand your co-workers better, which makes getting tuned into information channels easier. On the other hand, if you're seen as 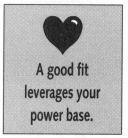 different or if you go against the grain of the group, you will find it more difficult to build cooperative relationships and to get information you need to perform.

A good fit leverages your power base.

Conduct a quick Corporate Culture Audit (see page 65) and use your Heart to test how attuned you are to the culture. The more you resonate with your company's culture, the more power you have and the easier it will be to get things done. With mergers and downsizing, cultures can change rapidly. Surveying the culture often and evaluating where you do or don't fit can be a matter of survival.

Ken Auletta describes a famous casualty of the clash between television's old show-business values and the hard-nosed corporate culture that engulfed them in his book *The Three Blind Mice.*

> ## REAL MEN WATCH TV AT DINNER PARTIES
> When General Electric took over NBC in 1986, NBC News President Larry Grossman, trying to ingratiate himself with his new bosses, planned a dinner party with Today Show stars and their spouses, for GE chairman Jack Welch on the night of the sixth game of the Mets-Red Sox World Series.
>
> It proved to be a disaster for Grossman, because he made two critical errors: the date and not bringing a TV. Both could have been avoided if he had known that brusque, combative Welch was a rabid Red Sox fan. Deprived of actually seeing the Red Sox first baseman let a ground ball through, Welch forever associated the horror of the game and the Red Sox's loss with Grossman, who is no longer with NBC.
>
> Ken Auletta
> *The Three Blind Mice: How TV Networks Lost Their Way*

If the NBC News President had surveyed the territory and its players, he would have known that the target of his efforts was an avid Red Sox fan and could have scheduled the dinner for a different evening, or at least made sure there were plenty of television sets present.

The Pathfinder's Interview

Pathfinders take initiative. People who take initiative are received differently in different companies. One way to Survey a prospective employer's response to pathfinding is to ask several pointed questions during the job interview. What will come across to the recruiter is that you won't take a job with just any company. You're looking for the company that's right for you.

> Communicate that you're looking for a good fit.

Your objective in the Pathfinder's Interview is to get a good picture of how things happen in the company. Don't settle for simple "yes" answers. Probe deeper, and ask for specific examples and anecdotes. Don't stop with interviewing the recruiter. Interview the receptionist while waiting for your appointment. Go to the cafeteria and talk to employees you meet there. The company "hangout" is another place to casually talk with people about the company ambiance.

Gifford Pinchot, author of *Intrapreneuring*, says one way to get company people to reveal what happens when people take initiative, make mistakes, or overstep traditional boundaries is to ask the person you are interviewing to provide an example of a person who took initiative, for example. Then follow up with the question: "What is that person doing now?" Whereas a person may be reluctant to say that the company treats mistakes harshly or thwarts initiative, what happens in such a circumstance is revealed when this question is answered.

THE PATHFINDER'S INTERVIEW*

- How much continuity will there be in my work? Will I work on projects from beginning to end, or will the work be passed on to the next person in line once I've completed my function?
- How much latitude will I have in deciding how to do my job? Will I determine the "how" of completing my job or will my boss do so?
- Will I be encouraged to take initiative in doing my work? How?
- What would happen if, in accomplishing my responsibilities, I exceeded my job description?
- What company resources (discretionary time, vendors, technology, funds) will be available to me for experimenting with and developing new ideas?
- What is rewarded in this company? What has happened when someone has tried something new? What is that person doing now?
- How are mistakes tolerated? What has happened when someone tried something new, but it didn't work as planned? What is that person doing now?
- How entrepreneurial is this company? Does it have many ongoing experiments, or does it concentrate on a few highly planned projects?
- What will my co-workers be like? Will they have job functions similar to mine, or will I be part of a cross-functional team?

- How much autonomy will my team have in accomplishing our projects?

* Thanks to Gifford Pinchot III, author of *Intrapreneuring,* for his input in the development of the Pathfinder's Interview.

Interpersonal Skills

Ability to develop rapport and put people at ease greatly increases power. Good communication skills, such as listening, empathizing and

In companies work is accomplished through people.

drawing people out, helps get things done. Being able to get cooperation, to delegate, and to manage people effectively builds important relationships. Remember, companies, associations, and communities are made up of people, and work projects are accomplished through people, which means that good people skills are the cornerstone of your power base.

Strategic Ability

Taking a Survey of your strategic ability is important. How you use your skills and information to achieve a particular objective is a question of strategic ability. Correctly discovering who really has power, assessing differences among people and their roles, and identifying directions of mutual interest involves strategic ability. It is the ability to "psych out" the situation, to know how and to whom to present things, to know what sensitive areas to avoid, and to develop win-win scenarios for getting cooperation and getting things done. Good strategic ability is essential for project managers and others who function outside the traditional chain of command system, such as association officers, fund raisers, volunteer coordinators, and community organizers.

A good fit lays the ground for your power base. But, let's face it, we don't always have the good fit we might wish for. Well-practiced strategic ability can take the rough edges off a less-than-perfect fit. I am reminded of a story told by a Zen monk and sometime cook at Tassajara (a Zen

Buddhist meditation center near Salinas, California), where one monk antagonizes the Abbot, but another uses strategic ability to win the Abbot's approval.

TWO MONKS WHO SMOKED

Two friends who enjoyed smoking became monks and joined a monastery together. They thought they would soon give up smoking, but instead discovered it a rare pleasure to light up, puff on their cigarets, watch the smoke curl and drift, and chat about the affairs of the day. One day, while they sat smoking, they talked it over, saying to each other that they really ought to find some way to integrate their religious life and their smoking.

So, shortly after this, one of them went to speak to the Abbot, saying, "I've been here a couple of years, and this religious practice has been very beneficial for me, and I am devoted to prayer. But there is one thing which I have not been able to give up. I still enjoy smoking, and I want all my activities to be part of my religious life; so I was wondering if it would be all right for me to smoke during prayer."

The Abbot was aghast. "Absolutely not," he responded. "Prayer is just for praying. You must never bring in any other activities."

Crestfallen, the monk returned to his friend and reported that the Abbot was completely unsympathetic, and that it would be useless to speak with him further on the subject.

Undaunted, the second monk said he would give it a try. So he went to see the Abbot and said that he really was grateful to be able to participate in the religious life of the monastery, but in fact, he still enjoyed smoking. "And I was wondering," he asked, "if it would be all right if I were to pray while I smoke?"

"By all means," replied the Abbot. "Whatever you are doing, you should also be praying."

Inspired by Edward Espe Brown
The Tassajara Recipe Book

Influence Skills

You can exert influence even though you may not have formal authority or be high up in the hierarchy. If you have responsibility without authority, good influencing skills are essential. These are the abilities we think of when someone speaks of "people skills." They include being persuasive, getting people to buy-in, presenting ideas in the other person's language, calling on other people's values, and so forth. Team members, especially those on teams with weak leadership, volunteer coordinators, community organizers and association officers who have good influencing skills find that their effectiveness, and consequently their power, are greatly increased by such skills. Your impact may be indirect and not very visible, and yet still be substantial.

Technical Skills

Another source of power that should be included in your Survey is your technical skill base. Being good in your field brings credibility and respect, which translate into power. When you have a crucial skill, others depend on you to get things done. Even if they may have greater status or more formal authority, they cannot accomplish what you can do with your technical skill. Having a multiplicity and wide range of hands-on skills gives you greater power, because such Jacks- or Jills-of-all-trades can do more and fill in during a crisis.

Proven Track Record

Rarely can you walk into a new territory and immediately be given a free hand. If you want your company to give you leeway in doing your

> **You must build trust before you can get leeway.**

work and to carry on projects of your own, you must develop trust and demonstrate loyalty first. Your boss must feel certain you will complete your assignments. Bosses want to feel that those they supervise are going to do what they want them to do, and not do anything that they don't want done. They are more confident of a person when they know that his or her personal goals are aligned with the company mission, and that the person will not get sidetracked by a personal agenda. As you show that you get the right things done, and do so excellently, you will gain more responsibility and latitude to decide on your own projects and to work under your own direction.

SURVEY THE STRATEGIC VALUE OF YOUR POSITION

A key part of the power-development strategy involves moving towards projects or jobs or departments that are strategically important to the organization. Positions in those areas allow one to control particularly important consequences for the firm, and this gives one power.
John Kotter
Power and Influence

As in sports, where it is easier to score from certain positions, so in organizations it is easier to get things done from certain strategic positions. You can do a lot to move yourself into such strategic positions, but first you must know what you want to accomplish and identify which positions give the best shot at doing so.

Kotter emphasizes that not every position is the same. Some jobs allow more leeway than others. Some bring more opportunity; others have more glamour. Having power in organizations helps you get cooperation, open doors and get things done. Power positions provide a composite of advantages. Power-development strategies involve moving toward projects or jobs or departments that are important to the organization. Positions in those areas are powerful, because they allow you to control important contingencies for the firm.

Project management is one such strategic position. Project managers oversee teams drawn from across departments, are exposed to important developmental information, usually participate in critical decisions, are flooded with unassigned problems, and have high visibility. Project teams are becoming increasingly important, because they are where a lot of innovation takes place. Increasingly, organizations are putting together special teams which often go beyond the boundaries of the company itself, to include members from other companies called "strategic partners." Unlike other organizational forms, which tend to be

bureaucratic and rigid, project teams are very fluid, taking the form
necessary to accomplish the project at hand and then disbanding when
their objectives have been achieved.

STAR PLAYERS OF TOMORROW

Most of tomorrow's work will be done in *project teams.* Project
teams will neither quash individualism nor blunt specialization.
To the contrary, individual contributions will be more important
than ever. Becoming expert—and enhancing your expertise—
will be imperative for almost all of us. . . . Though expertise and
specialization are more important than ever, developing "periph-
eral vision," a feel for the whole task, is essential. You will be
forced, routinely, to work/learn any job on the team. Though you
will be constantly investing in your own area of expertise, learning multiple jobs and understanding the entire function of the
team—*and* its relation to the enterprise—will be imperative. . . .
The lifespan of a project team can be life (very unlikely), or just a
few hours (not so likely). Dynamic, short-lived project configura-
tions will be commonplace. It will not be unusual to work on four
or five project teams in a year, or a couple of teams at one time—
but you may never work twice with the exact configuration of
colleagues, even in a 20-year "career." . . . The average project team
will have at least a 75 percent chance of including "outsiders"—
a vendor, a distributor, a customer, all of the above. Workers will
spend at least half their time on teams that include people from
the payrolls of others. . . . Who reports to whom will change over
time, and you will routinely report to a person for one task who
reports to you for another. Despite the muddle of "who reports to
whom," accountability for a goal will be far higher than in traditional organizations. . . . The "project manager" and "network
manager" are the star players of tomorrow! . . . Promotions will
go to those who are particularly adept at exercising such skills.

                                                    Tom Peters
               Liberation Management: Necessary Disorganization
                                 for the Nanosecond Nineties

Being a member of a project team is a strategic position in several ways. First, it allows you to get visibility from key people. Second, you have an opportunity to expand your experience. Third, and most importantly, you can get into a new kind

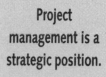

of career path. Traditionally, we learned that we should climb the corporate ladder to get ahead. The corporate ladder refers to the steps up the bureaucratic hierarchy. Unfortunately, for many this turns out to be a losing strategy in today's world. There are too many people on the ladder, which gets narrower and narrower with each rung up. In the late 1980s companies began cutting out the middle levels of the hierarchy in a process called "getting mean and lean" and "downsizing." "Plateauing" is another problem with climbing the ladder. Professionals, especially women, found that they could climb only so far and then they hit what came to be called the "glass ceiling," where, try as they might, they could not get promoted to the next rung.

Project teams are opening a new career path. Instead of climbing the ladder up the hierarchy, people are moving from one project to another. With each project you acquire experience, skills and allies. Climbing up no longer has much meaning. Your experience and relationships are more important.

STRATEGIC POSITIONS

Both traditional jobs and project teams can be looked at in terms of their strategic positions. It's not an either/or situation. In fact, you might have a defined position and also be a member of one or more project teams—but you can't do everything. So, before accepting a new position or volunteering for a project team, it is a good idea to Survey for strategic positioning. For example, Zeb was an engineer in Cisco Systems, a large, rapidly growing company that manufactures mutliplexers. For over a year he had been in customer service and was feeling burned out. Not only was customer service

Survey your power points.

extremely stressful, but it was a dead end. Zeb fancied himself as being an entrepreneur and wanted to get into marketing. He applied for many transfers but was rejected each time. When one of the project managers, Robin, a

mover and a shaker, invited Zeb to join his project team, his initial reaction was negative because it didn't involved marketing.

When Zeb stopped and looked at his options in terms of strategic positioning he was surprised. First, Zeb realized that his having been in customer service wasn't a total loss. Customer-service reps had to be able to help users of the company's sophisticated equipment over the phone. The reps had to be conversant in the workings of every product, even those no longer manufactured. For Zeb it was a double-edged sword. On the one hand, it had taken so long to train him and he knew so much that the company was reluctant to let him leave customer service. He was simply too hard (and expensive) to replace. On the other hand, it was precisely this breath of knowledge that made him attractive to Robin. When Zeb looked closer at Robin's team, he became more interested. The team was external, in that members came from several companies. The innovation they were working on was important and at the forefront of the industry. This meant important experience and important contacts. Zeb grabbed the opportunity.

Strategic Position: Exposure to Information

Having information draws people who need it to you. Information can be bartered for cooperation or access to resources. Information helps you have a better understanding of situations and enables you to make better decisions.

Positions that expose you to important information are more powerful than those that do not. You don't necessarily have to have a high-level job to have access to important information. Consider secretaries working for people in key positions, bookkeepers who see all the invoices and checks, or aides working for city-council members. Identify which positions in your company have high information exposure and what information exposure goes with your position.

Strategic Position: Access to Resources

Positions that allow you to access organizational resources provide power-building opportunities. You may be able to use the resources directly in implementing projects which move you toward your Vision. Alternatively, you may be able to act as a gatekeeper, providing access to others in exchange for their cooperation on your project. Sometimes resources you control can be bartered for resources you need. If you're self-employed, run a small business, or work as a volunteer, you won't have the multitude of resources available to those working in larger organizations. Consequently, identifying and using the resources you *do* have takes on greater significance. Business and social relationships are an important resource. Strategic alliances can open resources to you, because gatekeeping and bartering of resources often occur through networks and allies.

Strategic Position: Proximity to Decision Making

The closer you are to where critical decisions are made, the greater the power potential of your position. Outsiders looking in tend to associate you with important decisions. But, more importantly, you have an opportunity to interact with and learn from the decisionmakers. Should a position be vacated or a crisis occur, you might be just the one to step in—even if only temporarily.

Strategic Position: Exposure to Unassigned Problems

The more exposure to unassigned problems a position has, the more opportunities it affords the position holder. Unassigned problems represent the "U" in the SUIT-Analysis. They are needs, obstacles and

Problems that are unassigned are yours to take.

inefficiencies that haven't been assigned to anyone else. Change is a good breeding ground for unassigned problems. Departments that are new or undergoing restructuring are a reservoir of unassigned problems. Departments in crisis, like those undergoing change, offer many unassigned and unsolved problems.

When departments, or any kind of cohesive group, are in crisis or undergoing rapid change, requirements for qualifying and reporting tend to loosen up. People become less concerned with degrees and years of experience, for example. The questions become "Can you do something?" and "Are you willing to try?" Action takes precedent over asking for permission to act and awaiting formal approval. Finally, there's a tendency to throw out "This is the way we've always done it" thinking and embrace a "Do what works" approach.

Operating in a rapidly changing environment can be very exciting and fulfilling if you grab and ride the wave. Such environments are replete with unassigned problems. The strategic trick is to grab those unassigned problems that allow you to expand your skills and experience while fulfilling your Mission and moving you toward your Vision.

Strategic Position: Supporting Upwardly Mobile People

Movers and shakers tend to take those who help them succeed along with them when they move. Look for positions that put you close to such corporate heroes. If you can't get into a formal position that allows you to work with a go-getter, try volunteering to work on a committee chaired by one. Such strategic moves give you an opportunity to demonstrate your ability and become an essential player on the team.

Strategic Position: Get Visibility

You get more power when others, especially others with power, know who you are and are aware of your abilities and accomplishments.

Getting visibility involves positioning yourself in such a way that other people can see what you do. Serving as an officer of a professional organization puts you in the limelight. Volunteering to head a committee is another visibility position where others can see you in action. Project management is one of the most strategic positions available in today's workplace.

Sandra, whose story follows, was only an entry-level receptionist; so she grabbed a volunteer project to manage and as a consequence she was exposed to information, got access to resources, stepped into an important decision arena, and put herself in a position of high visibility.

■ **Strategic Positioning:**

Sandra was an entry-level receptionist with no college degree or technical training. She aspired to work in marketing, but her weak resume did little to catch the attention of the marketing manager. On the face of it, Sandra didn't have a chance, but she was a hard worker, and had corporate savvy.

Sandra positioned herself to get visibility. She read that a coordinator was needed for a children's fund drive her company was sponsoring for charity. Sandra volunteered and got instant visibility.

The company newsletter and the local newspaper ran her photograph and reported on her background. The news clippings were included in the PR packets sent to all the Divisions. Sandra became a key player in the children's fund planning committee where she worked with important managers and a few Division heads. She gave a pep talk at the kickoff. At the Awards Dinner, Sandra sat right next to the CEO at the VIP table.

By the end of the event, Sandra was known to almost everyone in the company. A month later, an entry position opened up in the Marketing Department, and Sandra submitted an application. As soon as the interviewer saw her name, Sandra had the job!

SURVEY THE RELEVANT PARTIES

Today's workplace is characterized by diversity and interdependence. To perform well, we must take others' priorities into consideration. Who are the relevant parties? What are the different perspectives of the relevant groups? What do they want? How do they look at the world? What are their real interests? Before you take on any self-assignments or start on any paths, analyze where various perspectives are in conflict. What are the important differences? What sources of power do they have, and to what extent will they use that power to help or hinder your course?

Identify who will be affected by your project. Who can make an impact, positive or negative, on your project? Make sure to consider everyone who might have a stake in the results of your actions, including people in other departments, even in other companies, and in some

cases, their families as well. People who feel that their concerns haven't been considered can get irritated and stand in your way.

With this analysis you can begin developing strategies for getting the support of those whom your project will affect; this is often called "getting your ducks in line." Lining up support for your project before you begin is an important secret of working smarter rather than harder. Always be thinking about whose cooperation you need. Pay particular attention to which people might resist cooperating, why, and in what ways.

■ **Steamrolling Consultants:**

I was part of a group of psychologists that trained teams of beat police officers who had "high credibility" among the other officers to be trainers in handling "415s" or "family fights," the most dangerous call that patrol officers face.

Problems in a program with a large East Coast Police Department began immediately, because we didn't identify who would be affected by our seven-week program and who might resist. To begin with, we were from California, and the men on the team had beards. It was the mid-70s and there was an immediate suspicion that we were "weirdos," if not full-blown "commie pinkos." But worse, there were women on the training team and the officers' wives were not at all happy with that.

We ignored early hints of trouble, and went steamrolling right on into the training, which was grueling, beginning at 7 a.m. and usually going to 8 p.m., often later. The guys we were training were expected to be at the training site—in a pair of hotel suites—most weekends to make video training tapes, as well as to devote a lot of time off-site studying and preparing for practice teaching.

By the end of the day, the guys were exhausted but too keyed up to go home. So just about every evening we'd all go down to the bar for a couple of beers to let off steam. These bull sessions frequently went until after 11 p.m. The wives had trouble understanding their men coming home so late, slightly snockered.

About three weeks into the program, two wives were threatening divorce. The guys weren't getting much sympathy from those back on the beat either. From the patrols' perspective, our guys were having a grand time over at that hotel with those California consultants.

We worked the guys into exhaustion. Their wives were furious. The other officers were putting them down. The success of the program was in jeopardy. It was our fault. Why? Because we hadn't surveyed who would be affected or how they might respond, or developed any strategy for dealing with such potential problems. Instead, we created a situation that undercut the guys' motivation and threatened to destroy the program.

We paid no attention to the fact that these men had responsibilities outside our program, and gave no thought to how the wives might feel when their husbands would be away from family routine for nearly two months. We never considered how we consultants might appear to the rest of the Department. There was a crisis, and we had to scramble to fix the damage. We brought the wives into the training site on weekends to serve as roleplayers for the video tapes to be used in the training and invited them to the evening get-togethers. Once involved, the wives became enthusiasts.

Next, we made a presentation to the Department, so that they would know what the training was all about, and invited the Chief to the training site to give the guys a pep talk. After that, there were few problems.

We didn't make the same mistake in the next police department. Instead, we took time to identify who would be influenced by our program and acted to get their support before beginning training.

IDENTIFY ALLIES

Consider who might be an ally. Don't fall into the trap of thinking in terms of "friends" or who you "like" when identifying your allies.

When people feel included they tend to be more cooperative.

Instead, ask; "Whose interests are similar to mine? Who could help me implement my project?" Don't restrict your consideration to "hot shots." Allies can come in many forms. An ally is somebody who can give you information, help you sort things out, open doors or speak up in support of your suggestions. There are lots of ways to be an ally.

IDENTIFY POTENTIAL FOES

If you haven't considered barriers other people might put across your path, your progress might come to a standstill. When you identify potential resistance, you can devise a way to handle it. Perhaps an ally can help you get the resister's cooperation. Deciding what to do begins with discovering who might resist.

Reasons for resistance are many. Maybe your adversary sees you as disrupting the routine. When things change, people are forced to change. Remember, change is stressful because with change comes fear, uncertainty, and doubt. Most of us resist change—especially when it feels foisted on us, and when we don't understand the purpose or see any gain for ourselves.

You can't argue people out of this resistance. When you argue about it, resistance tends to grow. Worse, if resisters think you're against them, they tend to get polarized and may develop a campaign against you.

Sometimes resentment is the cause of resistance. Maybe your adversary feels you're being too independent, getting too many perks, or taking away resources. For example, suppose you travel a lot, often working all weekend,

> **People who feel left out tend to resist.**

getting back late at night. Taking the next day off to sleep seems perfectly reasonable to you, but co-workers may feel resentment, because they don't see the long hours and weekend work. They just see that you get to travel and take time off.

Project Yourself into the Resister

Try to see the situation from the resister's perspective. Get into his or her shoes. One way is to use your Mental Theater. Project your adversary onto your Screen and zoom into the resister. Try to see and experience your project from that person's point of view. What does he or she want? How does he or she look at the world? What are this person's essential priorities? What are his or her sources of power? How are your own perspectives in conflict with this person's? What are the important underlying differences between you and this person? Similarities? How do you come across to this person? How does your project feel to him or her? What is important to this person? After identifying the potential resister and analyzing possible reasons for the resistance, you can develop strategies for dealing with the resistance.

Are You the Resister?

Sometimes you are the resister. Fearing change and the unknown, you think of every reason not to do something and dig your heels in. Don't try to argue yourself out of the resistance or to deny your feelings. Don't criticize yourself. Instead, recognize that you are resisting. It helps to step back and pretend that you are someone else doing the resisting. Put yourself on your Viewing Screen and watch what you resist and how you resist it. Notice what you resist, how it feels, and what you do. Use your Compass and Heart tools. It is possible that your resistance means that the project in question is wrong for you. If you come to this conclusion, perhaps you can bow out of the project. Alternatively, you can use your Heart and Mission tools to find a way to engage your values while working on the project.

SURVEY RESOURCES

Virtually any project is going to require a variety of resources for implementation. You may need photocopying capabilities for duplicating fliers, for example. Equipment such as computers or overhead projectors, telephone accounts, and meeting facilities are commonly needed resources. Survey what resources are directly available to you. This includes those you control or that you can gain access to fairly easily. These are resources you can use directly in implementing your project. They can sometimes be bartered for those you need. You can open doors to allow others to access resources you control and thus can build your power.

Think of the technology, equipment, facilities, expertise, person power, support systems, and funds available in a medium-sized to large company. When you are a member of the company team, all the company's resources are potentially there for you to use. Of course, bureaucracy can (and usually does) stand in the way of your access to the resources that you need in order to solve the problem you were hired to solve; so be creative in Surveying. Think outside of normal channels. What can you access informally or "through the back door"? Add these to your list. Also include resources available to you outside of work. Do you have a summer cottage on the river? Perhaps it can be used for off-site meetings. Add it to your list of resources. Do you have a well-stocked hobbyist workshop? Add it to your resource list.

CONSULTANT NETWORK

One of the most important steps in networking is analyzing your assets and skills. That is, make a list of all the people you know and the resources you bring to others.
Anne Boe and Bettie B. Youngs
Is Your "Net" Working?

Suppose you need information about software to complete a project. Chances are there is someone in the company who can advise you, and who probably would be happy to help you because you are a member of the company community. And there wouldn't be any consulting fee! Every person in your company is potentially your consultant. All you've got to do is to know who has the information you need and how to approach him or her. Even though these company "experts" are unlikely to give such "free" consulting to outsiders, it's okay to help you because you're an insider—one of them.

Every person in your company is potentially your (free) consultant.

Entrepreneurs have to hire accountants, advisors, marketing specialists, and management consultants. By comparison, virtually all these experts are available to you in the company. The same is true of support services, facilities, equipment, and all the other company resources. You may need a meeting room or need to access a computer in connection with a project. Chances are what you need is down the hall or on the next floor. Remember, you've been hired to solve a problem. If doing so requires certain company resources, most companies want you to use them. Locate the resources you need and develop a strategy for accessing them. It usually involves working through your network of allies.

By comparison, consider sole proprietors, freelancers and people working in start-up companies, which are usually undercapitalized. Such small ventures need accountants, for example, and accountants are expensive. Entrepreneurs and the self-employed have to hire consultants, and consultants cost a lot of money. Compare this to those working in large companies.

Freelancers, sole proprietors, and people in small companies generally have fewer resources, such as equipment and technology, facilities, funds, or in-house expertise and support systems available to them. If

Survey everyone
you know.

you're in this group, you'll have to rely even more heavily on an informal network of contacts to access resources and advisers. For you, your contacts, which I call your Consultant Network, are your most important resource. These are people you know professionally and socially who can give you advice, help you access resources, or direct you to someone who can. Your Consultant Network includes proprietors of shops and other businesses you frequent, as well as casual acquaintances. Approached properly, most people love to give advice. It makes us feel important, knowledgeable, and significant.

Think of every person you know through your work, your family, professional groups, recreations, and social life. Who can you approach for information, referrals, and advice? Analyze the kinds of things they know about and what resources they might be able to help you access. Since you know a lot of people, this is a big task. Using your Viewing Screen in your Mental Theater helps. Don't try to remember everyone all at once. Instead, come back to this list often and jot down names as they come to you. The resulting list is your Consultant Network, one of the major resources you have available for implementing your projects.

SURVEY OFTEN

Scanning the territory for problems and projects that can serve as vehicles you can ride toward your Vision is an ongoing process. The territory changes constantly. Like volcanoes erupting in the wilderness, there are frequent upheavals in our frontiers. Problems are solved and new problems appear, bringing new opportunities. People move in and out of your world. With the understanding that you should continually update your Survey, the next pathfinding tool is the Target, which allows you to set incremental goals along the way to your Vision.

CHAPTER 8

TARGET
SETTING YOUR GOALS

It's easy to dream; with just a little encouragement
you can close your eyes and conjure up a whole new life for yourself.
But if you want to make that life come true,
you will have to start by choosing one piece of it
and deciding that that's the one you're going to go for first.
Then you may still have to do a little work on that piece
to turn it into something that's really reachable
—not a mirage that keeps receding ahead of you.
Barbara Sher
Wishcraft

$\mathcal{V}$ision is your destination on the horizon, a picture of what's possible and where you want to go. But Vision is also the process of conceiving the picture. In other words, Vision is both a picture and the process of creating that picture. Ideas are plentiful. They are the stuff of Vision. But until ideas are implemented, they are little more than pie-in-the-sky dreams. Many a dreamer ends up on the rocks of burnout, because having a great dream and not being able to actualize it is a discouraging experience. After a couple of

Use the Target to go from vision to action.

disappointments you can come to believe that dreams are only receding mirages that you can never reach, and so you stop dreaming. When you let go of your dreams burnout is not far behind. Bliss comes when you follow a path with a heart. That path is found by dreaming. But as Barbara Sher says, if you want the dream to come true, you must take a piece of it and take concrete actions. It's with the Target tool that you take the first step to making your dreams come true.

The Target is the tool to use to go from vision to action, from idea to implementation. The Target is a goal or a step on the road to your ultimate destination—making your dream real. Suppose I imagine looking out from the peak of a mountain. To implement my Vision I must climb to the mountaintop, step by step. If I focus solely on the mountaintop, it seems far away, and I don't know which way to go. Now, suppose there is a meadow a short way along the trail to the mountain peak. I can imagine getting to the meadow. Reaching this Target becomes a step toward implementing my Vision of looking out from the mountaintop. When I begin moving toward this easy-to-reach Target of getting to the meadow, I have gone from vision to action.

FROM VISION TO ACTION

Results can be achieved by inverting our ordinary perception of the vector of time, from "I am **here** *and will, in the future,* **go there**" *to "I am already* **there**, *I came from* **here**, *and now I must recall how I did it. . . . The future is now." That is how leaders think.*
Peter Koestenbaum
Leadership: The Inner Side of Greatness

At the time you first tackle a problem, implementation of the solution lies somewhere in the future. In other words, there is a gap between now, the problem (the project; dreaming), and the future, the solution (implemented project; living your dreams). Getting to the solution requires bridging the gap.

With Vision you can bridge the gap between where you are now and where you want to be by projecting yourself into the future and picturing yourself having reached a particular milestone or, in some cases, having reached the goal you seek. This picture of a completed step in the project is the Target. Restated in terms of dreams, a picture of you living your dream is your Target. By using imagination you create a picture of what is possible and bridge the gap. But hold on a minute! You can't walk on a vision bridge! It's not real.

Work backward from the solution.

Plans for building the bridge are developed by working backward from the solution. What needs to be done is discovered by looking at the completed project and identifying each preceding step. When the action steps are identified, they are sequenced with deadlines to create a Map. Then implementation, building the bridge, is achieved by moving forward through the action steps, in real time, toward your Target. The chapter on the Map tool will give you specific examples of how to do this.

HOW TO SET POWERFUL GOALS

> *A goal is a basic unit of life design.*
> *A first target is a handy unit of commitment.*
> Barbara Sher
> *Wishcraft*

Research shows a consistent pattern in the worklives of people who use goals. They exhibit confidence, are action-minded, and expect to succeed. They tend to select activities where they have a good chance of succeeding. These goal-seekers seem to feel a strong need to tackle tough goals for themselves and to plan their lives ahead. They don't describe their success in terms of luck; instead, they see their success as a result of their having created their own luck.

A goal is a result toward which effort is directed. Although we tend to think of goals as explicit statements of what we want to achieve, often our goals are implicit and unstated. In fact, you may have a goal, a result you're putting effort toward, without being consciously aware of it! Such a goal tends to be weak and ineffectual. A powerful goal is one that exerts a strong, almost magnetic influence on your motivation, pulling you toward your desired result. It mobilizes your efforts. Powerful goals are easier to achieve and are more effective than weak goals. A powerful goal provides a compelling Target to aim at.

WHICH IS THE RIGHT TARGET?

> *Rowing harder does not help*
> *if the boat is headed in the wrong direction.*
> *Applying more muscle is no solution if the course is mistaken.*
> Kenichi Ohmae
> *The Borderless World*

Look for key factors for success.

Considering the work pressures that we face today and our limited time, resources, and energy, it's vital to concentrate on key operating areas that will be decisive for your success in moving toward your Vi-

sion. If you can identify the areas that really
hold the key to success in your work,
and can apply the right mixtures
of resources to them,
you might be able
to put yourself in a
position of great
competitive supe-
riority.

Use the 80/20 Rule

An old truism says that 80 percent of your results come from 20
percent of your effort. Sales provides a good example. The salesperson
doesn't get the same results from every sales call. Most calls result in no
sales or only small sales. But sometimes the salesper-
son hits it big. These big sales tend to come from
about 20 percent of the salesperson's efforts. The

> Work smarter,
> not harder.

depressing corollary is that 20 percent of your results comes from 80
percent of your effort. This high-effort/low-results work generally revolves around routine, busy work and meetings.

If you can identify the 20 percent activities that yield 80 percent
of your results, you can apply leverage to them and get a lot more results.

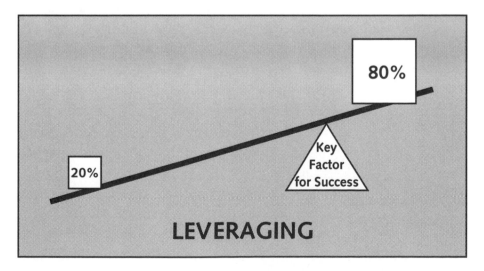

In leveraging we endeavor to use a lesser effort to lift a larger load than we could lift by simply picking the item up. The secret of leveraging lies in the 80/20 rule. These 20 percent activities are your key factors for success.

Identifying key factors for success can be difficult. Begin by dissecting your suitable projects, activities, major steps, and desired results as imaginatively as possible down into smaller pieces or segments. For example, a publisher who has a Vision of taking the lead among independent West Coast publishers may identify three segments: publishing books, direct mail order, and wholesale distribution. The next step is to rate each segment on how much impact it has on realizing your Vision. Stated another way, how much mileage do you get out of each segment in terms of moving closer to your Vision or destination? The higher the impact, the greater the mileage, the more results. The segments with the highest impact ratings are good candidates for Targets. In the example, the publisher might find that selling wholesale to bookstores leads to greater market share than does selling directly to book buyers by mail. Then the publisher would develop a Target around increasing the wholesale business.

MAKE YOUR TARGET COMPELLING

Not all targets are the same. Some are easier to hit. Some are more fun. Others are dull and boring. Compelling Targets have a magnetic force that pulls you toward them, making them easier to hit. The following guidelines work together synergistically to create the Target's magnetism or compelling power.

A positive Target draws you to it like a magnet does.

Guideline 1: Be Positive

We can mentally process positive information faster than we can process negative information. This probably explains why double negatives are so confusing. Consider the following: "I've never resisted that" or "Don't not call if you'll be late." Such statements make us stop and shake our heads in confusion while we attempt to decipher their meaning.

Along the same lines, if you say to a young child, "Don't touch the vase," the child is likely to become fixated on the vase. Why? Simply mentioning touching the vase creates an image of touching the vase in the child's mind. Chances are the child didn't hear "don't," but only "touch the vase" instead. The same is true of the subconscious. For example, consider the imperative "Don't think of a pink elephant." What comes to mind? If you're like most people, an image of a pink elephant is in your mind while you attempt not to think of it. Like the child, the subconscious responds to images, and tends to delete negative modifiers. How your subconscious responds to your goal greatly influences its power.

Your goal is more powerful when it is positive. A positive goal, such as spending at least one weekend a month in your lakeside cabin, is a Target that draws you to it like a magnet. In contrast, a negative goal, such as not working on Saturdays, does not function as a Target to shoot at, but as something aversive, to move away from or to avoid; yet, at the same time, it contains a hidden suggestion, continually reminding you of what you want to forget.

Your Compass and Heart Tools are essential for testing whether or not your goal is positive. Consult your Compass. Does imagining moving toward the Target elicit bliss feelings? Or is burnout indicated? Listening to your Heart reveals if the goal is attuned to your values.

Guideline 2: Establish a Timeline

Timelines help you to bring the pieces together. Goals with no specific completion time make setting timelines for action steps difficult. Such open-ended goals undermine motivation and encourage procrastination. But a deadline must be realistic if the goal is to be powerful. Unrealistically short deadlines can trigger panic, provoke the opposite "Why bother?" attitude, and generally generate a burnout climate. A deadline that is too short is usually better than no deadline at all, however. Unrealistic deadlines usually become apparent quickly, providing you an opportunity to readjust them to a more realistic time frame.

Guideline 3: Be Specific

Goals aimed at increasing satisfaction, having more fun, or improving communication are difficult, perhaps impossible to achieve. What is "improved satisfaction"? How do you know when you've achieved this goal? Does leaving work feeling good mean you've reached your goal of increased satisfaction? Or does increased satisfaction mean feeling you're making a socially beneficial contribution? How long, how much and what quality of satisfaction must you achieve before you can consider it to be "increased" satisfaction? Vaguely stated goals such as this one are frustrating and can lead to feelings of chronic failure or falling short in life. To be powerful, your Target must tell you what to shoot for and when you've hit it.

Go to the Doing Level

A specific goal is stated on the "doing level." It specifies *what you will be doing in the goal-state.* The "goal-state" is the time or situation in the future when you have reached the goal. It is the solution or end-point of your project.

The goal-state is the moment when you reach your Target.

The goal-state must be translated into the "doing level." The doing level specifies the actions, behaviors, or outcomes that will occur when you're in the goal-state, when the goal has been achieved. The following story will help illustrate.

■ Martin's Letter:

Martin's hands shook when he tore open the envelope and pulled out the letter. His breathing quickened as he read the brief note again and again. "What do they expect me to do?" he said aloud to no one. Suddenly he crumpled the letter up and threw it across the room into the empty basket.

Martin got up quickly, and as he did his chair rolled backward, hitting the wall with a thud. He went over to the window and looked out at the trees for a long time while rubbing his forehead. He was sweating in spite of the con-

trolled 68° temperature in the office. Martin walked back to his desk, took something out of the top drawer, and put it in his pocket.

Sitting back down in his chair, he scratched his head and stared at the clock. The phone rang and Martin jumped. He put his hand on the receiver, but didn't pick it up until the third ring. Taking a deep breath, he put the phone to his ear, and said, "Martin here." He listened to the caller while frowning and periodically saying, "I know! I know!" Then without warning, Martin hung up the phone loudly. Clenching his jaw, he said something under his breath. Martin looked at the clock again, got up, and quickly left the room without closing the door.

The table that follows lists two ways to describe Martin's reactions. Phrases in Column B describe Martin's actions, what he was doing. This is the "doing level." Descriptions in Column A tend to lead to argument among observers. Was Martin angry or was he afraid? Was Martin exhibiting immaturity or nervousness? On the other hand, probably everyone could agree on whether or not Martin frowned, or looked at the clock, or threw the letter into the basket. These actions can be counted. Actions have a beginning and an ending point. The items in Column A might be called generalizations or feeling states. These kind of descriptions speed up general communication and are wonderful for writing poetry and prose. If someone asks, "How's your boss today?" it would be laborious to answer, "She walked around the desk fifteen times, scratched her head eight times, and looked out the window three times." It would take a long time to convey. "She seemed frustrated all day." This kind of "shorthand" description is not helpful in setting goals.

TWO WAYS TO DESCRIBE MARTIN'S REACTION

A	B
Generalizations: Feelings	**Doing: Actions**
upset	waited three rings to answer phone
nervous	tore the envelope while opening it
lashing out	threw crumpled letter into basket
immature	left room without closing door
angry	scratched his head
anxious	crumpled up letter
worried	looked at clock
afraid	frowned
edgy	sweating

Consider it another way. What conclusions would you draw if you saw a man clasping and twisting his hands? Most people take these actions to indicate anxiety or nervousness. Now suppose the man clasps and twists his hands, then crosses his arms over his chest and pats his upper arms vigorously, while standing on one foot and then on the other foot. We usually read this body language as shivering due to being cold. Now suppose the man clasps and twists his hands while hunched over, squinting his eyes, and saying, "Hee! Hee! Hee!" under his breath. We generally read this as scheming. Clasping and twisting hands is a "doing" in each situation. The combinations in which the doings occur are what sends various signals about the meaning behind the behavior.

THE SAME ACTIONS CAN HAVE DIFFERENT MEANING

Action	Meaning
Clasping and twisting hands	Nervousness
Clasping and twisting hands, patting upper arms with opposite hands, while shifting weight from foot to foot.	Cold
Clasping and twisting hands while hunching over, squinting and saying, "Hee! Hee! Hee!"	Scheming

---

Powerful goals specify what you will be doing when you reach the goal-state. The more specifically you describe the doing, the clearer your Target will be. A clear Target tells you where to aim and what to do, which makes achieving your goal easier.

> When the goal is vague it is difficult to see your Target.

■ **Dialog with Bill:**
Bill: My goal is to learn desktop publishing by May 30.
Teacher: What do you mean by "learn?" What do you want to *do?*
Bill: To be proficient in using desktop publishing.
Teacher: What will you be *doing* when you are proficient?
Bill: I will make fewer trips to outside vendors.
Teacher: You are saying what you *won't* be doing. What will you be *doing* when you are proficient in desktop publishing?
Bill: I don't know.
Teacher: It will be difficult to achieve your goal, because you don't know what you will be doing or what you are aiming at.

■ **Dialog with Alice:**

Alice: By September 30, I will have all my files organized and current by setting aside the last hour of each Friday as my time to work on them.

Teacher: I suspect the files are not organized because you don't like doing it.

Alice: That's right.

Teacher: So your goal is negative. You are striving to do something that is not fun and is a chore. When the files are organized, what will you be *doing*?

Alice: I know what I won't be doing—going through twenty papers to find one I need.

Teacher: That's still negative. You are going to get those files organized in order not to have to go through stacks of paper. Such a goal is probably not compelling enough to motivate you to organize your files. When you've got the files organized, what will you be *doing*?

Alice: I'll be able to meet my friend at the spa and relax instead of having to stay late.

Teacher: Thinking of going to the spa with your friend is ever so much more motivating than thinking of organizing files.

Alice: I see! I should translate goals into things I find positive and motivating.

Teacher: Yes, good.

■ **Dialog with Allene:**

Allene: My goal is to prepare a list of the procedures and regulations for the doctors, but when I put myself into the goal-state, I saw myself using the list to tell a physician why he couldn't take a particular action.

Teacher: It sounds like your goal has to do with using the procedures and regulations rather than preparing them.

Allene: Yes, that's right.

■ **Dialog with Roger:**

Roger: My goal is to write a NIMH grant for a feasibility study of the benefits of facilitated support groups. But in the goal-state I saw myself going from group to group facilitating and making it happen. There were a lot of challenges, and everyone was saying that the facilitation was very beneficial.

Teacher: Interesting. Your experience is similar to Allene's. What you saw in the goal-state was not a written grant, but you facilitating the groups as proposed in the grant.

Roger: Yes, it's facilitating groups that I love doing, not writing grants.

Teacher: So your goal is facilitating the groups and writing the grant is a step toward doing that.

Guideline 4: Create a Compelling Image

> *Aristotle distinguised between efficient and final causation: the former is the finger that pulls the trigger and propels the bullet, and the latter is the target that caused the sportsman to fire in the first place.*
> Peter Koestenbaum
> *Leadership: The Inner Side of Greatness*

The purpose of a goal is to motivate, to get yourself moving. To get moving you need a compelling image, a picture that moves you, or more specifically, that draws you toward it. But, like Bill, who wanted to be proficient using desktop publishing, many goal-statements contain no clear picture. Consider the goal, "I will become a better time manager." What does better time

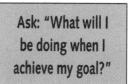

Ask: "What will I be doing when I achieve my goal?"

management look like? What does a good time manager *do*? When the goal-state is vague, it's difficult to see a picture which makes it difficult to see your Target or know which way to shoot.

How to Discover the Positive Image

A powerful goal contains a compelling positive image. A compelling image is a picture that elicits strong positive emotions. These positive feelings draw you toward the goal, like a magnet. Emotional response to the Target either compels us to move toward it or, when it's negative, repells us from it. The Target must have a Heart, and it should be based on seeking motivation rather than avoidance motivation.

Targets can attract or repell.

The way to uncover the positive image is to ask: "When I'm in the goal-state, what will I be *doing*?" For example, if Sylvia wanted to improve her time management she would ask, "When I've reached the goal-state and I'm a better time manager, what will I be doing?" She might love waterskiing, and see herself having fun with friends waterskiing on the bay on Saturday afternoon, instead of going to the office to catch up on back work. The image of waterskiing on the bay is more motivating than imagining filling out a daily planner. However, to go waterskiing on the

weekend, Sylvia may have to process a lot of paperwork efficiently and fill out a daily planner. The compelling positive image helps motivate her to do the disliked paper work and keeping the planner up to date.

Seeking to lose weight, like many self-improvement goals, has similar problems. To achieve the goal of weight loss, you have to eat less. Eating is fun, and eating less is not fun! Goals stated in terms of counting calories, fasting or eating a restricted diet are generally negative. The person setting a weight-loss goal should ask: "What will I be *doing* when I have lost weight?" The image of looking attractive, feeling good, and being envied is more compelling than a picture of turning down favorite foods to eat carrot sticks. For example, "to look great wearing a size-12 bathing suit by June 1st" would be a more powerful goal than "to lose 25 pounds by June 1st."

Barbara Sher, author of *Wishcraft*, emphasizes finding "the touchstone" hidden within the goal. The touchstone is the emotional core of your goal. Not too surprising, it is with the Heart tool that you find the touchstone.

Getting to the Heart of the Target

About your goal, ask yourself, "What do I love about this?" "What about this goal really matters to me?" Don't try to force an answer; instead, be receptive and notice what thoughts occur and what images come on your screen. Of these ask again, "What do I love about this?" "What about this really matters to me?" Continue asking these questions of the thoughts and images that come until you feel you've found the core. What do these images and thoughts have in common? Where's the core? From this create your compelling image of the goal-state. This is the picture of your Target.

Ask: "What do I love about this goal?"

MY GOAL

Write a goal-statement for your project that meets the four guidelines for a powerful goal. Make sure that the goal-statement is (1) positive, (2) has a deadline, (3) is on the doing level, and (4) has a compelling image.

■ **Dialog with Dr. James:**
Dr. James: For the next ten months, I will create and implement one successful marketing program for my medical practice, at two-month intervals, for a total of five marketing projects.
Teacher: That's very ambitious! Doctor, how do you feel about marketing? Using a scale of one to ten, with one being very negative and ten being very positive, rate your feelings about marketing.
Dr. James: Well, about 4, maybe 3.
Teacher: You are asking yourself to do something every two months for nearly a year that you rated as below five in liking! Your goal sounds positive, but is actually negative. Working on it could actually be aversive. Certainly it'll encourage procrastination.
Dr. James: Procrastination is a big problem with me.

■ **Dialog with Ralph:**
Ralph: By August 31, I will relocate my computer facility.
Teacher: The deadline is clear. It is specific because you can observe whether or not the facility has been relocated.
Ralph: The problem is that I don't want to

move. My boss's boss is after him to get this done and I
have to do it.
Teacher: How does the new space compare to the old
space? Which is more desirable?
Ralph: The old space is more desirable.
Teacher: Here again is a goal that seems positive at first but
is actually negative.

■ **Dialog with Wendy:**
Wendy: My goal is to increase my income by $10,000, half
in six months and half in twelve months.
Teacher: What is your source of income, Wendy?
Wendy: I'm a graphic designer, and I get paid by the job.
Teacher: How do you feel about making more sales calls
and quoting higher fees?
Wendy: Pretty uncomfortable. I hate asking for money.
Teacher: It sounds like stating your goal in terms of dollars
might be a hidden negative, because to succeed you must
ask clients for more money.

Aiming at negative Targets is surprisingly common. Sometimes it is
a goal imposed on us, as in Ralph's case, where he
has to relocate his computer facility to a place he
finds to be less desirable. Other times, as with
Wendy and Dr. James, the Target appears positive
until you check your Compass to discover that the

> **Aiming at
> negative Targets is
> common.**

doing level of the goal promotes burnout, not bliss. Dr. James doesn't like
marketing, and his goal specifies that he implement five marketing
programs. Wendy's goal requires her to bill her clients more when she
dislikes asking for money. As another example, time-management training often revolves around filling out a daily planner book. Using personal
planners increases record keeping and paperwork. People with time-
management goals tend to be poor record keepers who are already
overwhelmed by paperwork; so although a goal of improved time
management sounds positive, it can have negative images for a poor time

manager. If so, the person probably won't follow up and will fail to achieve the goal, because the picture of daily record keeping is aversive. In each example, the goal puts the person in a conflict situation, because success is defined in terms of activities or changes they dislike. Achieving these goals will be difficult and probably laborious.

MAKING YOUR GOAL MORE POWERFUL

It is important to get to the doing level of your goal. If you're not at the doing level you don't know what to do. Suppose you say "My goal is

Watch yourself in the goal-state.

to be more cooperative." What do you do? How do you start? If you are going to reach your goal, you must know what to do. Here's when your Mental Theater can help.

You can put almost anything on your Viewing Screen. You can go into the future or into the past. You can rewrite your history. You can stretch things, squeeze them, and get inside them. Your Viewing Screen is a fantastic tool for managing yourself and deciding what you are going to do.

Relax and go to your Mental Theater. Project the goal-state, the time when you have reached the goal, onto your Viewing Screen and

Identifying the doing of the goal-state.

observe it. Use your Eye to observe what you and others are doing. Remember to focus on specific actions, behaviors and outcomes. For example, if the aim is to "develop better communications," when you picture the goal-state on your Viewing Screen you may see co-workers asking one an-

other for feedback and making suggestions. In this case asking for feedback and making suggestions are the actions or the "doing" of bet-

Rework the picture to give a "bliss" reading.

ter communication and should be the focus of your goal-statement.

Consult your Compass. Notice how you feel when you imagine being in the goal-state. If it doesn't feel good, then change it. You can experiment. Work on the image of the goal-state until you notice flow feelings, where you feel energized and "one" with what you're doing. Remember, if you can't see an image on your Screen, then just imagine what the goal-state would look like if you could see it.

OBSERVE THE DOING OF THE GOAL-STATE

Imagine the moment when you achieve your goal. This is the goal-state. What does the goal-state look like? What are you doing? Look for actions and outcomes. What are others doing? What resources are used? What money? What people are involved? What technology? Just study the "doing" of the goal-state.

■ **Dialog with Wendy:**
Teacher: What did you see yourself doing when you had $10,000 more a year?
Wendy: I moved to a nicer, more expensive apartment. I saw myself spending more time and more money on leisure. I was surprised to see myself managing a staff. I didn't expect to see employees.
Teacher: Enjoying leisure and living in a nice apartment are images that are more compelling than "I will raise my income by $10,000." You can see yourself in these situations and they feel good. Seeing the doing of being in a nicer apartment, for example, makes it easier to move toward it.

Remember to create a compelling image. After you have identified your goal, what you actually want, the next step is to create a compelling image of the Target. For example, Wendy would see herself in the apartment and picture the details. Perhaps she would see a thick, cream-colored carpet. Perhaps it has a fireplace and bayview windows. Create an actual picture of your being in the goal-state and make it as real as you can. Wendy, for example, would see herself inside her new apartment; perhaps relaxing, perhaps entertaining friends.

■ Dialog with Ralph:

Teacher: What did you see when you were in the goal-state?

Ralph: I saw that I accomplished the move and I learned a lot about the hardware and bringing it together. I improved my relationship with the managing partner. He saw that I could handle the transition and was impressed.

Teacher: The move is still something imposed on you and a chore, but the compelling image is a picture of recognition. You said the managing partner was impressed. What did he do?

Ralph: He told several people that I'd pulled off a "near miracle."

Teacher: Good. This is a powerful image.

MY COMPELLING TARGET

Revise your goal-statement to make it more compelling. Use the "doings" that you observed when you pictured the goal-state—that time when you have reached your goal—to revise the Target you are shooting for. Remember to focus on the heart of the Target, what really matters.

PICTURE YOUR TARGET OFTEN

View your goal-state on your Viewing Screen many times. Each time shape your picture up a little more, much as a sculptor would. When picturing yourself in the goal-state, you are using your right brain. The right brain is a great mystery to science and psychology. No one understands why, but when we translate our goals into images and picture them often, the goal tends to manifest.

Our society tends to punish imagination. Teachers usually criticize kids who daydream. Fortunately, this is changing. We are beginning to understand the important role that right brain activities, such as making mental pictures, have in problem solving and creativity. The left brain, which is called on for speaking and doing arithmetic, functions much as a computer does. It's very logical and linear. Schools do an excellent job of training our left brains, but not of developing our right brain skills. We sat in school and said, "One and one is two. Two and two is four." We drilled. Even people who were not "brains" honed up these abilities in school. But most of us have had little or no training in right brain skills. Most of us are operating at a kindergarten level when it comes to right brain skills.

When you image, try to get inside your body to hear, feel, see, smell, and taste. The more senses you employ in your images, the greater their impact. Putting yourself into the goal-state and into your body using all the senses makes your images more compelling than just simply stating a goal.

■ **Dialog with Pam:**

Teacher: What were you doing when you pictured the goal-state, Pam?

Pam: I thought my goal was to be promoted, but now I realize that my goal is to be respected. I could be promoted to a dead-end job, and it would be no promotion at all.

Teacher: What is the doing of being respected? When you are respected what will you be *doing*?

Pam: Co-workers and managers will come to me for advice and will implement my recommendations.

Teacher: Good. You can translate being respected into "becoming an opinion leader within my department." An opinion leader is somebody who people seek out for their opinions when they are confronted with new situations or products. They use the opinion leader's opinions to help them form their own opinions.

Many times each day you are confronted with choices. A powerful goal helps you make those choices. Shall I do this or shall I do that? A powerful goal provides a sense of direction. Translating your goal into an image lets you compare where

Powerful goals help you to make decisions.

you are with where you are going. It's a beacon that lets you know you are moving toward something positive instead of away from something negative.

When you have a compelling Target before you, the next step in pathfinding is to draw a Map that shows the action steps to your Target.

CHAPTER 9

MAP

CHARTING YOUR COURSE

The first thing you have to do
before you find the treasure
is to find the map.
Barbara Sher
Wishcraft

You've sighted your Target. Now the route for getting to it must be charted. Should you take the freeway or a side road? Go along the river? Cross the plain? A Map must be drawn up, because without some kind of chart for navigation, you are likely to find yourself adrift on a sea of fear, uncertainty, and doubt. The conditions are ripe for burnout. Charting the route to your Target is Mapping, and defines the action steps to your goal. When you have a concrete plan with specific steps for reaching your goal, doubt gives way to confidence, and you feel in command, which are conditions that promote bliss.

BEGIN AT THE END

*A lovely way to understand the path ahead
and to make appropriate decisions
is to imagine that it is the future,
and that you have already made the choice.
Then you can look back and find out what you have chosen.
It is rather like one of these children's mazes where
if you start from the beginning you go down many false paths,
but if you cheat and start at the end it is
delightfully easy to see the way.*
Dina Glouberman
Life Choices and Life Changes through Imagework

It is tempting to leap into action as soon as your Target is in place. Watch out for this mistake. You may waste time on false paths, or you may

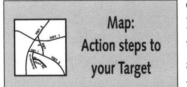

Map: Action steps to your Target

do the right things but in the wrong order. Instead, before starting on your journey, take your goal apart to discover what small, steady actions, in what order, will get you to your Target.

There's a curious paradox. When implementing a plan we move forward in time from the starting point to the goal. So it's natural to think that planning goes forward, too. But effective planning goes from the goal backward to the starting point, the present. To chart your course begin at the end, with your Target, and work backward, break your journey down into pieces, in order to discover the steps you must take to get there.

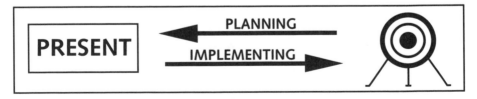

PLAN BACKWARD AND IMPLEMENT FORWARD

CREATE A FLOW MAP

Barbara Sher, author of *Wishcraft*, developed a simple method for identifying action steps; she calls it a Flow Map. Here's how it works. Shelly's Target was to set up an on-line database of health-care trends. To figure out the steps to her Target, she began at the end—the existence of the health-care-trends database—by asking, "Can I do this now?" The answer was no. So Shelly asked, "What do I have to do before I can set up the database?" She saw that the data had to be input first. Look at the illustration on the next page and you see that for the first step backward, Shelly drew a circle to the left of her Target and wrote "input data" in it.

EMPLOY THESE TWO IMPORTANT QUESTIONS TO UNCOVER THE STEPS TO YOUR TARGET:

- Can I do this now?
- If I can't do this now, what do I have to do first?

With one step identified, Shelly repeated the process by asking "Can I input the data now?" Again the answer was "no." Thinking of what she had to do before she could input the data, she identified "gathering the data" as the next step backward. When Shelly wondered if gathering the data could be done now, she realized that two simultaneous steps had to be completed first. The database had to be designed, and studies and product information had to be collected. Following the second of these, Shelly discovered that before she could gather the studies and product information, she had to identify the kind of information that would go into the database. Before doing this Shelly had to poll industry experts, before this she had to contact experts, before this she had to identify experts to poll. Identifying the experts to poll is something she *can* do immediately.

Returning to "gather data," Shelly began following the other path backward. She saw that a database program had to be selected before the database could be designed. Subjecting this step to questioning, Shelly realized that the data parameters had to be decided on before a database program could be selected. Before a program could be selected, the available programs had to be reviewed. But before she could do this, available programs had to be identified, and she had to survey suppliers to find out what programs were available. Before she could do this, Shelly had to identify suppliers—which she was able to do right away.

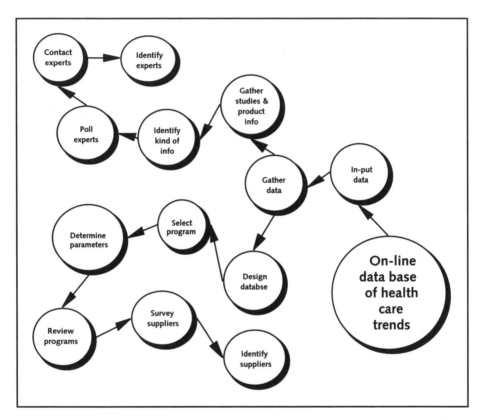

IDENTIFYING STEPS TO YOUR TARGET BY GOING BACKWARD

After identifying the steps backward from her Target of creating an on-line database of health-care trends, Shelly rearranged the steps from the starting point to her Target. Each of the activities she identified in the questioning process became an action step to her Target. With this process Shelly had created a Map for getting to her Target. The Flow Map resembles "flow charts" used in business planning; hence its name.

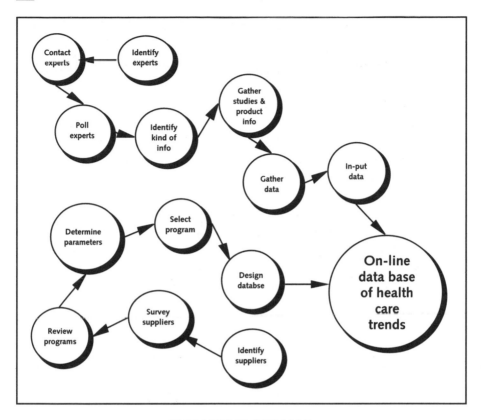

SHELLY'S FLOW MAP

Flow Maps are easy to make and the results are powerful, providing you with a step-by-step action plan for getting from where you are now to your goal. Try your own Flow Map. Draw a circle to represent your Target. Then ask, "Can I do this now?" and "If not, what do I have to do first?" Write your answer in a circle to the left of your Target. Continue until you get to a step you can do now.

Picture what you will be doing at each step.

Your Mental Theater can be helpful in this process. Imagine carrying out the particular step in question, then picture what you would be doing just before the step. Be careful not to create big steps or skip important ones. Continue the questioning process until you've completely bridged the gap between where you are now and the Target.

OUTLINES AS MAPS

Most of us learned how to use outlines in school. The outline starts with a main topic A. Under A we list sub-topics A1, A2, A3 and so forth. Each subtopic can have its own subtopic, so we get A1a, A1b, ... , A2a, A2b, ... , B1a, ... , B2b, ... , C2a, C2b, ... , and so forth until all the steps of the plan have been listed.

Outlining is a wonderful technique for organizing material and planning—provided all the steps have been identified. But outlining is not too useful in identifying the steps and actions. Our minds don't function in the linear fashion of an outline. Often, for example, while you're thinking through step C3a, something under step D2 comes to mind. Then you may think of something related to step G1. What do you do with these ideas? Probably you tell yourself to remember the point until you get to the section in the outline where it goes. If you're like most of us, by the time you get to step D2, you've forgotten the point. It can be frustrating. Once made, outlines can be great maps, but outlining is definitely not the optimal way to devise a Map.

MIND MAPS

Mind Mapping is a great tool for brainstorming steps and actions, because it draws upon our natural mental processes. I was introduced to this simple but powerful technique in Evelyn Wood Reading Dynamics. Later, Tony Buzan popularized Mind Maps in his book *Use Both Sides of Your Brain*.

Many projects demand implementing numerous steps simultaneously. Sometimes the order of the steps is flexible as well. With these
projects, brainstorming a Mind Map can be more effective than the
backward planning. Mind Maps allow you to
grab and build on out-of-sequence ideas, because, being nonlinear in structure, Mind
Maps have no sequence. Instead, Mind Mapping draws on associative thinking which is

> **Mind Maps help chart
> projects with many
> simultaneous steps.**

the way most of us think most of the time. One idea leads to another, not
by logic, but by a series of associations. Mind Maps enable us to capture
these associations. As ideas and steps are recorded on the Mind Map, they
take on a natural organization that can be transformed into an outline if
one is needed.

Here's how it works. Charles' Target was to display at the ARP
annual trade show. He drew a circle representing his Target in the middle
of a blank piece of paper and wrote "Display at ARP" in it. Then Charles
brainstormed major activities and interim accomplishments necessary
to get to his Target. These included materials, booth, travel and accommodations, appointments, registration, and, finally, parties. Next, Charles
drew several squares around his Target. He wrote one major step in each

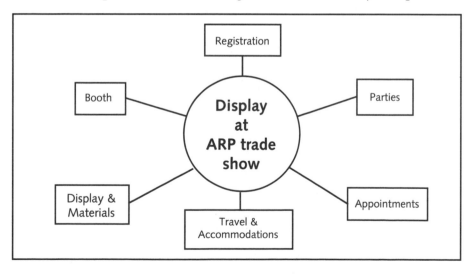

CHUCK'S PARTIAL MIND MAP

square. He drew a line from each square to the circle in the center representing his Target.

Next, Charles took each step one-by-one and brainstormed the actions needed to complete that step. For example, when he wondered what had to be done under travel and accommodations, Charles thought of making reservations, getting traveler's checks, and getting a phone calling card PIN code. He drew three lines out from the box representing travel and accommodations. He wrote one of the three actions on each line. Then Charles remembered he had to make several reservations. So he drew four lines perpendicular to "make reservations" and wrote "airline" on one line, "hotel" on another line, "car rental" on another, and "airport limo" on the last line.

Repeating the process, Charles focused his attention one-by-one on the steps in the boxes and indicated things that needed to be done on lines emanating from the box. For example, under "make appointments," Charles realized that he needed to meet with both old contacts and new prospects. Before appointments could be set with new prospects, Charles

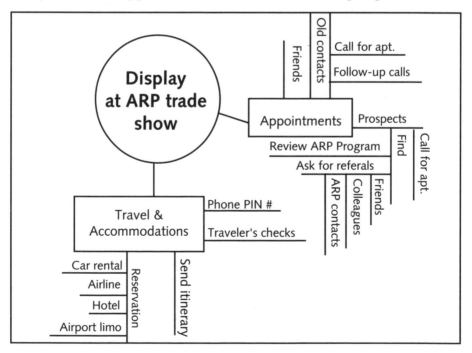

DETAILS OF CHUCK'S MIND MAP

had to locate prospects. Wondering where to find them, he thought of the ARP Program Guide, which listed all the other exhibitors. So he wrote "Review ARP Program" on a line extending from "Find."

> **Mind Maps enable you to capture ideas that come out of sequence.**

As Charles was working on items relative to appointments, an idea for sending an advance notice of his travel itinerary came to mind. Placing items out of sequence is easy with Mind Maps. Charles simply drew a line from travel and accommodations where he wrote "send itinerary." Then he returned his attention to "appointments."

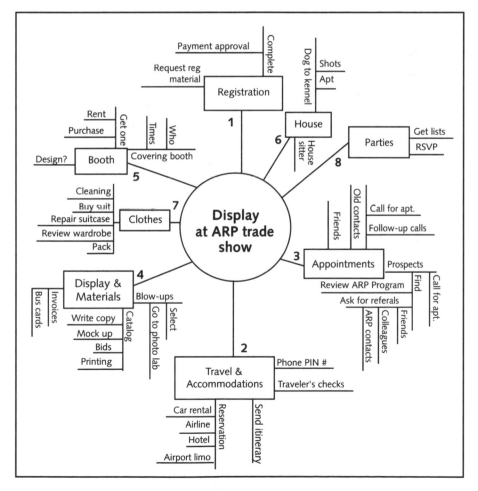

CHUCK'S COMPLETED MIND MAP

Charles had filled in activities under most of the steps in the boxes when he thought of getting his clothes together. This didn't fit under any of the steps, and he realized it was a step itself. So he made a box, wrote "clothes" in it, and connected the box to the Target circle with a line. Then he brainstormed all the activities he had to complete relative to clothes.

You can jump around from one step to another as ideas come to you. If you feel blocked in thinking of steps to accomplish for one activity, go to the next one, and imagine what steps are necessary to complete that activity. As ideas come to mind, find somewhere on the Mind Map to stick them.

As you fill in the Mind Map, you'll notice that it has a way of ordering your ideas, even though they may come to you in no particular order. Once you have a lot of material on your Mind Map, you can prioritize the steps and actions. Charles decided that registering as an exhibitor had to be done right away; so he designated that as 1. Then he realized that travel and hotel accommodations were a high priority timewise; so he designated it as 2. In a similar manner Charles ordered the remaining steps. Then he ordered the activities under the steps. From this he was able to create an outline.

Mind Maps organize your ideas.

DISPLAY AT ARP TRADE SHOW

1. REGISTRATION
- a. Request registration materials
- b. Complete registration forms
  - (1) Get payment approval

2. TRAVEL & ACCOMMODATIONS
- a. Make reservation
  - (1) Airline
  - (2) Hotel
  - (3) Car rental
  - (4) Airport limo
- b. Get phone PIN #
- c. Get traveler's checks

Lots of Uses

One of the nice things about the Mind Map is the large amount of information that you can put on one Map. By looking at it, you can get an overview of all the steps, which often can be quite complicated. Another nice feature of Mind Mapping is that you can put it away and come back to it later. Each time you come back and review the items you've already put on the Map, new activities and steps usually come to mind. Put these somewhere on the Map.

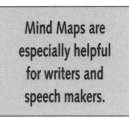

Mind Maps are especially helpful for writers and speech makers.

Mind Mapping is a quick and easy way to capture your ideas. A woman in one of my workshops called it a "brain dump." You can dump your ideas, then return to them later without fear that you'll forget things, which provides a certain feeling of control. Mind Mapping is an excellent device for writers. Instead of planning steps, writers use the Mind Map to brainstorm and organize material. It is particularly helpful in breaking "writer's block" and the "blank-page panic." The writer simply draws a circle for the topic. Then as ideas come, they are placed either in boxes representing major ideas, or on lines emanating from the boxes and representing material related to the idea.

Speechmakers find Mind Mapping to be a great tool for putting together their presentations. The Mind Map can replace awkward notes. The speaker can have all the notes consolidated on a single page. Mind Maps can be used very effectively for note taking from written material or while listening to a pre-

sentation. Try out this versatile tool, and see how you can make it work for you.

DETOURS, SETBACKS AND ROADBLOCKS

The best laid schemes of mice and men oft gang dry.
Robert Burns

If anything can go wrong, it will.
Murphy's Law

Remember the old saying, "The road to hell is paved with good intentions." In spite of our good intentions we sometimes stray from our course. Suppose Beth is working on a grant proposal

| Expect to get detoured and sidetracked. |

and, running out of steam, she sets it aside. Days and weeks go by without any work being done on the proposal. Beth has lost her way and doesn't know how to get back on course. Detours, setbacks, and roadblocks are those things that distract you and impede your progress, throwing you off the course toward your goal. Getting off course is virtually unavoidable; so be prepared for detours and distractions by planning for them before embarking on your journey to your Target.

THE APOLLO WAS MOSTLY OFF COURSE

We used to hear in the space program that on their flights between Earth and the Moon, the Apollo ships were off course more than 90 percent of the time. This spacecraft would wander off its trajectory and the crew would correct: wander off and correct, repeatedly. It was easy, mathematically, to come up with the perfect trajectory between here and there, but the lunar voyagers were actually on that trajectory only 10 percent of the time. And you know what? It didn't matter. What mattered was results. They did it by having the control to get themselves back on course, repeatedly.

Charles Garfield
Peak Performers

HOW DO YOU GET DETOURED?

Before you can make a plan for avoiding detours or getting back on course after the detour you must identify what distracts you and how it happens. When you have a clear understanding of how you are detoured, you can plan and practice course correction. Then when you encounter the distraction, you can enact your plan and get back on course.

There are two ways to identify detours: watching yourself in the moment and watching yourself on your Viewing Screen. Here's how it works. Go to your Mental Theater and project a situation onto your Viewing Screen where you were detoured or distracted and thrown off course. For example, suppose your Target is getting an MBA at night school. Although you intended to study last night, you got distracted and ended up watching TV instead. What happened and how did it happen? Put such a situation on your Viewing Screen and review it. The objective is to discover what detoured you and how. Use your Eye to mentally review the situation to find the moment when you became distracted. It may have been the sight of the TV. It may have been a thought or a feeling. It may have been something someone else did or said. Keep notes on your observations.

Study yourself getting detoured.

Watching yourself get detoured in the moment is essentially the same process as watching yourself on your Viewing Screen getting detoured. The only difference is that it's in real time. In some ways it's as if you were two people: you performing and you watching yourself perform. The you who is watching yourself uses your Eye tool. It is important to act as you normally would. Don't try to avoid the detour. Remember, the objective here is to identify and

observe the detour in action. When you watch yourself in the moment it is easier to notice how you feel and what you're thinking at the point of distraction. This is very important data. Again, keep notes on your observations.

Watching yourself getting detoured in the moment is also a good way to test theories about how you get detoured. For example, suppose  after mentally reviewing situations, you suspect that a particular self-defeating thought triggers the detour. If, when watching yourself in the moment, you notice the troublesome thought, and then feel yourself becoming detoured, you have added support to the theory that this thought is a critical event in your detour cycle. Then you can develop a plan for avoiding the detour or for getting back on course after being detoured.

TAKE SMALL STEPS

One way that many people defeat themselves is by demanding giant steps. They try to do too much too soon. Each step requires so much that they succumb to inertia. The laws of inertia say that a body at rest will stay 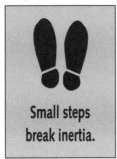 at rest. When you've Mapped out your course but have not yet started, you are a body at rest. You must break the inertia and get into motion. As with pushing a car with a dead battery, it's the first movement that's hardest. Giant steps in a plan are like pushing that car uphill. You'll never get started. Instead, break giant steps down into small easy steps. Small steps help you to get started. Then once you are in motion, the second law of inertia comes into play, it says that a body in motion tends to stay in motion. Get into motion and stay in motion by Mapping out small steps.

COURSE CORRECTION

> *On course does not mean perfect.*
> *On course means that even when things don't go perfectly*
> *you are headed in the right direction.*
> Charles Garfield
> *Peak Performers*

Getting off course is not a disaster and you're not a failure. We all get off course, again and again; so getting off course doesn't threaten your success. What's critical to pathfinding is effective course correction, which involves detecting when you've strayed off the course and then taking action to get back on course.

Once you've identified how you are likely to detour, the next step is to make a plan for getting back on course. One strategy is to *avoid the detour.* Suppose, for example, that seeing the TV is the distractor that detours you from studying in the evenings for your MBA. You could 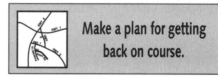 put the TV in the guest room or in a closet. Then, with the TV out of sight, you can avoid this distraction, and thereby avoid being detoured off course.

If avoidance isn't possible, maybe you can *counteract the detour by engaging in something else.* Suppose, for example, your time-management program is detoured by a co-worker who drops by your office on some pretense, because each time he shows up you end up getting sidetracked into office gossip. A substitution strategy might be to cut him off when he gossips and bring up a work-related issue instead.

Another strategy for handling detours is to *restructure your activities.* For example, Suzanne is a telephone saleswoman working out of her home. She finds herself detoured from making calls for appointments almost every day. Calling new prospects is vitally important. Suzanne knows this. Each evening she makes a plan to make such "cold calls," as industry insiders refer to them, at 8:30 A.M. the next morning. But in the morning she can't seem to get going. Sometimes she doesn't make the first call until 10 A.M. She often delays until after 11 A.M. Since the prospects are usually gone for lunch by then, she has to wait until 2 P.M. to make her calls. By then she is usually so depressed that on some days she makes no calls at all. The funny thing is that once she actually makes that first call she invariably thinks, "This wasn't so bad. This was easy." Then she makes the rest of her calls quickly, and leaves to keep the appointments she set up in the calls.

It isn't that Suzanne is lazy. Quite the contrary, she works feverishly each morning "getting organized." This involves logging all her notes from the day before into her file system, stamping the address on the brochures, and writing personal notes on her business cards, which she leaves with receptionists at prospective companies. This takes a lot of time. She believes her success with prospects depends on this good organization. Of course, Suzanne admits that if she doesn't call the prospect, no amount of organizing will result in a sale. She realizes that making the cold calls and making them early is an "A priority" activity.

> **Restructure your
> activities.**

The strategy that helped Suzanne get on course and keep on course involved restructuring her activities. By watching herself being detoured over and over, Suzanne began to realize that cold calls first thing in the morning are pretty hard to make. It's demotivating. She also realized that, while important, getting organized is really procrastination in disguise. Her self-observation yielded another important bit of information. When she is on the road and her pager beeps, she stops at a fast-food place or diner and returns the call. Making cold calls at these times is really pretty easy to do—almost enjoyable.

Taking all this into consideration, Suzanne devised a plan. When paged, she stops at a diner and makes at least one cold call before she calls back the person who paged her. Her objective is to fill the next morning with face-to-face appointments starting at 8:30 A.M. After making her calls, she sits in the back of the restaurant, orders a soda or snack and spends 15 minutes or so organizing. She has a "portable office," which is a basket filled with rubber bands, ink stamp, pads, and paper. Suzanne wouldn't think of being late for an appointment; so her plan works beautifully. She gets out of the house each morning for her 8:30 appointment. Since Suzanne enjoys face-to-face interactions she usually leaves the first appointment highly motivated, which makes cold calling easier to do.

> Having a plan builds confidence.

Having a plan for dealing with the detour is essential. A plan gives you a feeling of confidence, because you know exactly what to do when confronted with the detour.

Brainstorm ways that you can beat the detour. Return to your Mental Theater, and put the first detour situation on your Viewing Screen. One by one, try out the strategies you brainstormed for beating the detour. When one strategy works fairly well, refine it until it works very well in beating the detour. Repeat this process for each detour.

Practice is important. When you are caught in the clutches of distraction, it's difficult to remember good intentions. But when you have a plan and you have practiced your plan, it is easier to extract yourself from the temptation. Here's how:

MAKE A PLAN FOR COURSE CORRECTION

STEP 1. EXPERIENCE THE TEMPTATION:
Go back to your Viewing Screen. This time, watch the detour process start and allow yourself to *feel* the allure of the distraction. Read your Compass. Does it indicate bliss or burnout? Focus on what you're feeling. It is important to *actually experience the temptation* so that you are very familiar with how detour feels.

STEP 2. ENACT YOUR PLAN:
After you've experienced the temptation, enact your plan and watch it work in your mind's eye. If your plan doesn't work, rework it until the plan is effective in getting you back on course. See yourself and feel yourself getting control of your intention in the face of the distraction. See yourself getting back on course.

STEP 3. PRACTICE THE PLAN:
Mentally practice confronting the distraction and then using your

plan to get back on course. When you encounter the actual distraction you'll be prepared to act. The important thing is to practice the plan and see it succeeding in getting you back on course to your goal.

This technique is sometimes called "stress inoculation." Suppose you must confront something negative, such as having to fire someone. You don't want to do it but you can't avoid it. The tendency is to procrastinate, try to get out of it, or soften it; yet if you give in to these escapes, you fail to carry out your responsibility. Stress inoculation can help.

When you get a medical inoculation a weakened bacteria is introduced into your system which then produces antibodies. Later, should you come in contact with active bacteria, your immune system is prepared and can respond quickly. Similarly, you can emotionally inoculate yourself by *experiencing the distress* on your Viewing Screen and seeing your plan getting you back on course.

Imagine the dreaded situation and feel its distress. Then mentally practice your plan for handling the unpleasant or tempting situation.

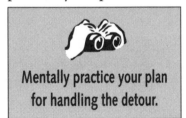

Mentally practice your plan for handling the detour.

This technique doesn't make you like the situation any better. You will still experience the distress or temptation. But you will be psychologically buffered by the inoculation and better able to handle the situation. Stress inoculation is a powerful technique. Encountering detours is inevitable. Mental inoculation helps you to get back on course quickly.

■ Dialog with William:
William: I know I have a problem procrastinating over the filing; so I let it pile up. I can see that this interferes with my working efficiently, because I have to spend so much time looking for papers. So then I just put my project aside, too.
Teacher: What are you thinking when you approach the filing, but before you actually start?

William: Well, I don't know about the words, but I often get this picture of an enormous mountain of files. It sounds silly to say it.

Teacher: It's not silly. We often think in pictures. I get the feeling that you are demanding that you do all the filing at once.

William: Well, yeah, I guess I am. I've got to get it done!

Teacher: When you procrastinate on the filing what do you do instead?

William: Phone calls. Talking to people is a lot more fun than filing!

Teacher: Yes. And you might be able to use that. Try this. Stop demanding that you do all the filing at once. Instead, tell yourself that you have to file only five folders, and then you can make a phone call.

William: Only five folders, hmmm. Well, I suppose I can do that. But there will still be a mountain of folders to file.

Teacher: Yes, but it will be five folders smaller each time you make a call.

■ Dialog with Yolanda:

Yolanda: I know that I'm getting fat from eating snacks during my breaks. But when I decide to forego the snack, I feel pulled into some kind of internal battle where I'm not going to be told what to do by anybody—not even myself! How can I conquer this detour?

Teacher: Avoid all or nothing thinking like, "I won't have any snacks at all any more!" Instead, you might think, "I can go without a snack **this** time." If that doesn't work, you might tell yourself, "I can have a small snack." Then you can stretch the time to include more and more breaks with no snacks or smaller and smaller snacks.

■ Dialog with Kent:

Kent: I sell airtime for KRZT-TV and have to call on a lot of merchants. A lot of times I get to the prospect's business and park, but then I leave without calling on them.

Teacher: Think of the last time you left without seeing the prospect. What happened?

Kent: I parked and as I was reviewing my notes, I got to thinking how the shop looked busy and probably wouldn't have time to see me and probably wouldn't buy. I'd be wasting my time. So I figured I'd come back later and left.

Teacher: So you were thinking of reasons why you wouldn't make a sale? What were you thinking at other times when you left?

Kent: Oh, that they don't have a budget. With one florist, I realized they are too risk phobic to buy TV ads.

Teacher: Sounds like the detour arises from what you think about before the meetings. Thinking can be a powerful detour. If you think, "They won't buy, I'm wasting my time," just before making a presentation, for example, chances are your thoughts will discourage you. This is demotivating. Even if you push yourself to see the prospect anyway, the pitch will probably be harder to give and less likely to result in a sale. Giving yourself a "pep talk" before the meeting might help you to beat this detour. Start by writing down the pep talk on a file card before leaving for the sales call. Then after parking your car, read it to yourself several times before going into your call.

With Map in hand, you know the steps to your destination. But there is still more to do before you actually begin on your journey. Next, you need to develop a method to measure your progress. To do this you use the Yardstick tool, which is the subject of the following chapter.

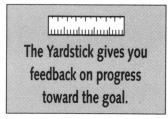

CHAPTER 10

YARDSTICK

MEASURING THE DISTANCE
YOU'VE TRAVELED

If you log consistently, you won't go crashing into icebergs in the fog.
Logs are the compasses. They tell us at a glance, all of us, where we are
and where we might be veering slightly from course, and they give us
information quickly enough so we can do something about the
situation before it becomes a problem.
Paul Hawkins
Growing a Business

Seeing progress toward achieving your goal is reaffirming and helps to keep motivation high. This is especially important when your goal is difficult or takes a long time to reach. Working for long periods of time with little evidence of progress can be very demoralizing and encourages burnout. On the other hand, when you have a sense of accomplishment, especially when you're striving to reach a difficult goal, experiencing moments of bliss is likely.

The Yardstick gives you feedback on progress toward the goal.

The Yardstick is a measuring device. In pathfinding it is used to measure the distance you've traveled toward your destination. It tells the progress you've made toward your Target, and indicates how much further you must go. With the Yardstick you can pinpoint where you are on the Map as well as decide when you're on course and when you must take corrective action

The Yardstick works in conjunction with the Target tool through a process called *feedback*. Feedback on progress toward your goal is tremendously important for sustaining motivation and achieving bliss. Feedback is an information loop where information about the result (output) of your actions feeds back to you, so that you can modify future actions (input), and thereby alter the future results (output). Consider this example. Suppose you were practicing archery with no target. You simply shoot into the air. Since there is no target, you don't get feedback on the accuracy of your shots. How fast would your aim improve without information on how well you are shooting? Chances are that you would show little improvement.

Suppose you set up a target and shoot at it, but can't see where the arrows hit. Your performance would probably not improve in this situation either, because you still have no information on your accuracy and don't know what adjustments need to be made. Feedback that is delayed tends to lose its effectiveness. Suppose you shoot at the target today and six months from now you find out that the shot went into the third ring from the bull's eye. Here, the information on your last shot is so slow in coming back to you that it will probably have little influence on your next shot.

Now suppose a friend with a cellular phone stands near the target. You shoot and seconds later your friend tells you that you've hit the third ring. In this situation you have immediate feedback on your performance, which enables you to make corrective adjustments on your next shot. Chances are you'll be hitting bull's eyes very quickly.

FEEDBACK

Information about errors and failure is valuable, because it lets you know whether or not you're making progress toward the Target. You've probably heard that learning occurs through "trial and error." This means that you make a trial, a shot at the target, for example, and then study your

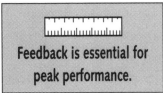

Feedback is essential for peak performance.

error. Informa-
tion on the error
helps you to
make an adjust-
ment in the next
shot. The sooner
you know when you've
been detoured and have encountered a roadblock, the
better. Without this feed-
back, you may think you're moving toward your Target when in fact
you're not. Or you may, in fact, be making progress without realizing it.
Without feedback you can get discouraged and give up.

Many people struggle toward their goals in a rather haphazard
fashion. They suddenly decide they need to improve this, reduce that, or
innovate here and then jump into a project without setting any method
to measure achievement of their goal. It's like shooting at the target
without being able to see where the arrow hit. Without a way to measure
progress, it is difficult to tell if there is progress. Without signs of
progress, it's hard to stay motivated. On the other hand, signs of even
small progress can keep you going. Seeing progress in one's quest is
rewarding, and rewards are what fuel motivation.

The Yardstick works by telling you where your shots are going now
as compared to where you want them to go. When you have an effective
method for measuring your efforts, you can evaluate progress. If you
discover you've been roadblocked, it is a lot easier to take corrective
action right away. In this way the Yardstick actually helps you to zero in
on the goal. It is through measuring and counting (a-count-ability) that
you take command of yourself to become the pilot of your ship.

SELF-MONITORING

Self-monitoring is an important process in leading yourself in
finding a path with a heart. But few people are in the habit of monitoring
their own performance. Self-monitoring involves paying attention to
your performance and the outcomes that result, then recording them. An

example is using a scale and weight chart to keep track of progress toward a targeted weight.

SPONTANEOUS CHANGE

Using effort to consciously practice an attitude or to cultivate a mood is unnecessary and can cause stress and strain. It is important only that we know what [the] attitudes are, that we know what the steps are, that we be aware of them. The more we become aware of them, the more this knowledge gets structured in our consciousness and awareness. Then it is more likely that our attitude and behavior will change spontaneously, without any effort on our part.

Deepak Chopra
Creating Affluence

Besides helping you to zero in on your Target, the Yardstick can improve your performance. Psychological research has demonstrated

Pay attention!

that performance can be improved simply by watching it and recording your observations. That is, you don't have to "try" to improve. When you pay attention in a systematic way to what you do, you'll tend to do what you want to do more and better. For example, a supervisor who wants to make more acknowledging statements to staff members would probably find that counting such statements helps. By counting acknowledging statements, the supervisor is continually reminded to make more of them. As Deepak Chopra points out, you don't have to try to change. You need only be aware of the principles and pay attention to what you do.

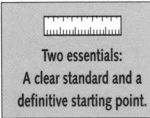

Two essentials:
A clear standard and a
definitive starting point.

DEVELOPING YOUR YARDSTICK

Begin by setting a "standard of achievement." Describe what you will achieve. This means making a clear statement of the conditions that will exist when you hit your Target or achieve a particular step toward your Target.

The next step after clarifying your standard of achievement is to identify your starting point, which is called *getting a baseline*, a measure of where you are when you start. With these two pieces—a clear standard and a definitive starting point—in place, you can

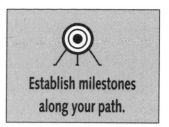

Establish milestones along your path.

use the Yardstick to monitor progress by measuring how far you've come from where you started, the baseline, and how far you have to go to reach your standard of achievement.

SET A STANDARD OF ACHIEVEMENT

Striving toward a goal, especially those that are ambitious and take years to reach, can be a long haul. Most of us have learned that the journey is easier when we break it into steps or milestones along the path. Reaching a milestone gives a sense of accomplishment, which refuels motivation and bolsters confidence to push forward. A milestone may be a small action, a larger step toward the Target, or achievement of the Target itself. The standard of achievement is a statement of the *results that will exist* when you achieve a particular milestone. It specifies a result, is measurable and attainable, and has a completion date.

A standard of achievement specifies a result, is measurable
and attainable, and has a completion date.

A Standard Specifies a Result

A standard of achievement specifies the result that you aim to
achieve during a particular phase of your journey. A result is the outcome

> A result describes
> the "what" but not
> the "how."

or end point you are shooting for to reach a
particular milestone. It describes *what* you aim to
achieve, but not *how* you will do so. *What* will be
achieved refers to an outcome or result, whereas
how refers to an activity or process.

It's easy to confuse results and activities, because we tend to think
in terms of activities rather than results. Most of us have been trained to
perform—to do our best—and than to wait for a boss, a teacher, or a
parent to tell us if we've succeeded. We've not been oriented to think in
terms of the *results* we aim to achieve. Instead we usually think of our
work as a job, a series of tasks or activities that we carry out repetitively
and routinely. Thinking in terms of activities and processes tends to keep
you locked into doing a job, performing a series of activities. Or worse,
sometimes when we focus on activities instead of the result we can get
something entirely different from what we were seeking. Take, for
example, the father who wants to be a "good" parent. For this reason he
works long hours and at a second job on weekends in order to earn
enough to buy his son all the things he never had as a child. Imagine the
father's confusion when he learns that the boy is a troublemaker at
school, and when the school counselor accuses him of being a neglectful
parent who cares more about his work than his son. Another example is
the administrator who wants to be more efficient. To accomplish this, she
spends hours and hours organizing, only to be told during her semi-
annual review that she is inefficient because she spends too much time
on irrelevant things like excessive organizing.

The problem is that we have not been encouraged to think in terms
of the problem we were hired to solve (or choose to solve, as with
individual projects, hobbies, and volunteer and aesthetic activities) or a
result we want to accomplish. But to be a pathfinder, you must develop

Vision and see where you want to go, see the solution to the problem you seek to solve. The important point to understand is that the solution you seek is a *result* and focusing on the result helps you to lead yourself, so that you can find the path with a heart—the path to bliss.

Focusing on the result helps you to lead yourself.

Activities are things you do to *achieve* results. An organized office is a result whereas filing papers is an activity that contributes to the office being organized. Being able to find a file in three minutes is a result, whereas coding files by product, then cross-referencing by client is a process. A process is the way in which something is developed or brought about. It refers to a particular method of making or doing something, in which there are a number of steps. Using a particular filing process results in a person's being able to find a specific file in three minutes.

A standard states what will be achieved...but not how.

■ Dialog with June:

June: My action step is to insure that our clients have marketable word processing skills. My standard of achievement for this step is to conduct weekly classes in word processing for twenty job applicants so that they will pass the data-entry exam by November 30.

Teacher: Your emphasis is on conducting a weekly class. Conducting a class is an activity. What is the outcome you are striving for?

June: The outcome is for them all to pass the data-entry exam.

Teacher: Good. So the standard should specify the outcome—passing the exam, not the activity—teaching one class.

June: Hmmm. Do you mean, "to prepare twenty job applicants so that they will pass the data-entry exam by November 30"?

Teacher: Yes, good. This standard states the result—what you will accomplish—but not how you will do it.

■ **Dialog with Lea:**

Lea: My action step is to revamp our antiquated office filing system to make it more effective.

Teacher: What is the purpose of the filing system?

Lea: The consultants must have ready access to information when they need it.

Teacher: Then your standard of achievement might be to be able to retrieve any information from the files within a particular number of minutes—like three minutes.

Lea: I also want the system to be current, and not clogged up with old useless stuff.

Teacher: What is old and useless?

Lea: Well, client cases and statistics more than five years old.

Teacher: Can you discard this information?

Lea: We never look at it. But, you know we might have to someday so we have to keep it. But it can be in deep storage.

Teacher: How about this one: to have only new files (less than five years old) in the active file system, and to have all client cases and statistics more than five years old in storage files.

■ **Dialog with Sebastian:**

Sebastian: My action step is to increase the speed of transcribing and editing the company newsletter. My standard for this step is to have no more than five percent of manuscripts returned because of misspellings for retyping per month.

Teacher: It could be difficult to identify when the return was caused by typing errors as compared to other errors. What are you really interested in?

Sebastian: Well, the number of manuscripts returned for rework.

Teacher: Good, so instead of specifying all the reasons that lead to rework, your standard should be more general, focusing on rework and not on each possible kind of error leading to rework.

■ **Dialog with Billie:**

Billie: My goal is to increase the professional image of the department. My action step is to maintain the Director's appointment schedule. My standard is to ask the Director each morning if she has made any appointments I don't know about.

Teacher: Asking the Director about appointments is an activity. In setting standards it is easy to become distracted by activities. Ask yourself: what is the outcome I aim to achieve?

Billie: That the calendar is current and on the Director's desk by 9 A.M.

Teacher: Asking the Director each morning about appointments is an activity. It's ongoing. There's no beginning or end. You can't tell when you've achieved it. By comparison, to have the appointment calendar on the Director's desk by 9 A.M. each morning can work as a standard. You can know whether or not you've achieved it.

A Standard Is Measurable

Accountability is important in pathfinding. At the heart of accountability is "counting" or measuring how close you are getting to your Target. The Yardstick provides a method for doing so. The Yardstick gives a method of a-count-ability. It is a tool that enables you to count your steps toward your destination, which gives a feeling of being centered and of knowing where you are. In addition to its bolstering effect, the Yardstick enables you to take corrective action quickly when you discover

The Yardstick provides a-count-ability.

you are off course. Without a Yardstick you can be deprived of a sense of progress, which can engender a sense of helplessness. This is especially true of people who work alone and who get little feedback from others. Being able to measure your progress, on the other hand, fosters a sense of control, and as we discovered earlier, feelings of control encourage bliss.

The Yardstick is a measuring system, with the demarcations being the units of measurement. These units change, depending on the nature

Measuring progress allows you to identify the need for corrective action.

of your Target. Sometimes the demarcations might be time segments such as weeks or months. With another Target, it might be numbers of units, like numbers of sales closed. Yet a third Target might use quality ratings. Deciding what the optimal measurement unit is, is easier when your goal clearly specifies the outcome that will exist when it is achieved. It is

much harder to establish the unit of measurement when the goal-state is vague. For example, suppose you have a goal to become more competitive. How can you measure progress toward this goal? What can you count or measure? By comparison, the goal to increase market share by 10 percent is specific and measurable.

When you've decided on the best unit of measurement for evaluating progress toward a milestone on the way to the goal, then you establish your standard of achievement. The standard indicates at what point along the Yardstick you've reached your milestone.

Kinds of Measurements

There are five kinds of measures: **cost and income, quality, time, frequency** and **quantity.** Cost and income refer to money and expenses, such as overhead, net income, and dollar amounts. Quality refers to how well something will be done, and involves judgments, such as poor versus better, or high versus low. Time refers to how long something will occur, and involves hours, minutes, delays, or speed of reactions.

KINDS OF MEASUREMENTS:

- ■ 1. cost and income
- ■ 2. quality
- ■ 3. time
- ■ 4. frequency
- ■ 5. quantity

Frequency refers to how often, and involves counting such things as the number of sales, the number of returns, and the number of complaints. Quantity refers to how much there will be of something and might be in terms like pounds, dozens, or hundreds.

A Standard Is Attainable

A standard that makes you stretch a little is good, but unattainable standards are frustrating and diminish motivation. For example, a perfectionist's standard is perfect performance. Of course, such a standard is not usually attainable. If you're always falling short of the standard, your self-esteem suffers, and you can develop an attitude of "Why bother? If I can't reach the standard, then why should I try to do so."

> Set a standard with a little stretch.

When setting a standard, follow the example of the yogi. In yoga, you put yourself into a particular posture, like bending at the waist and reaching with your hands as far toward the floor as you comfortably can. Then you stretch a little bit. Each time you assume this posture, you stretch a little more. Eventually, you can bend over and place your palms flat on the floor without strain.

Set a standard that, with a little stretch, is attainable and you'll gain in confidence and experience a boost in motivation when you achieve it. Instead of demanding a giant step, set a series of stretching standards that you can meet, and avoid demanding the unattainable of yourself.

■ **Dialog with June:**

Teacher: You said that your standard of achievement is to prepare twenty job applicants so that they will pass the data-entry exam by November 30. Are you setting a standard that requires 100 percent success in order for the standard to be achieved?

June: Of course, I want them all to pass.

Teacher: I understand. But is it attainable? Or are you setting yourself up in such a way that you'll be unable to achieve your standard?

June: I see what you mean.

Teacher: What is a realistic number of passes?

June: Well, I'd say 19 out of the 20.

Teacher: Ok, that's 95 percent. Put this into your standard.

June: That 95 percent of the job applicants I prepare will pass the data-entry exam by November 30.

Teacher: Yes, good.

A Standard Has a Completion Date

A completion date provides a clear point in time to achieve the result. This part of the Yardstick helps you to decide if you are on time,

| Set yourself up |
| to succeed. |

ahead of schedule, or late. Like the other elements of a standard, the completion date can be motivating when it is realistic or discouraging when unattainable. Targets are achieved in real time. The completion date enables you to schedule activities and to pace yourself. If you fall behind, the Yardstick reveals this quickly so that you can take corrective action before things get hopeless.

EXAMPLES OF STANDARDS OF ACHIEVEMENT

EXAMPLE 1: *Contribute to the sales staff's understanding of doctors' needs.*

This standard is too vague and has no completion time. "Contribute to understanding of needs" doesn't specify a measurable result. What kind of contribution and how much contribution is not clear. It doesn't provide any guide for knowing when the standard has been achieved.

EXAMPLE 2: *Poll doctors' needs and preferences, identify the sales staff's difficulties in selling to doctors and review existing training. Develop a three-session training module, including audio and video models, on calling on and talking with doctors, present it to the sales staff by December 15 and evaluate its impact on number of cold calls made, quotas reached and sales staff's perceptions.*

This standard has a completion time and is probably attainable but it is too detailed. It describes the "how" rather than the "what." In fact, it is more of an action plan describing several steps.

EXAMPLE 3: *To have a training module on communicating with doctors developed and presented to the sales staff by December 15.*

This standard is better. It describes what will be achieved but not how. You can tell whether or not it has been achieved.

GET A BASELINE

Once you've developed your Yardstick by establishing a standard of achievement which specifies where you'll be when you reach the mile-

> **Baseline is your starting point.**

stone and how you will measure it, then go to the next step which is to use this Yardstick to measure where you are starting from. This starting point, or "baseline," is used as the base or point that you measure from. It helps you to measure your progress relative to a beginning point, whereas the standard of achievement helps you to measure progress relative to a particular end point.

In weight loss, for example, the baseline is your weight before going on the diet. The baseline tells you where you started and provides a

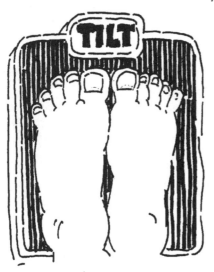

reference point. Always gather information on a baseline first. By knowing where you've started from, you can see the distance you've traveled.

MONITOR PROGRESS

Use the Yardstick to monitor progress. Sometimes this may mean measuring on a daily, or even hourly basis, while other times the measuring may be less frequent. It all depends upon the nature of your project and what you are trying to achieve.

GUIDELINES FOR USING THE YARDSTICK
THE SOONER, THE BETTER

Feedback that comes too late or too long after performance loses its effectiveness. This is analogous to shooting an arrow at the target and then being told six months later that it went into the third ring from the bull's eye. When there's a long time delay before measuring, it is difficult to remember the situation well enough to learn from it or to take any corrective action. At six months, how can you remember the tension you used when pulling the bow or where you aimed? Which feedback will have more impact on a runner's performance: running time given immediately after the race, or running time given two weeks later? Immediate feedback has a greater impact, because the runner can correlate running time to his or her performance and make adjustments. By comparison, two weeks after the race the runner has probably forgotten most of the specifics of the run. Feedback that is delayed provides little help in making improvements.

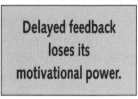

Delayed feedback loses its motivational power.

Whenever possible, feedback should be immediate. Think of ways of measuring that yield information while you are still performing or shortly afterward. The sooner the feedback, the sooner you know when you strayed off course, and the sooner you can take corrective action to get back on course.

PORTABLE AND EASY

Feedback systems that require a lot of effort to record tend to be pretty ineffective because we just don't bother doing it. The recording apparatus must be present when the behavior occurs. There are many kinds of portable recording devices you can experiment with.

Logs

Every ship's captain and airplane's pilot keep a log of each voyage. This is something like a diary where you can periodically record progress along with significant events, measurements of various sorts, and subjective evaluations. Later, when you read over the log, you can see patterns and draw conclusions. You can find a variety of notebooks, some pocket size, in office-supply stores. Alternatively, you might keep your

log in a computer. However, unless it's a lap-top, the computer is less practical, because it isn't portable.

File Cards

Three-by-five file cards are great for collecting data of all sorts. They can be easily carried in a shirt pocket or purse. You can draw columns on them to create times of the day or days of the week. Or they can be used to jot down notes or cross-hatches when counting things. File cards come in several colors, too.

Counting Devices

There are a variety of inexpensive counters available that can be used to count things. Golf-stroke counters that look like watches and can be worn on the wrist are available in sporting-goods stores. Knitting-row counters that can be slipped on to the end of a pencil can be purchased in yarn stores. These counters can be used to count anything. Your imagination is the limit. Behavioral psychologists teach their clients to change thinking styles by counting particular thoughts, for example. If you're adventurous you might use an abacus, which is a frame on which beads slide back and forth on wires. They are available in Chinatown and toy stores.

Another method for counting is a pocketfull of coins. Each time you observe the event or item in question, you move one coin from your left pocket to your right pocket. At the end of the observation period, you count and record how many coins are in your right pocket. Finally, you can use the traditional cross-hatches, which consists of four vertical lines and a fifth line that crosses and connects the vertical lines. Each line represents one event or item counted.

Timers

Stopwatches can be purchased in sporting-goods stores. Cooking timers are available in housewares sections of department stores. Or, if you prefer, you might experiment with an hourglass.

Scales

The bathroom scale is one of the most familiar measuring devices. You can step onto the scale each day and monitor your weight. When you notice that you've gained a pound or two, you can take action to lose the unwanted weight. If you're on a diet and see that you've lost a couple of pounds, you probably feel elated by this feedback on the success of your dieting. Scales of all kinds are available in variety, discount, and department stores.

Rulers

Rulers are another measuring device that most people have had much experience using. In many homes with growing children you'll find marks on the kitchen door frame indicating each child's height. The child and other family members can see at a glance how much the child has grown since the last measuring. Rulers and yardsticks in inches and other measures can be purchased in office-supply stores and variety stores.

MEASURE KEY FACTORS FOR SUCCESS

> *What gets measured gets done.*
> Guy Kawasaki
> *Selling the Dream*

Measuring the wrong variable can lead to focusing on improving the wrong thing. There is a natural tendency for us to focus on the things that we're getting feedback on and to ignore other things. This can slow your progress, even throw you off course. For example, if you wanted to increase profitability it could be a mistake to count the number of sales. Counting the number of sales will encourage salespeople to focus on the number of sales rather than the amount of sales. The result is often that easy-to-obtain small sales increase, but profitability goes down,

We pay attention to what we measure.

because small sales are always less profitable than large sales. Each sale may require producing an invoice and bookkeeping. These steps are time consuming. Consequently, it costs the same to process a large sale as a small one, but there is more profit in the large sale. A better measure for assessing profitability might be daily or weekly net sales, which would be the amount of sales minus operating costs.

FOCUS ON THE POSITIVE

Always strive to measure the feedback positively, not negatively. The glass contains the same amount whether it is half full or half empty. However, feedback on how "full" the glass is is more motivating than feedback on how "empty" the glass is. For example, measure uptime, not downtime. When you measure uptime, you're paying attention to times when the system is functioning. Your focus is on success and you feel good when you see it. By contrast, when you measure downtime, your focus is on the negative. It's easy to overlook success—uptime—and to be constantly looking for failure—downtime. Such emphasis on the negative can give you the feeling that you're always failing. Needless to say, this is very demotivating. Instead, stress the positive side over the negative side.

■ **Dialog with Sebastian:**

Teacher: Your standard specifies the number of manuscripts sent back for rework. It focuses on manuscripts needing rework, with the emphasis being to reduce that number. This standard is stated in the negative. What is the positive that you really want to achieve?

Sebastian: To increase the number of manuscripts that don't require rework.

Teacher: Yes. Reframe your standard in terms of this positive that you wish to achieve. Remember to keep it attainable.

Sebastian: That 97 percent of the manuscripts will move to production without rework.

Teacher: Good. But is 97 percent a realistic level?

Sebastian: Our current rework level is 15 percent rework rate which is 85 percent passable without rework. But I think that can be brought down—ah, brought up considerably. And that's my Target.

Teacher: It is easier to make a change when you focus on small steps or on reaching intermediate milestones. What would be an intermediate step?

Sebastian: Well, 92 percent without rework. But I wouldn't be satisfied with that!

Teacher: Yes. However, small steps are easier to achieve than giant steps. As you reach each small step, you set another, higher standard.

Sebastian: Yes, I understand what you're saying, but it still seems as if I'd be accepting less than adequate work.

Teacher: Of course, that's true for the short term. However, right now you're accepting 85 percent passable.

Sebastian: I'm not accepting it. I'm complaining about it!

Teacher: Is it helping?

Sebastian: Well, no.

Teacher: What would be a small step improvement?

Sebastian: Well, I suppose 88 percent passable without rework.

Teacher: Okay, good. Achieving 88 percent error free manuscripts is a step toward your goal. How would you state your standard?

Sebastian: That 88 percent of the manuscripts will move through production without rework.

MAKE FEEDBACK VISUAL

Putting feedback onto a graph gives a picture. Charts and graphs can be very motivating, because you can see how close you are getting to your Target. You don't have to translate abstract data to see your progress. So experiment with ways of putting your data onto charts and graphs. Try posting it on a wall or bulletin board where you can see it often.

Seeing progress is itself a reward.

CHECK YOUR YARDSTICK OFTEN

There is a tendency to act and move through the steps to your Target without measuring progress. This is a mistake. The Yardstick lets you know what progress you're making, and it's reaffirming because seeing progress is a reward in and of itself. So check your Yardstick often.

MONITORING YOUR
PATHFINDING SKILLS

Becoming skilled as a pathfinder is an ongoing, lifelong process. Pathfinding is complicated with many steps to learn. Sometimes you will advance quickly in one area, other times it will seem as if you're making little progress. It helps to periodically review your personal leadership skills. The Pathfinding Checklist (page 333) summarizes the pathfinding process with all its many steps and components. It can help show you where you are skilled at leading yourself and where you have areas to improve.

When embarking on a project use the Pathfinding Checklist as a quick reminder of the pathfinding steps. It can also be used with the Yardstick for measuring your personal leading skills. Of course, rating your personal leadership skill is subjective. You decide if you engaged in a particular activity to a satisfactory degree or if you could have done it more. You can use the Checklist to identify pathfinding activities to concentrate on. Remember, developing your pathfinding skills is a life-long process.

The next important step in pathfinding is getting your ducks in line. It's important to build cooperation and to assess who might resist and why before launching into your project. For this you use the Team tool which follows.

CHAPTER 11

TEAM

ELICITING COOPERATION

Leaders know they can not do it alone.
It takes partners to get extraordinary things done.
James Kouzes and Barry Posner
The Leadership Challenge

*W*hen struggling with burnout we tend to withdraw from others both at work and at home. If the burnout persists, we usually experience interpersonal conflict, because we are irritable, moody and depressed. Problems with others tend to become a vicious cycle: as we withdraw from others, we become more difficult to deal with, then they withdraw from us. On the other hand, if you are going to make your way from burnout to bliss you've got to invest time and energy in other people in your world since it is next to impossible to accomplish much of consequence without others' support. Giving attention to others can be very hard to do when burnout has depleted your energy and enthusiasm.

Your project's success depends on others' support.

Social support is important for many reasons. For one thing friends and family can buffer you from the effects of stress and burnout. Building social support is one of the paths to personal power and beating burnout. You will be happier and more productive, and experience more moments of bliss, when surrounded by supportive friends, family and colleagues. Social support is also important in your endeavor to find a path with a heart.

Remember: No project operates in a vacuum. Whether your project is at work, a volunteer activity, a political or community issue, or recreational, it probably takes place in a social environment—which means that other people can make or break your project. So it is well worth the effort it takes to enlist the support of all those whom you need to make the project work and of all those who may be affected by it. Above all else, this requires cooperation and attention to the needs of others. By developing these qualities, you will be laying the necessary groundwork for a strong social support system. Not only will such characteristics earn you respect and enhance your reputation as a team player and a person who gets things done, it will also increase your own personal power, your ability to attain goals and influence events. When things go well for you and you have a supportive situation, your moments of bliss will be many.

COOPERATION IS THE KEY

There's one phrase that I hate to see in any executive's evaluation,
no matter how talented he may be, and that's the line:
"He has trouble getting along with people."
To me, that's the kiss of death.
Because that's all we've got around here.
No dogs, no apes—only people.
Lee Iacocca
Iacocca

Traditionally, there's been an emphasis on being the star performer, and people generally feel that it is soloing that really counts; so we shouldn't be too surprised that most people tend to compete rather than cooperate. However, in today's world it's next to impossible to accomplish much without the help of others. Other people can open doors or slow things down. They can give you information you need or let you go out on a limb. In a real sense, your success depends on cooperation from others. If you focus on your own individual achievement too much, you'll appear overly competitive, which may make getting others' cooperation difficult. Getting cooperation doesn't just happen. It takes time and effort to get others onto your team.

RECIPROCATE

Reciprocity or an I'll-scratch-your-back-if-you-scratch-my-back scenario is an effective strategy for creating cooperative relationships. Although people can sometimes rise to the top by running roughshod over their com-

Act like a partner.

petition, chances are their hold on power will be tenuous. Their very means of ascent will make them a target, and when they fall, they fall hard. In today's political and social climate, networking, cooperation, and reciprocity is proving to be a more effective combination than the Machiavellian doctrine of expediency and manipulation.

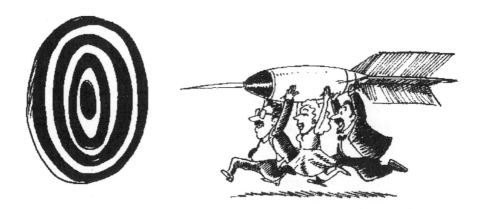

PARTNERS GET THINGS DONE

Yoshitaka Suzuki was a sales rep with Nihon Electric Company (NEC) and had a large securities firm as his sole client. Suzuki took his account from almost zero business in 1978 to a constant $10 million annually by 1987.

Suzuki started by selling a small system to someone relatively far down in the organization. He didn't stop with the sale. Instead, he thought of himself as a "partner" and helped his customer to use the computer to get visibility. As a result, the customer reciprocated by introducing Suzuki to others who decided to use NEC. Continuing his win-win approach, Suzuki worked up to the division level, and to introducing the president of NEC to the president of the client company. As he put it, "From that one sale of a small computer came the next one thousand sales." Suzuki's first "partner" became managing director. As Larry Wilson, founder of Wilson Learning Corporation, who first reported Suzuki's story, put it, "They came up the organizational chart together."

Larry Wilson
Changing the Game: The New Way to Sell

Suzuki acted like a partner to his customer, helping him to get visibility and to succeed. In return, his customer helped him with strategic introductions. They established a win-win scenario based on cooperation.

A winning approach for establishing reciprocity is to cooperate first, then ask for reciprocity. An incentive for someone to help you is knowing that you will help in return. Begin by setting an example. Look for ways to help others. Be generous with information. Extend yourself to others. The best time to ask for cooperation is when you've just provided support to someone else. People are inclined to cooperate with those who help them. The rule of thumb is to help first then specifically ask for support.

Help first, then ask for support.

Giving support doesn't have to be time consuming or take you away from your priorities. Moral support where you show interest in and empathy for other people's concerns, is the easiest. Being a sounding board, listening to a person's dreams and worries, and giving feedback can help tremendously. Another way to give support is to acknowledge your allies. Mention their good ideas, successes, and ways they've helped you. This is particularly powerful when you share this kind of acknowledgement with co-workers and supervisors. Backing up others' ideas in meetings is another easy way to be supportive. Your support gives their suggestions more weight. Think of the people whose cooperation you need as being allies and on your team. In sports, you set teammates up so that they can make the shot. When your team wins, you win. It's the same thing.

GET OTHERS INVOLVED

When people feel involved they tend to be more cooperative, whereas you're likely to run into resistance from people who feel excluded. When people feel involved, they tend to buy into your project and support it. Two simple but powerful ways to involve others is to keep others informed and to ask for their opinions and advice.

Keep People Informed

You can get tremendous mileage out of the simple act of keeping people informed, particularly those who are influenced by your project. Above all, avoid surprises. In the workplace, people tend to resist surprises, because they can be unnerving and create insecurity. "If this happened, what next?" When you inform people of small developments, even when they are problems or discouraging events, they will accept them much more

Keeping people informed builds trust and fosters involvement.

easily than hearing about the accumulation of events all at once. It's easier to accept something when you hear about it as it develops, blow by blow, which allows you to adjust to each small change. Keeping people informed builds trust and fosters a feeling of involvement. Nothing creates suspicion and distrust more than to find out about something that affects you through the grapevine after the fact. Strive to prevent such information leaks to those influenced by your project and those whose cooperation you need by telling them what's going on soon and often.

Communicate up, down and sideways. Don't forget the support staff and people below you in the hierarchy. Let them know what's going on, too. Management consultant Dr. Keshavan Nair said, "To get things done, it is important to have friends in low places." And it's important to keep them informed, too. When you take the effort to inform people in modest positions of what's going on, they feel important and respected. With this small effort, you can make valuable allies in low places.

Ask for Opinions and Advice

Another way to get people involved is to ask for their opinions, ideas, and feelings and to listen to what they say. When you ask others for their advice, you communicate that you value their opinion. This can have an almost irresistible effect, because the person whose opinion you've solicited will feel important and in the know. All too often in today's world we feel insignificant and ignored; so anything you do to communicate to other people that they are valued and important brightens their world and promotes their moments of bliss.

Once a person has given you his or her advice, that person has an investment in your project. They have made a contribution and will usually be curious as to the outcome. All of this predisposes the advice giver to be supportive of this project in particular as well as your future projects.

HOW TO ASK GOOD QUESTIONS

Surprisingly few people know how to ask good questions, and instead ask questions that are actually statements, or that "lead" the answers. When you have good skills at asking questions, you can get quite a bit of information even when you have little or no prior information. In fact, with good interview skills, you can get more information in ten minutes than someone with poor questioning skills could get in half an hour or more. Following are several guidelines and techniques for asking good questions.

QUESTION-ASKING GUIDELINES

Guideline: Establish Rapport

For people to be open enough to share opinions, ideas and feelings, they must feel accepted and free to express themselves without judgment or recrimination. Being relaxed promotes open-ness. So put the person at ease so that he or she will feel comfortable with you.

Put the person at ease.

Avoid negative nonverbal feedback. If, while a person is expressing his or her opinion you start shaking your head, you communicate disapproval. Such feedback can destroy rapport and cause the person to suppress ideas and opinions. Nonverbal behaviors that send a negative message can be subtle. A look of disparagement, a yawn, exaggerated surprise, or a stern gaze can be taken as being judgmental and discourage the speaker from being open.

Instead, give positive feedback, which encourages openness. Smile and give the person your undivided attention. Use your nonverbal behavior to communicate "I am listening, I am interested, and I am making an effort to understand your point of view." Look at the person, nod approvingly, smile, lean forward, and encourage the person to speak with "un huh," "hum," and saying things like "I see," "I understand," and "Oh, really!"

Guideline: Don't Argue

When you ask people for their opinions, ideas, and feelings, and then argue with them, they feel judged. Arguing implies that what they have said is wrong, silly, or somehow inappropriate. This undermines rapport, and people will clam up or simply tell you what they think you want to hear. Not only is arguing unproductive in terms of getting information you need, it can turn allies into resisters. So avoid arguing. Instead, strive to communicate that you want to understand the issue being discussed from his or her perspective. Understanding what a person thinks and feels does not mean that you agree with that position.

Avoid using the word "but," which sounds as if you disagree and tends to provoke an argument. Suppose, for example, a person says "The staffers want to get involved." You sound as if like you're disagreeing or correcting the speaker if you say, "Yes, but involvement at the top is essential." Practice substituting "yes, and" for "yes, but." For example, "Yes, and involvement at the top is essential, too," communicates support while still making your point about the importance of top-level involvement.

> **Avoid the words "but" and "yes, but."**

Guideline: Don't Talk Too Much

If you're going to find out what the person thinks and feels he or she has got to do most of the talking while you do most of the listening. The rule of thumb is an 80/20 percent split with the other person speaking about 80 percent of the time. If you catch yourself speaking more than 20 percent, you've probably strayed from asking good questions to telling your own opinions and feelings instead.

> **If you're doing more than 20% of the talking, you're talking too much!**

Guideline: Avoid Leading Questions

A leading question is one phrased in a way that it leads or influences the person to answer in a particular way. The problem is obvious. You're biasing the answer. Nonetheless, leading questions are surprisingly hard to avoid. In fact, most of our questions are leading because we tend to phrase questions with the answer we think the person will make in the question. For example, "Don't you think funding will be a problem?" is a leading question. The asker thinks funding will be a problem, and the question is worded in such a way so as to focus on the funding issue. A better question would be, "What problems do you see?" The question "This design is flawed, isn't it?" also leads the answer. A question that doesn't lead might be, "What is your opinion of this design?"

Guideline: Avoid Yes/No Questions

Avoid questions that can be answered with "yes" or "no," which are called "closed questions." There are several problems with yes/no questions. For one, they are inefficient in getting information, because the person can give one-word answers of "yes" or "no," which gives little information. So you can easily find yourself talking more and more as you ask long questions and get only yes or no answers. In the extreme, it can become something like an interrogation. Interrogations usually emphasize closed questions. "Can you … ?" "Isn't it true that you … ?" "Did you … ?" If you try to elaborate, the interrogator snaps, "Just answer the question. Yes or no!" The object of interrogation is to push the subject into an admission, usually a 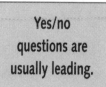 particular admission. Clearly, such an approach destroys the relaxed atmosphere and feelings of trust needed to promote openness and sharing of views.

Another problem with questions that can be answered with yes or no is that they are usually leading. Take the question, "Do you think we will have trouble getting support?" for example. You guess that the person thinks the problem is getting support, then phrase the question to confirm it. Of course, the person can disagree. But closed questions like this tend to restrict the field of possible answers by focusing on confirming or disagreeing with the answer implicit in the question. The closed question has put a frame around the answer, a context in which it is understood.

Guideline: Don't Jump to Conclusions

It seems obvious that we should avoid jumping to conclusions, but the problem is that we're usually not aware of when we are doing it. We all see things from our own perspective and interpret things within our own frame of reference. So when something is vague or ambiguous, we usually fill in the blanks without realizing it and, in the process, draw unwarranted conclusions. The best way to avoid jumping to conclusions is to get specific information and check out your understanding of what the person has said.

QUESTION-ASKING TECHNIQUES

Technique: Repeat

Most of us tend to speak ambiguously. We make generalizations, use technical words and speak in jargon. Suppose a person says, "I see a number of problems getting this project off the ground." With the repeat technique you can clarify what the person means and get more specific information. Here's how it works: Pick out the key word in what a person has said. Here the key word is "problems," or "number of problems." Repeat the key word or phrase with a slight inflection. You say, "Problems?" or "Number of problems?" The person will almost always elaborate more specifically on the word or phrase you repeated. The beauty of this technique is that you can interject your repeat into the people's flow of conversation without their feeling interrupted.

The repeat technique is great for clarifying technical phrases, jargon and slang. "I'll have to check with The Big D first." You repeat, "The Big D?" The person replies, "Yea, you know, the Director." The person says,

"It was an ATM problem." You repeat, "ATM?" The person replies, "You know, automatic transmission mode." You repeat, "Mode?" The person answer, "You know, my usual way of doing it."

Technique: Probe

The probe is an open-ended question beginning with who, what, when, where, under what conditions, or in what way. Like the repeat technique, the probe encourages the speaker to be more specific. Following the example from above, the speaker says, "I can see problems getting this project off the ground." A probe would be, "What kind of problems?" Such an open-ended question can't answered with "yes" or "no," because such an answer doesn't make sense. Instead, the person will usually give more specific information. Consequently, when using a probe you tend to talk less while getting more information.

It's a good idea to avoid the word "why." The word "why" implies a request for justification and tends to put people on the defensive. Feeling judged and being defensive destroys rapport and makes people clam up. Instead of "Why?" you can ask, "What happened?" or "What was the reason for that?"

> **Avoid the word "why?"**

Technique: Silence

Silence can be a good information-gathering technique. When the person is talking and pauses, resist the urge to leap in with a question. Instead, just remain silent for a few seconds while using nonverbal behavior, like smiling and nodding, and prompts like "un huh," and "Go on." The person will usually to pick up where he or she left off. If not, you can follow with a probe, "What other problems do you see?" or "What happened then?"

Technique: Check-Out

Jumping to conclusions is tremendously difficult to avoid because we are constantly making judgments and drawing conclusions about all kinds of things in our environment. So it takes conscious effort to override this tendency.

When you think you understand what a person has said, don't assume you understand, because you may be jumping to conclusions. Instead, check it out. Here's how the check-out works. Take the conclusion that you are drawing, which is your understanding of what the person means, ask, "Do you mean + (your conclusion)?" You'll notice that "Do you mean . . ?" is a yes or no question. When checking out you want a clear "yes" or "no" answer. When the answer is "yes," you can feel confident in your conclusion. Simultaneously, you've communicated that you are listening carefully to make sure you understand, which builds rapport.

On the other hand, when you are incorrect in your conclusion, the person will almost always correct your misconception. "No, what I mean is . . ." So, in a funny way, the check-out provides more information when you are wrong than when you are right, because if you use the check-out correctly, by beginning with "Do you mean," "Are you saying," or another phrase that elicits a yes or no reply, you can be wrong, and still communicate that you are making an effort to understand the person's view.

> When checking-out you can get more information when you're wrong than when you're right.

A common mistake is to phrase your check-out as a simple closed question like, "Do you think … ?" or "Do you feel … ?" These questions do not clearly communicate that you are checking out your understanding. Another mistake is to *tell* the person what he or she means *instead of asking*, by saying, "Oh, what you mean is . . ." or "So you feel . . ." These questions tell the person what he or she is thinking or feeling. If the person is too shy or annoyed to want to correct your misunderstanding, you can draw the wrong conclusion. Most people are put off by being told how they feel or what they think, instead of being asked. Practice beginning questions with the straightforward phrase of *"Do you mean that you think…?"* for checking out opinions and *"Do you mean that you feel…?"* for checking out feelings.

Technique: Review

The review is an extremely powerful technique that communicates you are listening carefully and really care about what the person is saying.

> Review and sum up when people ramble or you've been interrupted to get back on track.

Here's how it works: Summarize the main points (point 1 + point 2 + point 3) and follow with "Is there anything else?" For example, "To summarize, you see trouble with getting support (point 1), finding the funds (point 2), and turnaround time (point 3). Is there anything else?" If you've gotten it all, the person will usually say, "No, that's about it." If, on the other hand, the person has more to say, the answer will usually be, "Yes," followed by more information. Again, you'll notice that the review uses the closed question, "Is there anything else?" to elicit a yes or no reply. It helps to make sure you've really gotten what the person is saying and that you're not cutting him or her off.

Sometimes you will miss or forget a point. When your review leaves out a point the person made, the question, "Is there anything else?" prompts the person to restate the missing point. If it is not restated, the overlooked point probably wasn't too important.

The review technique is an excellent way to deal with people who ramble off the topic. Instead of getting irritated, interrupt and summarize what was on the topic, then follow with a probe that is on the topic. For example, cutting in on the rambler you could say, "Let me see if I understand. You anticipate problems in getting support, with money and with turnaround time. What other problems do you see with this project?"

Finally, when you've been interrupted by a phone call, for example, or otherwise distracted, reviewing is an excellent way to get back to what you were talking about. Simply review what you recall and follow with a probe.

BE PERSUASIVE

Just because you have a great idea, don't expect people to immediately buy into it. They've got to be sold. Every encounter with people who may have a stake in what you do is an opportunity to promote your Vision.

> Avoid the
> word "try."

Be positive and optimistic. Avoid the word "try" which means to expend effort that may not succeed in its objective and implies the possibility of failure. "I'm trying to start the car," means I'm making efforts to start the car but so far it hasn't started. "I'm trying to lose weight," means that despite my efforts, I've not yet lost weight. A statement such as "I'll try to get to the accounting today" or "I'm trying to get more resources for our project" is not very convincing. People want to be on a winning team. When you use "try"—especially if you use

it often—you sound weak and prone to failure. This puts people off. By contrast, affirmative statements like "I will get to the accounting by closing today" or "I will push hard for more resources" project confidence.

Express your enthusiasm, smile, use gestures, move your body, speak more clearly, make eye contact. Communicate that you are excited about what you say. Use as many forms of expression as you can to transform the intangibles of your Vision into a picture they can see. Enrich your language with stories, metaphors, analogies.

SHOW LEADERSHIP

> *You need to have been a lieutenant leading your squad into battle*
> *before you can be a general and send others into battle.*
> Keshavan Nair
> *Beyond Winning: The Handbook for the Leadership Revolution*

You need to show you can perform before others will follow your lead. You're more likely to get cooperation if you're perceived to be a person of action—someone who takes charge and gets things done. It conveys success and achievement, which tend to be attractive to others, especially go-getters.

Most people do not see you making decisions on important things. It is decisiveness about small things that influences their opinion of you as a person of action. At meetings make an effort to be the person who

> **Decisiveness in small things communicates leadership ability.**

summarizes. Just before the meeting breaks up you might interject, "Let's summarize what we've accomplished today." Then use the review technique to summarize the main points of discussion and decisions made. Another strategy for showing leadership is to end the meeting with a decision being made by you.

OVERCOMING RESISTANCE

The causes for resistance are numerous but generally the reason people will resist is that they perceive what you are doing to be a threat or at cross purposes to their interests. Sometimes this is true; other times it is based on lack of knowledge and misunderstanding.

Clearly the first step is to uncover the person's reasons for opposing your project. Ask questions and listen carefully. If you have a direct conversation with the resister be extremely careful not to be reactive. It is very easy to be defensive and try to rebut each point. Remember, your objective is to find out how the resister sees the situation and not to offer criticism or rebuttals. Being detached in this manner is not easy by any means.

When you've gathered what you believe is a good understanding of the resister's objections and concerns, make sure you check it out, because you could easily be jumping to conclusions. Get into the resisters shoes, so that you can see your project through his or her eyes. Go to your Mental Theater, put the resistant person on your Viewing Screen, then project yourself *into* the person. Notice how this person sees you, and how what you want to do impacts on him or her.

See the situation from the resister's eyes.

Try to identify what it is about your project that is bothersome. Notice how this person feels. Strive to actually experience these feelings. Discover what this person wants from you. Identify mutual priorities and areas of interest you have in common with the resistant person. These can be built upon.

The next step is to discover ways to get around and beyond the person's resistance. The strategies for getting cooperation are doubly important with a resistant person. Lack of information and misunderstanding are the most common reasons for stonewalling.

You can overcome much resistance by anticipating potential objections and planning in advance. It is easier to prevent resistance than to undo it once it gets started. The best way to accomplish this is by

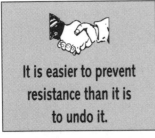

It is easier to prevent resistance than it is to undo it.

involving people as early as possible, preferably before launching your project, and then keeping them informed. Find out the ideas of people whose cooperation is critical to your project, and strive to integrate them into your Vision. Ask potential resisters for criticism and shortcomings in your ideas. While asking for

cooperation, offer the person a choice in the way he or she might help. People are more cooperative when they have a choice, because it conveys a sense of control.

Sometimes it helps to use a third party. Perhaps there is an ally who can be a go-between to soften the resistance. But even the most resistant persons will be helpful if they see that helping you helps them. Although you can't overcome all resistance, you can usually reduce it by planning ahead.

WHO MIGHT RESIST AND WHAT TO DO

Survey all the people who are touched by your project, even indirectly, and all the people whose cooperation you need to succeed. Identify who might resist, even a little. Don't make the mistake we consultants made when we launched into the intensive seven week training with the police without giving a moment's thought to how long training days that went on into the night would impact their families. If you recall in Chapter Seven that oversight nearly destroyed the program when wives and co-workers rebelled.

After you identify who will be affected by your project, go to your

Mental Theater and, using the deep breathing technique, open your Viewing Screen. One-by-one, project each potential resister onto your Screen, and zoom into the person. Notice how the person sees you and your project. Discover what it is about your project that bothers the person and how he or she feels about it. Finally, look for areas of commonality and mutual priorities. Zoom out of the person and leave your

Picture yourself as the resister.

Mental Theater. Review what you discovered about the person's reasons for resisting and what you have in common.

Talk with potential resisters and ask questions to uncover possible conflict and mutual priorities. Next, brainstorm actions you can take to avoid or reduce resistance. Keep notes on your ideas. When you think you have a good plan, go to your Mental Theater and play it out on your Viewing Screen. Keep refining your plan and practicing it in your imagination until you come up with a plan you feel is workable. Then try it with the potential resister.

BUILD TEAM SPIRIT

When you know The Story,
and the story is yours,
you are part of the group.
If you don't know The Story,
you just don't belong.
Linda Ackerman
"Flow State Leadership in Action"
Transforming Leadershp

Team spirit refers to the enthusiasm behind a joint effort. It is rooted in shared ideas, values and goals and characterized by feelings of camaraderie. You can promote team spirit by reminding members of their commonality. One way to accomplish this is by telling stories about the team.

Every group has a history.

TELL "THE STORY"

Two or more people who have a relationship always have a shared history, which is a story that arises out of their experience together. It recounts how everything got started, how things are around here, and where it may all may end up. For example, suppose two strangers ride on a bus that breaks down. The two people take on a shared history involving the bus's breakdown. In telling the bus story, they would use the word "we." All groups have a story about how they got started. It can be as unglamorous as the bus-delay example, or it can be dramatic. But because they have a shared history, at least relative to the story of their experience together, the individuals become a "group."

Newly hired people are usually told the company's story during their orientation and old-timers often take them aside to tell the "real story." These stories are essentially myths of the corporate culture and help create the spirit or the *esprit de corp* of the group. One of the clear signs that you are hearing the myth of a group is when a story about them is told with awe and excitement.

INITIATION

A friend took the 13-week H & R Block tax-preparer course. On several occasions when he told me about the course, he never mentioned anything about Block as a company or its history. Subsequently, he was hired by Block and after one week of training he enthusiastically told me Block's history. Beaming with pride, he relayed the story of how the Block brothers had a thriving bookkeeping service and prepared taxes only as a courtesy to their customers. Word spread, and people sought out the tax preparation. Overwhelmed by so much demand, the brothers made a business decision to drop tax preparation altogether and focus on bookkeeping only. The outcry was unexpected. The decision to drop tax preparation was reversed, and H & R Block was born.

I listened with fascination to his telling the company myth as his eyes flashed with excitement. My friend had been initiated into Block. They had told him The Story and he retold it as his own.

Simple though it may sound, stories are a powerful tool for pulling people together and defining them as a group. Stories act like a bonding agent, because their telling and retelling underscores the "we" of the group. Listen for stories about the group or project. How did it get started? Be especially alert for stories about times when they rose to a challenge, beat a tough deadline, and performed against odds. When talking with others in the group, use these stories as illustrations of how things work and who succeeds.

An excellent illustration of a company telling its story is Genentech, a fast-paced San Francisco Bay Area biotechnology company. To commemorate their new research headquarters, called the Founders Research Center, Genentech commissioned a lifelike, lifesize bronze sculpture depicting the first meeting of its founders, Bob Swanson and Herb Boyer in a tavern where they shared a beer and discussed their vision. A company press release tells the story: "They had a beer, and decided what no one else believed—the practical value of recombinant DNA

Genentech's sculpture in the Founders Research Center, tells the story of the founders' first meeting in a tavern when they agreed to found the company.

(commercial gene-splicing) technology. They formed Genentech by giving their brainchild its name, **Genetic-Engineering-Tech**nology, and putting up an initial $500 each. It was the first biotechnology company, and effectively launched the industry." In the following 17 years Genentech's revenues grew to $516 million. Swanson, who was the venture capitalist, became chairman of the company, and Boyer, who left his position as a biochemist at the University of California at San Francisco when Genentech was born, became director.

The statue, which is seven feet long and four-and-one-half feet tall, weighing about 600 pounds, remains permanently in the courtyard among the Founders Research Center's three buildings, which is the world's largest facility devoted solely to biotechnology. Anyone entering the center for the first time can't help but wonder what the story is behind the sculpture. Whenever employees pass by it, they are reminded of the founders' story.

Genentech's CEO, Kirk Raab, explained the story associated with the statue of Swanson and Boyer's first meeting in the tavern: "The statue is our way of permanently remembering the enthusiasm and risk taking necessary to make innovation happen, as well as Bob's successful leadership in making it happen here. There isn't much we respect more than that at Genentech." This is a strong message to people working in Genentech that innovation is paramount and that they should take risks to make it happen.

Build a Story Database

Recall stories about your project or the activities you're undertaking to accomplish your Mission, and about your team or the people helping to make your project succeed. Be alert for stories about the history of your project and how it got started, and about the history of your team and how people came together. Look for stories about significant events and how barriers were surmounted, as well as humorous situations and mistakes. Then brainstorm points it can be used to illustrate.

Emphasize Commonality

You can promote team spirit by referring to the others as "we" because it emphasizes inclusiveness and reminds people of their bonds and what they share. Sprinkle your discussions with "we," and use

> Sprinkle your conversations with "we."

"I" sparingly. When you say "we," people feel included and sharing in the credit. You can use this phenomenon to promote team spirit.

CREATE MEANING

There is a deep human yearning to make a difference. We want to know that our life means something, and that there is an important purpose in what we do. The yearning to be part of a successful and worthwhile enterprise is one of the most fundamental of human needs. The meaning we derive is a source of self-worth and pride. Work can satisfy this yearning.

But the importance of some work is not always readily apparent, and many people don't know how to find purpose in their work. In the

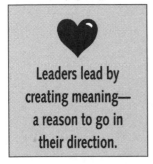

Leaders lead by creating meaning— a reason to go in their direction.

extreme, feelings of meaninglessness can lead to job burnout and damage motivation. Generally, people will gravitate toward meaningful activities, which gives a sense of worthiness and enlivens them. Remember that engaging in meaningful activities increases the likelihood of experiencing bliss. You can enlist people to support your efforts and to join your team by creating

meaning. To create meaning, tie your Vision to their values, show how your Vision fulfills their mission, and communicate shared values with metaphors and stories.

Tie Your Vision to Values

Show concern for what is important to people and they will usually respond with concern for what's important to you. When your Vision is attuned to a person's values, he or she will tend to see helping your project along as important and meaningful.

People talk about what's important to them.

The first step is to find out what is important to those whose cooperation you need. Don't assume that you know what is important, because you can be quite mistaken. One approach is to study their conversations. People tend to talk about what they're most concerned with. For example, someone who highly values relation-

ships will talk about social events, people, and other socially related topics, people who are concerned with recognition will talk about their own achievements: people concerned about community activism will tend to talk about social ills.

Identify the themes that run through the conversations of those whose cooperation you seek. Notice what issues they frequently speak about. Ask questions and listen carefully to get an idea of their perspective as individuals. Use your Mental Theater to project yourself into their positions to see things from their point of view.

Once you have gotten a feel for what is important to those whose cooperation you need, you can speak to these issues. The key is to tie a statement relating to the person's values to the action you would like to have carried out. If the person's area of concern is recognition you could mention possibilities for increased visibility, for example. If the person's concerns revolve around relationships, you might mention networking benefits, whereas to the activist you might mention benefits to co-workers or the community.

Going one step further, try to uncover the essential purpose or mission within the company mandated to those whose support you seek. What are the problems they were hired to solve? If supporting your project moves them closer to accomplishing their purpose, then you have great potential for a win-win strategy. When you've discovered the problems they've been hired to solve, you can tie the support you need to their purpose.

Share the Vision by Telling Stories

Stories are rather like maps; not much in themselves,
but very helpful when crossing strange territories.
Harrison Owen
Spirit: Transformation and Development in Organizations

Your Vision is a picture of a desired future. To make that future a reality you need the cooperation of others, which means that the Vision must be communicated to those whose help you need. Describing the Vision in a story is an effective way of doing this. The process is called "sharing the vision." It is communicating the Vision in a way that others "buy into it" and see the Vision

Share the Vision.

as a future they want to work toward. At first, the notion of leading through telling stories sounds frivolous, but there's more behind the word "story" than meets the eye. A Vision is a "picture" of a desired future. Remember that old cliche, "A picture is worth a thousand words." The corollary is that it takes a thousand words to describe a picture! Which means it takes a lot of words to convey your Vision. Fortunately, there is a linguistic short cut: metaphors. Metaphors are like picture-words. Take the metaphor "time flies," for example. An image is created with only two words, yet it is a picture that says a lot about the experience of time.

You can use metaphors to give vividness and tangibility to abstract ideas. The richness of figurative speech can paint word pictures to portray the meaning in your Vision. Leaders use stories and metaphors to encourage the values and actions that promote their vision. In other words, stories and metaphors are powerful leading tools.

Employ Metaphors

Use of metaphor pervades our thinking. So many of the concepts that are important to us, such as time, emotions, infinity, and ideas, are either abstract or not clearly delineated in our experience. We can get a grasp on them only by means of other concepts that we understand more clearly. A metaphor is a way of speaking in which a simpler concept is used to communicate a more elusive concept. For example, we say being happy is "up" and being sad is "down." We can understand spatial orientation from direct experience, then use it to communicate about the emotions of happy and sad, which tend to be elusive and difficult to describe.

> Metaphors are picture words that make abstract ideas tangible.

Time is hard to grasp and can be difficult to think about, whereas flying is a concept that is easier to understand. We've all seen birds flying, and most people have flown in a plane. We can use flying to comment on the speed at which time seems to pass so quickly that it seems to fly.

Metaphors We Live By Lakoff and Johnson shows how metaphor plays an extensive role in the way we function, the way we conceptualize our experience, and the way we speak. Metaphors are plentiful in our daily conversations. Metaphors and analogies are as common in business as numbers. We talk of computers having "memory" and ships "plowing the sea." We talk about love as "magic." We talk about knowledge as "power." We talk about business as a "game." Military metaphors are commonly used to communicate corporate strategy. The sports vernacular is heard daily in business meetings.

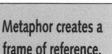

Metaphor creates a frame of reference.

Using a story to communicate values is what Watson, the son of IBM's founder, was doing when he told the story about a naturalist who fed wild ducks so much that they stopped flying south for the winter. Watson always ended the story with the point that you can make wild ducks tame, but you can never make tame ducks wild again. According to corporate culture experts, Deal and Kennedy, Watson told this story again and again to impress upon people the value of deviance and tolerance for outlaws in a company known for conformity and standardized ways.

A metaphor creates a frame of reference that suggests other aspects of the concept we're communicating about. The "time is money" metaphor, for example, creates a frame within which to think about time. You might ask, "How do you spend your time?" Or say, "You are wasting time. You need to budget time." Once an image is suggested, you can fill it in. Leaders often use compelling metaphors to communicate their vision. Not only can others "get it," but they can help create the story themselves. Returning again to Watson and his duck

story, after he created an idea of wild ducks in IBM an employee reportedly told him that "even wild ducks fly in formation." This rejoinder quickly became part of the wild-ducks story, precisely because it made another important point about IBM's culture: we're all going in the same direction. In other words, the employee picked up on the wild-duck metaphor and took the lead himself to express the necessity to balance individual performance with teamwork.

In *The Way of the Ronin,* I used the free samurai as a metaphor to convey how to be self-mastering like a warrior while functioning within corporate feudalism—a mindless bureaucratic system that prevents you from doing what you are there to do and threatens to destroy your spirit. People resonate with the idea of being a warrior struggling with self-direction and excellence within the constraints of bureaucracy. I remember a man who had just been promoted to a senior position in Becton-Dickinson, an international biotech company. He said following the way of the ronin helped him move into the role and make needed changes. When I asked him how it helped he said, "I'm using the windmill technique. I'm going in with two swords swinging!" I'd never described any sword fighting techniques in the lectures or book. Nonetheless, the metaphor spoke to the medical director's challenge in a meaningful way. He fleshed out the image of the samurai when he used the ronin as an aid in thinking about the complex problems he faced.

Leading yourself and others is an abstract process to talk about. On the other hand, the metaphor of pathfinding is more familiar, and in the United States we resonate with it. It's part of our culture. Columbus "discovered" the New World, and settlers pioneered the wild west. We've seen countless movies of explorers, scouts, and trailblazers. There's a commonality between self-leading and pathfinding. Both head into unknown, uncharted territory. The pathfinding metaphor makes available an enormous vocabulary, such as roads, maps, destinations, time tables, stay the course, horizon, compass, and mission, for example, to draw from in describing the abstractions of self-leading. You understand the pathfinding images, and can readily use them to describe your own experiences and discoveries.

Finding metaphors that click takes a while. A good metaphor resonates with the people in the situation. For example, GTE Strategic Systems employs many retired military people; not too surprisingly, military metaphors are commonplace there. On the other hand, military metaphors might not be an effective way to communicate to the League of Women Voters, who 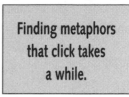 have probably had little military experience. Images that the metaphor elicits should be engaging and inspiring. The rock group The Grateful Dead has spawned an enormous cult following of "Deadheads" who use all kinds of skull and skeleton images to communicate.

Experiment with using metaphors to express your feelings and ideas. Notice how people react and which are effective in getting your point across. You will probably find that different metaphors work with different groups of people. You might introduce 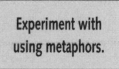 your image in a story, like Watson did with the wild ducks. You know you're on to something when others use your images. For example, while consulting at GTE Strategic Systems I used a story about an experiment with dogs on an electric grid floor to describe the burnout process. In one situation the dog had a lever to turn off the shock, in the other situation there was no lever. The dog without the lever became helpless and gave up. Later, the dog that had learned to be helpless was given a lever too, but it couldn't (or wouldn't) learn to use it. People resonated with this image. I frequently heard them say things like, "We've got to look for the lever" and "I was the dog on the floor." That story "took." They got it and understood the complicated existential process that leads to the loss of spirit that we call burnout.

BUILDING COOPERATION IS ONGOING

Getting cooperation is so important that it can mean the difference between success and failure of your project. It is next to impossible to accomplish anything of importance in an organization without cooperation, and a strong social support group acts as a buffer against job burnout. Building team spirit and getting support is an ongoing process. The more time and attention you invest in helping your allies and building your team, the more benefits you'll reap in terms of cooperation when you need it. So far we've covered several ways to get others' support: reciprocating, keeping people informed, asking for opinions, telling "The Story," and sharing your Vision through picture words.

Getting cooperation and giving support to colleagues calls on a different mindset than does evaluating progress with the Yardstick tool. In the next chapter, we'll explore the impact of different mindsets, sometimes called "changing Hats."

CHAPTER 12

HAT

CHANGING YOUR ATTITUDE

Just as an explorer needs some plan of procedure,
so the thinker needs some organizing structure.
Edward DeBono
The Six Thinking Hats

*I*t is hard to imagine that anyone would choose to remain in burnout, but burnout does tend to become a self-perpetuating process. It is through the way that we think and view the world that burnout gets a stranglehold on us. Experiencing bliss is unlikely when we feel helpless and unable to influence events around us. Without realizing it you can get trapped in your own negativity by telling yourself that there is nothing you can do.

Hat tool: Assuming the mindset optimal to the function at hand.

There is no one right view of the world. You can approach a given situation with a variety of attitudes. With a negative attitude, you point out why things don't work. At other times, you can have an open-minded attitude and consider wild possibilities. Sometimes a critical attitude is most effective: at other times having an open mind is the optimal approach. Using the various pathfinding tools effectively calls upon different mindsets. For example, the Yardstick tends to draw on critical thinking to determine how you measure up, whereas the Vision tool works best when you think of what might be possible. Going from one mindset to another is often called "changing hats." With the Hat tool you assume the attitude that will best facilitate your objective at the moment.

SPECIALIZATION AND ONE-HAT THINKING

Traditionally in the workplace there have been three general management functions: leading or setting direction, implementing or making things happen, and regulating and keeping things under control. Each function calls on a different mindset or thinking style. People usually spent most of their work lives in one function. As a result they tended to develop and use only one thinking style. This mental restriction tends to limit one's ability to cope with the kind of changes that are happening in the way people work. The result is too many moments of feeling inadequate and too few moments of bliss.

Let's take a closer look at each function and the kind of thinking it encourages. Upper level managers have generally been responsible for

Leading, implementing and regulating call on different thinking styles.

setting the course, choosing the direction the organization should go. These are the people we usually think of as the leaders. Lower-level managers, on the other hand, have been responsible for traversing the course and getting where the upper level say they should go. These are people who coordinate the implementation of the leader's vision. They supervise workers who assemble products and provide services. In between are middle managers, whose responsibility it is to stay the course. They are the regulators who monitor progress and contain deviation from the course. According to Stanford Graduate School of Business Professor Harold Leavitt who describes these three functions in his book *Corporate Pathfinding,* leading, implementing, and regulating involve different day-to-day activities that draw on different capabilities and thinking styles. Thus it is common to find that a person may perform outstandingly at one function, such as supervising people, and poorly at another, such as making strategic decisions.

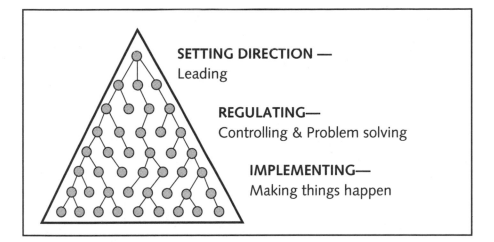

TRADITIONAL ORGANIZATIONAL STRUCTURE

SETTING THE COURSE—SEEING DIRECTION

By comparison, setting the course involves little direct contact with the people who actually do the implementing. At the upper level, managers are expected to be visionaries who see what's possible. Their task is to fashion values, forecasts, and the bottom line into a driving

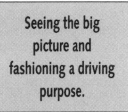

Seeing the big picture and fashioning a driving purpose.

purpose. But visionaries often ignore rules, act impulsively, and wave off what they see as trivial details, because they are more concerned with the future and the big picture.

TRAVERSING THE COURSE—IMPLEMENTING

Implementing is the nitty-gritty hands-on work supervised by lower-level managers. It is doing, changing, and influencing. It is about action and making things happen, where the

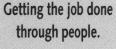

Getting the job done through people.

rubber meets the road. Implementing is getting the widgets assembled, the services rendered, and the products delivered. This type of management is a social activity in which things happen through people. Since managers must change people's behavior, implementing is an emotional activity which draws upon intuition and gut responses, such as pride, ambition, and loyalty, not intellectual reasoning, to persuade and cajol people into performing.

STAYING THE COURSE—REGULATING

People in middle management approach things in yet a different way. Mandated with regulating the organization to stay the course set by the top, they are concerned with accountability for those below. Middle managers check people, products, and markets for errors. They organize, plan, solve problems, and make decisions. Detailed job descriptions and standards of performance are the tools of their trade. Unlike implementers, who deal with emotions and social interaction, and the leaders who envision possibilities and forge a driving purpose, regulators catch and correct errors in order to stay on course.

> **Accountability— catching and correcting errors.**

CHANGE

We are leaving what historians call industrialism and moving rapidly into what futurists call the information age. The nature of work and the way people work together is changing. There are ever more new products and services where information has become both a resource and a product. Increasingly, people trade in information that may have no form at all. Instead of assembling widgets, people may be working with blips on a fiber optic miles away on the information superhighway.

> **Today we must lead, implement and regulate—all three.**

For most of us, work is no longer simply a repetitive routine activity dictated by a supervisor. You probably do things in your job that no one else in your position has done before and in which you may have had little or no training. This means you must discover your work while teaching yourself how to do it. You must choose a direction, implement your strategies, and stay on course, all three. Whereas in the past people specialized in one of the functions—implementing, regulating, or leading—and had to excel at the kind of thinking that that function required, today you are likely to have to perform all three functions to get your job done. This means that just to stay abreast, *you must be fluent in several different thinking styles.*

Visionary thinking, which is needed to set direction, for example, is nonlinear and controlled by the right brain, whereas the analytic thinking needed when monitoring and solving problems, calls on the left-brain abilities. Different yet is the intuitive thinking that goes into motivating people and facilitating cooperation.

It is popular to believe that most people have a dominant thinking style and that they can't really effectively engage in the other styles—

> You must be fluent in several different thinking styles.

yet in today's workplace that is exactly what you need to do to be successful. You must call on visionary thinking to envision possibilities for solving the problem you were hired to solve. You must call on intuition and empathy to get people's cooperation and motivate them to perform. You must use logic and reason to make decisions and solve problems in the process of implementation. Too much analytic thinking can squelch visionary thinking and overrule the gut-level thinking needed to work with people. Too much visionary thinking is pie-in-the-sky and nothing gets done. Too much intuition is touchy-feely and pollyanna, and hard to take seriously.

When you are proficient in the three functions and apply them to your work, your job can become a vehicle for finding a path to your bliss. When you have the flexibility and skill to assume the mindset optimal for the task at hand, you

SETTING THE COURSE

STAYING THE COURSE

TRAVERSING THE COURSE

PATHFINDER'S VEHICLE

can take on ever more interesting challenges, while feeling confident that you can rise to the challenge. When you have meaningful challenges that match and stretch your abilities you feel empowered. Potential for many moments of bliss is high.

THE THINKING HATS

> *We need pathfinders. Vision, values, and*
> *determination add soul to the organization.*
> *Without them organizations react but do not create;*
> *they forecast but do not imagine;*
> *they analyze but do not question;*
> *they act but do not strive.*
> Harold Leavitt
> *Corporate Pathfinding*

You've probably heard the phrase "put on your thinking cap." Well, to be effective at pathfinding, you must have different thinking Hats and know which one to wear when. If you're going to find a path with a heart—a path to your bliss—you must be skilled at different thinking styles, be able to decide which style is needed at any particular time, and be able to change from one Hat to another.

Edward DeBono's work on thinking styles is particularly helpful

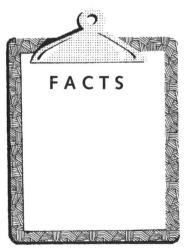

here. In *The Six Thinking Hats* Dr. DeBono describes six distinctly different thinking styles. He uses hats and colors as metaphors to facilitate understanding and remembering the different thinking styles. Each Hat or thinking style has a particular way of conceptualizing. When you understand the Hats and are skilled at using them you can get the maximum gain from your efforts. Following is a description of each Hat and how you think when wearing it. You'll notice that each has a memory association. These are images or catchphrases that capture the essence of the thinking style, and facilitate understanding and remembering the Hats.

THE WHITE HAT

When you wear the White Hat you assume an objective mindset. Sergeant Friday in the 1950s television series *Dragnet* captures the essence of the White Hat when he says, "Just the facts, Ma'am. Nothing but the facts."

When wearing the White Hat you strive to be neutral and ask for facts and figures without preconceptions or emotions. Reporting only relevant information and avoiding opinions and extrapolations is the core of White-Hat thinking.

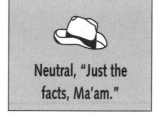

Neutral, "Just the facts, Ma'am."

THE RED HAT

When wearing the Red Hat you assume an intuitive mindset. When you use red-type thinking, you express emotions, reactions, and preferences. Red-Hat thinking is concerned with values and hunches rather than being logical. Inconsistency is accepted and justifying feelings is avoided when wearing the Red Hat.

Seeing red, burning desire.

THE YELLOW HAT

When wearing the Yellow Hat you assume a positive and optimistic mindset. This is when to probe for benefits in ideas and use logical thinking to explore feasibility. Yellow-Hat thinking is supportive and nurturing, as it searches for ways to strengthen and improve ideas. Trying to find alternatives or ways to change is avoided when wearing the Yellow Hat. Instead the focus is on how to make the idea happen by increasing its effectiveness and quality.

Sunshine, support.

THE GREEN HAT

When wearing the Green Hat assume a creative mindset. Search for

Growing, germination.

alternatives and new approaches. Think of ideas as stepping stones to get from here to new ways of looking at things. Green-Hat thinking actively tries to escape from old ideas, sometimes by making illogical or even absurd suggestions, sometimes by exploring vague or silly ideas. When wearing the Green Hat being judgmental or thinking about why things won't work is always avoided.

THE BLACK HAT

When wearing the Black Hat assume a judg-

Judge's black robe.

mental mindset. It is with Black-Hat think- ing that you evaluate how the idea com- pares to what has

worked in the past. This is when you look for what's wrong and why it won't work, and strive to uncover risks and dangers. Black-Hat thinking analyzes and uses logic to criticize while avoiding emotions. This is where negative questions are asked, but attacking and arguing is avoided.

THE BLUE HAT

When wearing a Blue Hat assume a detached mindset. It is with

Blue sky overhead, cool
blue water, blue uniform.

Blue-Hat thinking that you orchestrate prob- lem solving by defining the parameters of the problem, setting the focus, determining the subject of thought, and monitoring think- ing. Blue-Hat thinking pilots projects by observing, asking the right questions at the right time and providing an overview. It is the Blue-Hat mindset that summarizes, draws conclusions, structures, and controls.

CHANGING HATS

We switch hats all the time without thinking about it. Sometimes we are simply reactive, especially with emotions, which is Red-Hat thinking. Sometimes we believe we're wearing one Hat when we're actually wearing another. For example, a woman might be insisting that she's just telling the facts (White Hat), when she's actually using facts to advance an argument (Black Hat), for example.

The Hat tool helps pathfinders to be more effective thinkers. Practicing changing Hats makes us aware of the way we tend to wear one Hat, usually black, most of the time and helps us to be more flexible and agile in our thinking and able to call on the thinking style optimal for the task at hand.

One approach to practice is to take an idea or situation and think about it while wearing the Hats, one at a time. Each Hat has a basic question, such as "What are the facts?" for the White Hat, which you can use to begin the process.

THE WHITE HAT

You can get into the White-Hat mindset by asking the basic question: "What are the facts?" Facts include quantity, quality, number, color, shape, sequences, time frames, names, objectives that must be achieved, deadlines, conditions that must be met, conditions that exist. Facts can include

What are the facts?

other people's opinions and beliefs, but your own opinions are never facts. For example, "Joe has stated that he believes…" would qualify as a fact. A belief is a fact here because it is a fact that Joe believed something, even if the belief itself is incorrect. Joe's state of mind at a point in time is a fact. Following this same logic, your own state of mind at a time in the past can be a fact, even though the opinion or belief itself is not a fact. It can be a fact that you held a certain opinion at a certain time. For example, a statement like, "When Joe said that, I felt put down," describes how you felt at a particular time, and so would classify as a fact. On the other hand, a statement like, "John was running a power trip on us," is not a fact. It is your belief about John's motives. It would be more accurate to say, "It felt as if John were running a power trip on us."

DeBono says that in the beginning, wearing the White Hat is probably the hardest to master, because it is difficult to separate facts and neutral information from extrapolations and preconceptions. It can be easy to confuse feelings with facts because we often feel so strongly about certain things that they seem to be facts.

THE RED HAT

Red-Hat thinking delves into your psyche, which is the root of your individuality and uniqueness. With the Red Hat you explore your feelings and personal responses (or those of others) to ideas and situations.

You can get into a Red-Hat mindset by asking the question, "What's the feeling?" Feelings include physical sensations like butterflies in the stomach, aching back, numbness, and pins and needles, as well as emotions like anger, depression, joy, and anticipation. Another category of feelings are hunches like, "I bet he's late again," or "I sense that..." Also included are insights, intuitions, attractions, repulsions, beliefs (such as John's power tripping), and suspicions. Values, motives, and self-interest fall into the domain of Red-Hat thinking. The most difficult aspect of wearing the Red Hat is resisting the temptation to justify the feelings you express and suppressing the desire to make them consistent. Feelings are not rational and are often contradictory.

THE YELLOW HAT

The memory association for the Yellow Hat is sunshine. You can think of the sunshine as nurturing and supporting growth. When you wear the Yellow Hat, you assume a supportive mindset and ask "What's right about this?" The object is to explore what's positive and feasible about the idea. Focus on the merits of the situation. Avoid being critical and looking for what's wrong and won't work, which is Black-Hat thinking. Instead, think of

What's right?

ways that the idea can be improved upon. Remember to be particularly careful not to slide into thinking about problems with the idea. When wearing the Yellow Hat, your outlook is idealistic; you tune into dreams and hopes as they relate to this situation. Look for opportunities, and consider how the idea can be fleshed out and nurtured. It is when you wear the Yellow Hat that you make positive speculations and proposals.

Keeping your focus on the positive is the most difficult part of wearing the Yellow Hat because most of us have a tendency to look for what's wrong with ideas and proposals and to avoid appearing unrealistic. When you catch yourself doing this, just remind yourself that it's okay to romanticize about what is right about the idea, since you'll explore the problems later with the Black Hat.

THE GREEN HAT

You can get into a Green-Hat mindset by asking the question, "What's possible here?" Pose "what if" questions and challenge yourself to push the limits. Try turning the idea or situation into its opposite. For example, if you are thinking about a person who has wronged you, look for ways that the person is an ally, and how the supposedly wrong act is actually a benefit. Dream up preposterous alternatives, then use them to germinate new ideas, even if they seem silly. Try thinking about the situation from the end, and move backward in time.

Suppressing the urge to evaluate the ideas is the most difficult part of Green-Hat thinking.

What's possible?

The challenge when wearing the Green Hat is to break out of your usual way of thinking about the situation, and to use novel ways of looking at it in order to move into new territory.

THE BLACK HAT

You can get into a Black-Hat mindset by asking the question, "What's wrong with this?" This is where you look for what is missing and what is wrong with the idea or situation. Play the devil's advocate, and list ways this idea could fail, by identifying risks and dangers. Think of ways the idea doesn't make sense, and be alert for inconsistencies. Point out the problems with the idea, but don't suggest solutions, which would be Yellow Hat thinking.

Most people feel pretty comfortable wearing the Black Hat, especially those with a lot of college training or scientific backgrounds. Education generally focuses on teaching us to use logic and reasoning to develop arguments and advance critiques. Once on, the Black Hat is the hardest to take off. After you see the deficits in an idea or proposal, it's hard to see the positives. For this reason, DeBono advises that you push yourself to do Yellow and Green thinking before moving to criticism.

In biotech and other science-based industries there is the notion of

What's wrong?

the "killer experiment." This is the study that goes to the heart of feasibility. If the results are negative, further product development is killed without additional investment. Curiously, instead of the scientist, it is the business interests that push for the killer experiment. The scientists who lead the product-development effort tend to stay with the Yellow-Hat question, "What's right?" They are often seen as being overly optimistic, even romantic about their research. The business focus, on the other hand, is on the bottomline: maximum profit while curtailing risk.

THE BLUE HAT

You can get into a Blue-Hat mindset by asking the question, "What's the next step?" This is where you assume a broader perspective and think strategically in order to figure out the next step and what attitude will facilitate accomplishing it. What generalizations and conclusion can you make about the idea or situation? Consider if a particular aspect of the idea needs more thought. Analyze which questions should be asked now. It is with Blue-Hat thinking that you decide which Hat to wear while doing which step. When wearing the Blue Hat you are like the master mind who coordinates and decides what happens when and how.

What next?

The hardest thing about the Blue Hat is remembering to wear it. It's easy to respond without stepping back to objectively evaluate progress and think strategically. Once mastered, the Blue Hat is worn simultaneously with the other Hats, so that you both act and direct your actions.

PRACTICE CHANGING HATS

Select an idea or situation for practice. One by one, imagine wearing the six thinking Hats, and put yourself into the mindset of the Hat being worn. Begin thinking about your idea or situation by asking the basic question for that Hat. Don't rush. Go through the process slowly, and allow your mind to mull over the question. The objective of this exercise is to learn to differentiate the mindsets that the Hats represent. Strive to maintain the mindset of the Hat you are practicing. If you catch yourself slipping into another Hat, stop and put the Hat being practiced back on.

THE RIGHT HAT WITH THE RIGHT TOOL

Finding a path with a heart, a path to your bliss challenges and expands all your thinking capabilities. Wearing a particular Hat enhances the effectiveness of particular tools. For example, the Heart tool is used to identify values and what is really important. Tuning into your unique self calls upon Red-Hat or emotional/intuitive thinking. At other times, when deciding on your destination, you use the Vision tool and need to switch to the Green Hat to explore what is possible. And at yet other times, when evaluating the suitability of potential projects, you use the Survey tool and wear the Black Hat, so that you can evaluate options critically. If you habitually wear a particular hat, such as a black one, as many people do, it will be harder to use the other tools effectively. No one style of thinking is better or worse than others. Each has its valuable contribution.

The more you practice changing Hats, the more you will be able to

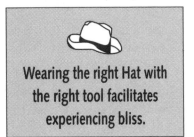

Wearing the right Hat with the right tool facilitates experiencing bliss.

reap the benefits of each kind of thinking. When you understand which Hats facilitate the use of which tools, you'll be able to use them more effectively and gain a better understanding of each tool. Interestingly, each tool draws upon the thinking capabilities of two Hats. Sometimes the Hats seem to be complementary, at other times to conflict. Ability to use the tools effectively increases with the ability to change Hats.

THE COMPASS

Your personal response is the substance of the Compass, because it

Red and White.

is with the Compass that you get your bearings by checking your internal responses. The Compass is calibrated by recalling and studying burnout and blissful experiences. These experiences are identified by how they feel. It is with the Red Hat that you experience your personal response. The important thing when studying burnout and bliss situations is to be aware of how you respond without trying to change it in any way.

However, to simply experience feelings would not be productive. With burnout experiences, you'd risk becoming immobilized or depressed. So a switch to the White Hat is needed, in order to step back, like a scientist, to objectively study how you react to the situation or idea. When you are wearing the White Hat your focus is, "What are the facts, Ma'am?" as you gather data on the situations to find out where you were, what was going on and what factors were critical in making the situation burnout or blissful. To summarize, the Compass is a tool to help you get your bearings. You do this best by first wearing the Red Hat to experience your response, then switching to the White Hat to study the "facts" of your response.

THE HEART

Essential to finding a path with a heart is to clarify your values in order to understand what really matters to you. The object is to identify *what* is important to you, without justifying *why*. The Heart tool tunes into subjective responses to decipher your values. You can most effectively explore your responses and discover your individuality by wearing the Red Hat.

Red and Black.

Sensing what's important and what you dislike is only half the challenge of the Heart tool. The other half is making sense of your responses and extrapolating your values. It takes the logic of Black-Hat thinking to identify patterns and commonality that are clues to your values. Remember the memory association for the Black Hat is the judge's black robes. It is with the Black Hat that you make value judgments—this is good, and is bad.

THE MISSION

A path with a heart provides meaning. Meaning is born of a purpose that engages your values. The first step in developing your Mission is to identify the problem you seek to solve. Critical in this process is *seeing the problem*. It takes Green-Hat thinking to imagine "what if"— what would happen if the problem went completely unsolved—and to exaggerate the image sufficiently to get a clear picture of the hole, the absence of

Green and Red.

attention to this problem. Filling this hole with a solution to your problem is your purpose in the organization, the reason you were hired.

To find a path with a heart, this purpose and your values must be aligned. Accomplishing this requires changing to the Red Hat. It is from alignment of your values and your purpose that you generate the enthusiasm and passion characteristic of a Mission.

THE VISION

Your Vision is a picture of your destination, where you want to go.

It is a concept of what is possible—an excellent solution to the problem you seek to solve. Generating such an image takes brainstorming alter-

Green and Yellow.

natives and new approaches, which call on Green-Hat thinking. But effective use of the Vision tool doesn't stop here. Once you have gathered many alternative possibilities, it is necessary to put on the Yellow Hat to nurture and grow your ideas into useful and workable proposals. The challenge is to uncover the feasible aspects of your green ideas and shape them into a clear picture that you want to work toward—a path with a heart.

THE SURVEY

The Survey tool is used to get the lay of the land—a sweeping picture of your situation. The objective when doing a survey is to gather the facts

White and Black.

of the situation. This is accomplished by first wearing the White Hat to gather a list of problems, available resources, allies, and potential enemies. Keep an objective mindset in order to look for what's a problem, what doesn't work, what's inefficient and too costly.

The second step in surveying is to analyze the data you have collected. Analyzing calls on Black-Hat thinking. For example, when you conduct a SUIT-analysis, to determine which problem is SUITable for you to tackle, you weigh each potential project against the four criteria of suitability: Can I solve it? Is it unattached and available for me to assume? Is it attuned to my values? Is it on target with my Mission? Black-Hat thinking helps in making judgments of this sort.

THE TARGET

An effective Target has a compelling image. Put on a Green Hat to create a picture of the time when you have achieved your goal. Remember, it is with Green-Hat thinking that you dream the big dream and brainstorm what's possible. Once you have a general picture of what you want to achieve, the challenge is to shape it into a powerful goal. It takes Black-Hat thinking to work

Green and Black.

out a precise statement of your goal that includes a deadline, is stated on the doing level, and is positive. The fact that the goal must be positive does suggest Yellow-Hat thinking. However, it is through the logic and critical analysis of Black-Hat thinking that you identify and discard hidden negatives.

THE MAP

Hills, rivers, and valleys are the "facts" of the terrain. A map is, essentially, a picture of these facts. In creating a Flow Map of your project, you begin at the end, your Target, and work backward to identify the steps necessary to reach it. Put on the White Hat when asking the two questions, "Can I do this now?" and "If not, what must I do first?" In Mind Mapping you ask, "What steps lead to the Target, and what actions are needed to complete those steps?"

White and Yellow.

Once the Map is drawn, switch to the Yellow Hat to decide how to use it most effectively. Maps show you the topology, with the highways and backroads, but they don't choose the route. You select the path that is best for you, the path to your bliss, which takes Yellow-Hat thinking.

THE YARDSTICK

Just as athletes measure their performance to track improvement, so too you can benefit from feedback. Using the Yardstick is an evaluative process where the distance between the current shot and the Target is

Black and Yellow.

measured. It takes Black-Hat thinking to look for errors and judge progress. But the Yardstick can be detrimental if you wear *only* the Black Hat. It can lead to perfectionism, where your focus is solely on the errors, which you then use to flagel-late yourself. This is demoralizing and erodes self-esteem.

The trick is to use error information in a supportive way. To accomplish this put on the Yellow Hat and use the Yardstick to help improve performance, so you can reach your Target. Instead of looking at the distance by which you missed the Target, focus on the positive and look at progress you've made toward your goal.

THE TEAM

The Team tool is used when working with people to get them onto your team. Wearing the Yellow Hat facilitates getting the support of allies.

Yellow and Red.

Reaching out, helping first, reciprocating to build cooperation, encouraging others in their projects, and developing win-win strategies are all prod-ucts of Yellow-Hat thinking.

People are emotional and don't necessarily respond logically or rationally. Red-Hat thinking taps intuition, hunches, and empathy to help you better understand other people's viewpoints. Motivating people takes the Red Hat to call on pride, ambition, and loyalty, which are emotional not rational.

Often when working with people you need to ask questions to get facts and figures. Wear the White Hat when seeking information. It keeps you neutral and without preconceptions. White-Hat thinking helps avoid leading questions and jumping to conclusions.

THE HAT

The purpose of the Hat tool is to be able to employ different thinking styles for different pur-poses to support your pathfinding efforts. This calls on the Yellow Hat, because the objective is increasing effectiveness. In this mindset you focus on what works and how to make it work even better.

However, it takes Blue-Hat thinking to decide which Hat to wear, because it is with the Blue Hat that you think about thinking. With Blue-Hat thinking you are like a conductor orchestrating the use of the various tools. And it's with the Blue Hat that you get an overview, draw conclusions, and decide what to do next.

Yellow and Blue.

THE WAND

The Wand is a transformational tool used to get around roadblocks and to escape from paralyzing paradoxes that diminish motivation and pull us into burnout. Wear the Green Hat to break out of habitual ways of looking at things. Sometimes transformations come from what seem, at first, like absurd alternatives. Green-Hat thinking generates lots of ideas, including those that seem silly or far-fetched.

Green and Blue.

A list of ideas, especially wild ideas, doesn't accomplish much of anything if you stop there. The Wand is effective only if you switch to the Blue Hat, which helps you to step back and use the breakthroughs and absurd possibilities strategically in order to get around the roadblock.

THE EYE

The Eye tool plugs into your "higher consciousness." With the Eye you pilot your journey. When you wear the White Hat, the Eye watches objectively, like a scientist, gathering data on how you function, what you do, what you think, and what you

White and Blue.

feel. This, of course, is difficult to do, because all kinds of shoulds and shouldn'ts get in the way. White-Hat thinking focuses our attention on the facts and away from judgments and rationalizations.

When you wear the Blue Hat, the Eye decides where you are at any point in the pathfinding process and which tool to use. Pathfinding tools are often used jointly and simultaneously. For example, it's with the Eye that you watch your feelings when calibrating the Compass. And it's with the Eye that you objectively and dispassionately study people projected onto your Viewing Screen. While wearing the Blue Hat and using the Eye tool, you lead your pathfinding adventure to finding a path to your bliss.

BEATING BURNOUT

There are objective factors in a situation that render it bliss promoting or burnout promoting. But we all know people who seem to be able to rise above the most dreary situations and others who constantly project doom and gloom. If you get stuck in one mindset, wearing one Hat, you will be vulnerable to burnout. This is especially true for those of us who tend to always be wearing the judgmental Black Hat and seeing

all the ways in which things could go astray. Remember: there are many different ways to view any particular situation. All you have to do is change your Hat and things will look very different.

So push yourself to practice changing Hats and you will discover a freedom and power you didn't realize you had.

When you've developed your skill in switching Hats you're almost ready to begin your journey. No journey is without problems, detours and other obstacles. The next chapter will show you how to use the Wand tool to transform the obstacles into opportunities.

CHAPTER 13

WAND

TRANSFORMING OBSTACLES IN YOUR PATH

*Bureaucratic practices set limits
to the assertion of power of individuals in the organization,
but the possession of power in organizations
reduces the harmful consequences of bureaucracy to the individual.
Therefore, survival in bureaucracies falls to those individuals
who know how to negotiate a double bind situation,
and advancement in bureaucracies falls to those individuals
who know how to make an opportunity out of a paradox.*
Abraham Zaleznik, Manfred Kets de Vries and John Howard
"Stress Reactions in Organizations"
Behavioral Science

*L*ife is replete with paradoxes, those contradictions that stop us in our tracks. Immobilized and confused, we lose our way and find ourselves heading straight into burnout. With the Wand you can transform obstacles blocking your path into opportunities. It is when we grab opportunities and rise to challenges that we are most likely to experience bliss.

The Wand helps you
to transform obstacles
into opportunities.

CONTRADICTIONS BETWEEN INDIVIDUALS AND ORGANIZATIONS

> *The inherent preferences of organizations*
> *are clarity, certainty, and perfection.*
> *The inherent nature of human relationships*
> *involves ambiguity, uncertainty, and imperfection.*
> *How one honors, balances, and integrates*
> *the needs of both is the real trick . . .*
> Richard Pascale and Anthony Athos
> *The Art of Japanese Management*

There is always a certain degree of tension between individuals and the organizations they work in. There is tension between supervisor and subordinate, between cooperation and competition, between short- and long-term agendas, between tangible and intangible rewards, to mention just a few of the common conflicts inherent in our modern workplace. The contradictions can be subtle and complicated. You can get ensnared in dilemmas of this sort and find yourself feeling immobile, unable to accomplish what you are expected to accomplish.

Organizations are made up of individuals, for example, yet they tend to be environments that are hostile to individuality. Organizations

> **Organizations are threatened by individual power.**

want predictability and certainty but individuals are ambiguous and unpredictable. As people, we are naturally subjective and emotional, but the organizations where we work expect us to be logical, rational, and able to control our emotions. Of course, a few prima donnas can get away with throwing fits, but, for most of us, emotional displays at work are considered unprofessional.

Another way in which organizations are alien to us individuals is that organizations tend to be mechanistic systems that treat employees like "interchangeable parts" of a corporate "machine." But we're alienated by being made into standardized human parts to be popped in and out like replacing a carburetor in a car. We think of ourselves as unique. But unique people are irreplaceable, which threatens organizations.

Differences such as these between individuals and the organizations where they work result in mind-boggling contradictions for those working in organizations—which includes most of us.

THE PARADOX OF INDIVIDUALS AND ORGANIZATIONS

Individuals are:	Organizations expect:
Ambiguous	Certainty
Unpredictable	Predictability
Imperfect	Perfection
Unique	Standardization
Emotional	Reason
Subjective	Analysis

Bliss is most likely experienced when we're engaged in purposeful activity—which is usually when at work. When we get ensnared in paralyzing contradictions of the sort described in this chapter our potential for experiencing bliss declines. Grappling with these paradoxes can generate feelings of powerlessness, and start the negative spiral of job burnout. That's the bad news. The good news is that your potential for flow—experiencing bliss—is not fixed. You can change it. You can increase bliss potential when you take on challenges that match your ability; when what you are doing is meaningful; and when you can influence events at hand. With the Wand tool, you can transform these obstacles to create blissful conditions. Like the medieval alchemist who transformed lead into gold, you can turn paralyzing paradoxes into opportunities and immobilizing contradictions into challenges.

CRAZYMAKING DILEMMAS

Irreconcilable contradictions make us feel crazy and can't be solved by working harder or being smarter. The phenomenon is so strong that Gregory Bateson, Paul Watzlawick and others from the Mental Research Institute in Palo Alto proposed a model of "mental illness" that points to the paralyzing power of paradoxical communication as the cause of aberrant behavior. For example, a mother says to her child, "Billy, come give your Mamma a hug or I'll be very unhappy." But when the child reaches out to the mother, she snaps, "Don't touch me, you filthy brat," while recoiling in disgust. According to these psychologists, the contradictions at the core of such a paradox are created by conflicting messages about what's expected of Billy and what he can expect from others. However Billy responds he fails to meet his mother's expectations. If most of the messages Billy receives from his world are of this mutually exclusive nature, Billy will probably begin exhibiting "craziness" and eventually be given a psychiatric label.

> Crazymaking dilemmas make us feel powerless and lead to burnout.

These same crazymaking paradoxes are commonplace in everyday work situations. We all know that contradictory communication can make us "feel crazy." When the situation is important, such as our perceived job security, for example, we can become immobilized in conflict which sends us into the vicious cycle of burnout.

The MRI group identified four categories of crazymaking paradoxes:

(1) **Be Spontaneous!**

(2) **Either/Or**

(3) **Damned-if-you-do, Damned-if-you-don't**

(4) **The Game Without End.**

All of these mind benders are commonly found at work, at home and in recreation. Wherever you find people you can run into these crazymaking situations. Fortunately, each of these paradoxes can be transformed into an opportunity with your Wand. To achieve this, you must be able to recognize the paradox and understand the nature of its central contradiction.

DILEMMA: BE SPONTANEOUS!

A contradiction that is sure to cause you to feel crazy is being told to "Be spontaneous!" You can't meet a command to be spontaneous, because spontaneity doesn't operate on demand. A "Be spontaneous!" paradox is one in which attempting to meet the demand makes it impossible to do what is demanded. Insomnia presents such a dilemma. Sleep can't be forced. Those times when we have difficulty in going to sleep are often due to trying to force sleep. Sexual arousal is a similar phenomenon. It can't be demanded.

CENTRAL CONTRADICTION IN BE SPONTANEOUS!

The central contradiction in the "Be spontaneous!" paradox is an "impossible demand." Typically, the dilemma arises in interpersonal situations in which one person demands or expects of another person a behavior which can arise only spontaneously. Suppose, for example, your boss demands that you volunteer. You can't meet the demand, because doing what you are told is compliance, not volunteering.

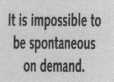

It is impossible to be spontaneous on demand.

TRANSFORMING THE BE SPONTANEOUS! DILEMMA

The strategists have a saying:
"If I cannot be a host,
then let me be a guest.
But if I dare not advance even an inch,
then let me retire a foot."
Lao Tzu
The Way of Life

Let go! Stop trying to meet the impossible demand.

The only way to transform the "Be spontaneous!" dilemma is to let go and to stop "trying" to meet the demand. When you stop trying to fall asleep, for example, you usually go right to sleep. As another example, when impotent clients are told by their sex therapists to simply enjoy fondling and to stop trying to get sexually aroused, they tend to get very turned on.

Let Go of Attachments

Attachment is holding on to the way things "used to be" and to ideas of how things "should" be. If, for example, you have an incompetent boss you might lament, "My boss should be skilled and should give me direction and shouldn't be so critical." You are attached to the way the boss "should be." Eastern philosopher Krishnamurti said "attachment is the root of all suffering." Attachment causes suffering by creating discontent and unhappiness with the way things are. When things change, most people tend to resist it. We keep wishing things were the way they were in the past. Our attachment to the past causes us suffering. Acceptance, or surrender, frees us from this suffering. When struggling with insomnia, instead of thinking, "I've got to go to sleep!", let go, surrender and accept being awake. "It'd be nice to go to sleep, but I'm awake; so I'll just lie here and rest." Chances are you'll be dreaming soon. Returning to the unskilled boss, according to psychologist Albert Ellis, who fathered "rational-emotive psychotherapy," it is not the boss's ineptness itself that causes your distress but your "irrational thoughts" about it. Ellis says that what you're thinking about the boss is "My boss is critical and doesn't give direction. *And that is terrible.* My boss *shouldn't* treat me so poorly." This catastrophizing is what Ellis calls irrational. Both Ellis and Ken Keyes,

Be detached, like a mirror.

author of *Handbook to Higher Consciousness,* advise us to let the irrational demand go and accept the situation as it is. So instead of lamenting about the boss's shortcomings, for example, you accept her and think, "I'd like it if my boss gave me direction and if she were appreciative of my work, but she's not."

Accept it! Let go! Surrender! This is heresy to those of us want to be assertive and in command of our selves. Surrender! Are you kidding? Achieving freedom by surrendering is another paradox. The secret of transforming paradoxes lies in using nonlogic, doing the opposite—and doing something (seemingly) absurd. In the case of "Be spontaneous!" fighting, resisting, and trying are results of attachment and entrap us, whereas surrender or acceptance of the contradiction is freeing.

Alan Watts used the mirror to explain how to let go. Step in front of a mirror and it reflects you. The mirror doesn't say, "I don't like your looks; so I'm not going to reflect you." The mirror simply reflects, because it's not attached. It doesn't take your reflection personally. Step away from the mirror, and it lets your reflection go. The mirror doesn't say, "I don't want you to go away. It's not fair. I'll keep reflecting you anyway." The mirror simply lets your reflection go.

IS THAT SO?

A young woman who was pregnant was afraid when her brother demanded, "Who did this to you?"

"It was the old man up on the hill," she lied.

Furious, her brother stomped up the hill to the old man's cottage, and said, "You dirty old man. Look what you've done to my sister."

And the old man said, "Is that so?"

Time went by and the baby was born. The brother took the baby up to the old man's cottage and banged on the door. When the old man answered, the brother said, "This baby is your responsibility. You take him."

And the old man said, "Is that so?"

The old man took care of the baby and loved the baby. The baby brought the old man much joy as he grew. But one day the young girl began wanting her baby back and confessed to her brother. Shamefaced, the brother trudged back up the hill to the old man's cottage. "Old man," he said, "I'm sorry I wrongly accused you. I'm taking the baby back."

And the old man said, "Is that so?"

IS THAT
SO?

You'll be amazed at the freedom that using the phrase, "Is that so?" can provide. You're not saying you're happy with events. You're not saying you agree with what's happening. You're not promising to do nothing or anything about it. You're simply asking, "Is that so?"

A story about Mother Teresa, the Nobel Laureate nun, provides another example. When asked, "Mother Teresa, you work with sick and dying children, and they die anyway. How can you stand it?" She answered, "We love them while they're here."

Mother Teresa gave the sick children the love they needed while caring for them. But if they died, she didn't protest life's unfairness. She wasn't attached. She surrendered and let them go.

The closest most of us come to understanding nonattachment is sportsmanship. Good sports get out on the field and put all they've got into the game. They play hard to win. But if they lose, they don't kick lockers and swear. They accept the loss and let it go. A good sport says to the victor, "You played a great game. Congratulations on your win!"

Sports teach us to be detached.

Don Juan, the Yaqui Indian sorcerer said: tie your shoe laces impeccably here, now! Live fully in the moment. Be mindful of what is happening here—now. An old Zen saying captures the idea: "When walking, just walk. When sitting, just sit. Above all, don't wobble."

Be here now!

When you encounter a "Be spontaneous!" paradox where trying to satisfy what is demanded of you negates your efforts, use your Wand to transform it.

Instead of striving to meet the impossible demand, work impeccably here and now, and let go of your attachment to winning. You'll discover a certain freedom in the ravines of life.

TIE YOUR SHOESLACES IMPECCABLY

Carlos and Don Juan were walking in a ravine when Don Juan stopped to tie his shoelaces. Just at that moment, an enormous boulder fell from the cliff above and landed right where they would have been had they not stopped. Shaken, Carlos exclaimed, "If we hadn't stopped we would have been killed!"

"Yes," Don Juan calmly replied, "by stopping we gained a precious moment that saved us. But suppose on another day in another ravine we stopped to tie my shoelaces and in doing so we lost a precious moment and were crushed by the falling boulder."

Confused, Carlos asked, "What should we do?"

Don Juan answered, "The only possible freedom in that ravine consists in tying your shoe laces impeccably."

Don't worry about trying to avoid the boulder because it will fall or it won't fall. Instead, be here now and focus on tying your shoelaces.

Inspired by Carlos Castaneda
The Teachings of Don Juan

DILEMMA: THE EITHER/OR CHOICE

What the philosophers say about reality
is like a sign you see in a shop window,
which reads, "Pressing done here."
If you brought your clothes to be pressed
you would be fooled, for the sign is only for sale.
Søren Kierkegaard
Either/Or

Either/or paradoxes are everywhere. The phrase "You can't have your cake and eat it, too" catches the flavor of the either/or dilemma. Having your cake and eating your cake are both positive and desirable, but you can't do both. You can either eat the cake and then you won't have it, or you can have your cake but only if you don't eat it. Women who want to pursue a career and have a family and who are told that they can take either the fast track or the "mommy track," face an either/or dilemma, for example. They are faced with two mutually exclusive options. Constantly encountering either/or situations, especially when the stakes are high, can lead to feeling trapped and helpless. Blissful moments are few and burnout is close behind.

The process of pathfinding itself presents us with either/or situations. Stanford University Business School professor Harold Leavitt,

Each pathfinding tool takes wearing a different Hat.

author of *Corporate Pathfinding* says, pathfinding activities fall into three broad functions or categories: *setting the course, traversing the course, and staying the course.* Each process calls on a different mental attitude—wearing a different Hat—to optimally carry out the activities involved. Setting the course requires visioning and takes a creative mental attitude, or wearing the Green Hat. Traversing the course, by comparison, refers to implementing, and involves getting people to cooperate, and maneuvering through roadblocks and detours, which requires a supportive attitude and flexible thinking, or wearing the Yellow Hat. Staying the course, on the other hand, involves

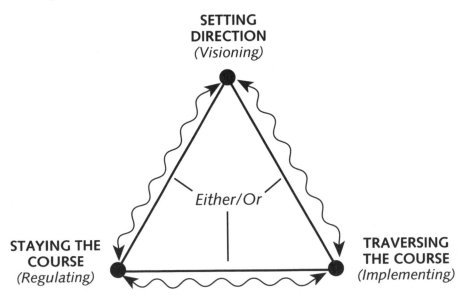

looking for deviation from the plan and taking corrective action which requires a critical mental attitude or Black-Hat thinking.

Moving from one function to the next can be confusing. You have to cross the ambiguous terrain between vision and plan, between plan and action. The process is replete with contradictions. The conflicting activities and mindsets required to set the course, traverse the course and stay the course could ensnare pathfinders in three either/or dilemmas.

EITHER SET THE COURSE OR TRAVERSE THE COURSE

Setting the course requires seeing the big picture and deciding on a strategic direction. To accomplish this you must break out of restrictive mindsets, to create a Vision of what could be. Creating such a Vision occurs in the imagination, but making it real must happen within the limits of the materials, the organization, the people, and the resources available. Some pathfinders feel uncomfortable with visioning and rush right into implementation. But without a Vision to act as a beacon, they risk unproductive action that goes nowhere. Others are impractical dreamers and resist practical action. They get stuck with a pie-in-the-sky idea. Negotiating the dilemma between setting the course and traversing the course means being both a dreamer and a doer.

Another facet of this dilemma is that envisioning tends to be an individual activity but making the Vision a reality usually takes the efforts of many people, which means being a team player during implementation and brings up the dilemma of being either an indi-

vidual contributor or a teamplayer. Along this same vein, setting the course is pointing the way, but getting people to work together as a team to traverse the course takes people skills. When to see or when to do, when to lead or when to manage, when to contribute individually or when to teamplay, these are all part of the either/or dilemmas between setting the course and traversing it.

EITHER TRAVERSE THE COURSE OR STAY THE COURSE

Leavitt's research indicates that pathfinders face another either/or dilemma when grappling with the challenges of traversing the course (implementing) while staying the course (regulating). Staying on the course focuses on accountability, so that deviation from the plan is detected and corrected. But implementation or traversing the course takes place in an imperfect and changing world, in which things rarely proceed according to plan. There are always roadblocks and detours to get around, which takes compromise, innovation, and flexibility. But too much flexibility can find you way off-course.

Implementing takes getting participation and consensus, which are social processes involving alliances, power, and persuasion. When regulating, on the other hand, you exert control by solving problems, making decisions and formulating plans, then tracking output and checking systems and performance to make sure the plans are implemented.

Another facet of this either/or dilemma lies between deciding and acting, for many a decision is a fixed and final act, but traversing the course is a continuously unfolding set of events. Making the shift from deciding to acting can be paralyzing, since we want to base our decisions on all the facts, but all the facts are not available until the end of the journey.

EITHER SET THE COURSE OR STAY THE COURSE

A third either/or pathfinding dilemma occurs between staying the course, or regulating, and setting the course, or envisioning. Setting direction involves seeing what could be and pushes toward innovation, whereas staying the course involves checking and correcting deviations from the plans. Staying on the course is a regulatory

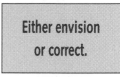
Either envision or correct.

process that requires being cool, systematic, and analytical (Black-Hat thinking); whereas setting the course takes intuition and imagination (Green-Hat thinking) and tends to stimulate your passion. Regulating is repetitive and systematic, aiming toward continuity. In contrast, envisioning moves people into uncharted territory by inspiring them to take on new challenges and to develop new ways of doing things.

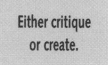
Either critique or create.

This classic either/or dilemma is often played out between a visionary company founder, such as Steve Jobs of Apple, and the professional manager, such as John Scully, who was brought in to shape things up. Conflict was inevitable. The professional manager is a regulator who systematizes and finds the capricious, autocratic style of the founder appalling. More often than not, the dilemma is resolved by

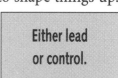
Either lead or control.

insisting that "entrepreneurs are good at starting companies, but not so good at running them" and easing the founder out.

CENTRAL CONTRADICTION IN THE EITHER/OR DILEMMA

A "false dichotomy" creates the central contradiction in the either/or paradox. A dichotomy refers to two mutually exclusive categories. Man or woman, dog or cat, and apples or oranges are examples of dichotomies. An individual can be in one group or the other, but not both. Either/or situations make us feel that we must pick one of the alternatives but not both, because there is no middle ground. We're told that we must choose either an apple or an orange—when in fact we could ask for a fruit salad.

TRANSFORMING THE EITHER/OR DILEMMA

Aristotle in his *Ethics* proposed that the secret to transforming the either/or dilemma lies in finding the balance or "golden mean" between the two extremes of either/or. The golden mean is a balance point somewhere along the continuum between the two extremes. Aristotle says that the golden mean is "the right action at the right time to the right

Find the Golden Mean—the balance between extremes.

degree." For example, good money management is somewhere between the extremes of being miserly and being extravagant. The balance point does not have to be in the middle. In fact, it changes. Exactly where the golden mean is at any particular time depends on the situation. During a recession, for example, good money management might move closer to the miserly extreme, to encompass saving more and being tighter in spending. In planning an addition to your home, on the other hand, good money management might move closer to the extravagant extreme because when purchasing tile for the floor, for example, a more expensive, higher-quality tile might be smarter than the cheapest tile available.

> **OVERCOMING THE POWER PARADOX**
> Overcoming the power paradox means making it easier for your opponent to say yes *at the same time* that you make it harder for him to say no. Making it easy to say yes requires problem solving negotiations; making it hard to say no requires exercising power. You don't need to choose between the two. You can do both.
>
> **William Ury**
> *Getting Past No*

Balance is the optimal action between the extremes presented by the either/or dilemma. The career woman who wants children and who is

told to choose either the fast track or the mommy track might devise her own track. She might take the fast track job, then delegate, delegate, delegate; enlist her husband's help in "mothering"; hire a housekeeper; and make weekends off-limits to the job, for example.

The table shows several examples of either/or extremes and the golden mean between them. For example, being decisive is somewhere between being impulsive and being ambivalent. Assertiveness is somewhere between being passive and being aggressive.

> The balance point is the optimal action in the situation.

BALANCE: FINDING THE MEAN BETWEEN EXTREMES

GOLDEN MEAN	EXTREMES	
Decisive	Impulsive	Ambivalent
Assertive	Passive	Aggressive
Adventurous	Fearful	Rash
Money Management	Miserly	Extravagant
Self-Confident	Self-deprecating	Bragging
Self-Management	Self-denying	Indulgent
Autonomous	Conforming	Rebellious
Friendly	Obsequious	Surly

Finding Balance Between Extremes

Balancing can be compared to surfing. When surfing you ride on the balance point, which is slightly ahead of the wave. Move out too far and you'll lose contact with the surge which is propelling you. Fall back too much and you'll be over thrown by the wave's crushing power. The Wand allows you to find balance. This balance point is constantly changing. Bicycle riding is a similar phenomenon. If you were a Martian looking at a bicycle, you'd probably say it's impossible to ride, because the bike would fall over. Chances are the first time you attempted to ride a bike, you probably did fall over; yet if you solve the either/or dilemma and discover the trick of balance, you don't fall over. Instead you can ride much faster than you can walk.

> The balance point is constantly changing.

Examples of either/or traps are plentiful. For example, Bruce felt stuck and oppressed by demands from his partner to act, but he didn't have enough information to make a decision. Without realizing it Bruce was caught in an dilemma to decide or to act. When he challenged his notion that a decision was an all-or-nothing proposition he realized that he could make incremental decisions when he had enough information to decide on the next small step but not enough to decide once and for all. He realized that with incremental decision making, he could act and decide both. This enabled him to escape the either/or dilemma and get on with his project.

> Either/or traps pull us into burnout.

EITHER MILLWRIGHT OR POET

One day the millwright (at Herman Miller) died. My father, being a young manager at the time, did not particularly know what he should do when a key person died, but thought he ought to go to visit the family. He went to the house and was invited to join the family in the living room. There was some awkward conversation—the kind with which many of us are familiar.

The widow asked my father if it would be all right if she read aloud some poetry. Naturally, he agreed. She went into another room, came back with a bound book, and for many minutes read selected pieces of beautiful poetry. When she finished, my father commented on how beautiful the poetry was and asked who wrote it. She replied that her husband, the millwright, was the poet.

It is now sixty years since the millwright died, and my father and many of us at Herman Miller continue to wonder: Was he a poet who did millwright's work, or was he a millwright who wrote poetry?

Max DePree
Leadership Is an Art

Courtney was a project manager responsible for coordinating an important biotech project. Although she was responsible for making sure that all the details of the project were done, she wasn't the official boss of any of the team members, some of whom were high powered scientists. Her ambiguous position of authority threw her into a stressful dilemma when she endeavored to get people to follow through and get the job done. In the beginning, she was very "nice" in her approach, as she asked, almost begged, them to get their progress sheets in. This approach failed. Worse, she felt a subtle sense of contempt for her. So she took a hard-line approach only to be called a "drill sergeant" by the lead scientist on her team. When she attended my workshop on managing authority, Courtney learned how to be a coach and break out of the nice-guy/ drill-sergeant dilemma. A coach is both demanding and supportive. With her new approach Courtney's team was more productive and she was more respected.

DILEMMA: DAMNED-IF-YOU-DO, DAMNED-IF-YOU-DON'T

A damned-if-you-do, damned-if-you-don't paradox, sometimes called a "double bind," creates feelings of powerlessness, which can destroy motivation. It is a forced choice with each

> **Both "options" are negative.**

alternative leading to equally negative outcomes. For example, suppose you are told to innovate or you'll be passed over and at the same time warned not to rock the boat, because you'll be viewed as a troublemaker and passed over. Two mutually exclusive actions are demanded; both have negative consequences. No matter which you elect, you are "damned." Also known as Catch 22, these paralyzing situations tend to make people "feel crazy."

> ### CATCH 22
> There was only one catch and that was Catch-22, which specified that a concern for one's own safety in the face of dangers that were real and immediate was the process of a rational mind. Orr was crazy and could be grounded. All he had to do was ask; and as soon as he did, he would no longer be crazy and would have to fly more missions. Orr would be crazy to fly more missions and sane if he didn't, but if he was sane he had to fly them. If he flew them he was crazy and didn't have to; but if he didn't want to he was sane and had to.
>
> **Joseph Heller**
> *Catch-22*

Damned-if-you-do, damned-if-you-don't situations can have a paralyzing effect. Since both alternatives result in negative outcomes, it is hard to choose either. Responding to sexual harassment on the job is a good example. If the sexually harassed person does nothing, then the harassment continues. But if charges are filed, then the person is publicly

ridiculed and ha-
rassed by co-work-
ers for speaking
out. The dilemma
some minorities
face is another ex-
ample. Minorities
want to be recog-
nized for their
merit. With affir-
mative action their
success may be dis-
counted as token-

YOU'VE GOT TO CHOOSE

ism and not a result of merit, but without affirmative action their
opportunities for recognition are greatly diminished.

CENTRAL CONTRADICTION IN DAMNED-IF-YOU-DO, DAMNED-IF-YOU-DON'T

An "illusion of an alternative" is the central contradiction in the
damned-if-you-do, damned-if-you-don't paradox. The well-known
expression "Heads I win, tails you lose," illustrates the paradox. It sounds
as if you have alternatives, but if you think about it, it becomes apparent
that you lose in either case. That there is an alternative to your losing is
an illusion. The reality is that the situation does not allow the possibility
of your winning.

TRANSFORMING THE DAMNED-IF-YOU-DO, DAMNED-IF-YOU-DON'T DILEMMA

*In every conflict situation there are basically two ways of defending
oneself against the opponent's thrusts: to react with a counter-thrust of
at least equal force or to yield, thereby letting the other's attack fall
into the void and making him lose his balance.*
Paul Watzlawick
The Language Of Change

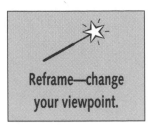

Reframe—change
your viewpoint.

In the damned-if-you-do, damned-if-you-don't paradox choices appear to exist, but in actual fact they are not true alternatives. Although the options presented to you seem different they actually constitute only one pole of a pair of opposites. As long as you seek a solution within the apparent alternatives presented to you you will remain entrapped.

You can transform the damned-if-you-do, damned-if-you-don't paradox by using the Wand to "reframe" your options in the situation.

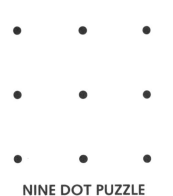

NINE DOT PUZZLE

Instruction: Connect all the dots with four straight lines, without picking up your pencil between lines.

The supposed alternatives in a damned-if-you-do, damned-if-you-don't paradox are presented to you within a particular frame of reference. The Wand helps you to go beyond current boundaries to look at the situation differently, through a new frame of reference. Sometimes it is called "thinking outside the square." The Nine-Dot Puzzle demonstrates the problem

Most people make assumptions about the nine-dot puzzle that are not actually in the instructions. They try to solve it by staying within an invisible box around the dots. This box is assumed, and not part of the actual instructions. The solution lies in going outside the dots, and is found by examining the *assumptions about the dots*, not the dots themselves. Solving the puzzle requires challenging these unseen assumptions, then reframing them by looking at the problem differently.

When first looking at the black and white image to the left it resembles a

chalice, but as you continue looking at it, two faces emerge. Of course, many people see the faces, then the chalice. Once both have been seen, you can make the image go from one to the other.

HOW TO CATCH A MONKEY

Monkeys are supposedly caught by burying a narrow-mouthed jar of nuts in the ground. A monkey comes along, puts his paw into the jar, and grabs a handful of nuts. But the mouth of the jar is of such a size that it will admit only an empty paw, not a clenched paw full of nuts. The monkey is unwilling to let go; so he is trapped.

Edward DeBono
Lateral Thinking

Like the monkey, DeBono warns that we can get trapped by our reluctance to let go of a particular way of looking at a Catch-22 situation. The monkey could grab the nuts and, when he can't pull out his hand, realize that holding the nuts is a trap. A human being could let go of them and find another way of getting at the nuts, perhaps by digging up the jar and emptying it out. But the monkey doesn't let go; so he is easily captured.

HOW TO REFRAME

Problems that remain persistently insolvable should always be suspected as questions asked in the wrong way.
Alan Watts
The Book

Like the monkey, we can become trapped by the obvious and not know it. The key is realizing we may need to escape from a particular way of looking at a situation. Escape from the damned-if-you-do, damned-if-

| Change the way you look at the problem. | you-don't paradox lies in reframing the problem. In this strategy you search for a new way of looking at the dilemma. A new interpretation of the situation needs to be made. |

Identify Assumptions

> *What makes the world so hard to see clearly*
> *is not its strangeness but its usualness.*
> *Familiarity can blind you, too.*
> Robert Pirsig
> *Zen And The Art Of Motorcycle Maintenance*

The challenge is to identify your assumptions about the situation. This is surprisingly difficult because we tend to be blind to assumptions that underlie our beliefs and actions. Of each alternative, ask, "What are my basic assumptions about this situation?" Be a detective. Search for hidden assumptions. Don't overlook the obvious. In the nine-dot puzzle, for example, the assumption most people operate under, usually without realizing it, is that you must stay within the "box." In the "be innovative but don't rock the boat" dilemma, there is an assumption that being passed over for promotion is bad. Another assumption is that there is a right action that will lead to a promotion. It may be that you will be passed over no matter what you do.

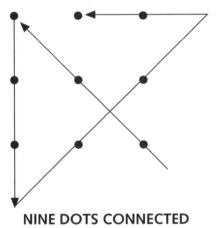

NINE DOTS CONNECTED

Challenge Each Assumption

Confront what you have taken for granted with the simple question, "Why?" Instead of accepting the first answer, demand the reasons for it and persist in asking "Why?" to each answer you give. Repeat four or five times in succession in order to get to the guts of the issue where the fundamental illusions hide. When you challenge the assumption that you're supposed to stay within the "box" you've made a breakthrough that could lead to solving the puzzle.

> Old college saying: Question authority.

Returning to the innovation versus not rocking the boat example, you might ask what is bad about being passed over. You might answer that you don't advance in the company. Asking what is bad about not advancing in the company, you might answer that you don't look successful. Asking again what is bad about not looking successful, you might answer that it's bad to look unsuccessful, because you feel bad about yourself. Continue in this fashion until you've challenged every assumption. Again, don't overlook obvious, or silly, assumptions.

Actively Change Your Viewpoint

> *A mistake is not a mistake.*
> *It is a chance to improve the company.*
> Paul Hawkins
> *Growing a Business*

It is very easy to get stuck in a damned-if-you-do, damned-if-you-don't situation. Often you create the Catch-22 yourself because you are stuck in one way of looking at the situation. There are always multiple ways of looking at any situation. By changing your view of the situation, you may be able to escape from the double bind. There are several techniques for getting at hidden assumptions. The first that you might try is stating the assumption differently.

Rephrase Assumptions

Remember that for every half-empty glass there is a half-full glass. If the assumption is that there is a problem, rephrase it in terms of the opportunities presented. Most problems provide opportunities to develop skills, build allies, and get visibility, for ex-

Change Hats.

ample. Every cloud has a silver lining. Change Hats, and push yourself to look for the positives, the challenges. This ability to see things from many different perspectives is particularly important when eliciting cooperation and building your Team.

Look Through Others' Eyes

Look at the situation from the viewpoint of the people presenting you with the illusion of alternatives. Your Mental Theater is the ideal place to do this. Put others on the screen, one at a time, and review their priorities and the dilemma from inside their heads.

Remember what Tom Sawyer did when he didn't want to paint the fence. Even though he thought painting was a boring chore, he made it appealing to his friends. He said fence painting was a lot of fun and they were lucky to have the opportunity to do it. His friends not only painted the fence and enjoyed doing so, but they also paid him for the opportunity to paint it! The fence had not changed, the paint had not changed, the labor had not changed. Only the perceptual frame had changed. Tom was able to accomplish this feat because he looked at the painting from his friends' viewpoint to discover what motivated them to paint.

Martial arts such as judo, in which a woman can throw a large thug trying to attack her, offers an example. Instead of resisting, the woman uses the thrust of the attacker for momentum and then "throws" him, seemingly without effort, by redirecting his movement. The force of the attacker is redefined as an aid rather than as something to resist.

CREATING NEW PRODUCT IDEAS

A new product can consist of technological innovation or simple repackaging. It can come from an improvement in quality or a decrease in cost. New products can result from renaming, restyling, recombining, or giving old products new advertising slants. A new product can be an actual thing or service, or it can be a different promotional strategy for an existing item. There are several techniques for generating new product ideas:

■ Apply new technology in an unrelated field.
■ Think of an accessory for the latest technology.
■ Find a simpler solution.
■ Put an existing product to another use.
■ Improve an existing product.
■ Invent a new type of package.
■ Make something out of waste.
■ Synthesize two or more services.
■ Present information in a new way.
■ Make something safer.
■ Adapt an existing service.
■ Do something faster.

Tony Houch and Cynthia Foust
That's A Great Idea

Let It Percolate

Another approach to uncovering hidden assumptions is to stop trying to "solve" the dilemma. Instead, review the assumptions about the situation that you identified and your challenges to each assumption. Then set it aside. Relax. Enjoy a hobby. Daydream. Work on something else. Let the possibilities percolate in your unconscious. When you return to the situation, new ways of looking at it will probably come to you.

Turn It Upside Down

Turn the situation around, inside out, upside down, back to front. Find ways to make undesirable results into beneficial outcomes. Think of obstacles as "teachers" that provide lessons to learn from. Instead of thinking about what you can't do, think of what you can do. Another

trick is to restate the assumption in terms of its opposite. A half-empty glass, for example, is the opposite of a half-full one. Shift your approach from negative to

Put on a Green Hat.

positive. When a situation presents a negative, push yourself to uncover its hidden positives. If a situation involves different priorities between you and an adversary, for example, brainstorm priorities that you share and ways that you and the adversary are similar.

A GOOD BUSINESS HAS INTERESTING PROBLEMS

Business will always have problems. On an autumn Saturday several years ago, I was working in my office while the rest of the world was enjoying the Indian summer. I forget the particular problem I was trying to solve. It was one of hundreds and I was proceeding in my usual fashion: solve that problem once and for all. For years I had been the greyhound chasing the rabbit of permanent solutions. I knew that if I worked just a little harder, a little longer, a little more creatively, I would finally catch that rabbit and have a perfectly running business at last. I would experience commercial nirvana, and emerge from the dark of the night of the ledgerbook into the clear dawn of administrative beatitude. Monday morning would always be a pleasure. I was wrong.

I had my nirvana, all right, but it was the opposite of what I had been seeking. On that pretty afternoon the actual truth finally struck me. I would always have problems. In fact, problems signify that the business is in a rapid learning phase. A good business has interesting problems, a bad business has boring ones. Good management is the art of making the problems so interesting and their solutions so constructive that everyone wants to get to work to deal with them.

Paul Hawkins
Growing A Business

When Paul Hawkins demanded that his business be free of problems he created his own burnout conditons. Problems were viewed as bad and indicators of failure—his inability to eliminate problems. Because problems are inevitable, he probably experienced a sense of powerlessness. When Hawkins reframed he transformed burnout potential to bliss potential. Problems were not signs of failure, they were signs of success—that he had created a good business. As a result of this transformation Hawkins found bliss in problem solving, not burnout.

Reframe with Metaphors

> *New metaphors have the power to create a new reality.*
> *Language does not so much reflect reality as create it.*
> Richard Pascale and Anthony Athos
> *The Art Of Japanese Management*

Metaphors are a powerful linguistic device for creating and changing meaning. Metaphors use images or pictures to focus attention on one set of properties about a situation rather than on others. Meaning is not fixed; it is relative to the person's way of looking at the situation. What's meaningful to me does not depend on rational knowledge alone but on my past experiences, values, feelings, and intuitive insights. When you change the metaphor you use to describe your dilemma, you change the focus of your attention, which effectively reframes the way you view it. To illustrate, consider the following statements:

Metaphors change "reality."

- A sexy blonde joined our group.
- A renowned scientist joined our group.
- A bestselling mystery writer joined our group.
- A socialist joined our group.
- A lesbian joined our group.

If you're like most people, you had a different reaction to each statement. In each case the phrase describing the person who joined the group triggered a host of associations, assumptions, feelings, and memories. A "sexy blonde" might bring to mind a woman with a Marilyn Monroe look, for example, whereas your image of a "renowned" scientist might be someone in a white lab jacket wearing horned-rimmed glasses. George Lakoff, a University of California at Berkeley linguist who studied the impact of metaphors on meaning, emphasizes that every description highlights, downplays, and hides. For example, suppose all five statements about the person joining the group refer to the same person. Each description focuses on one set of properties, and shifts attention away from others, resulting in a different impression. Describing a woman as a sexy blonde focuses attention on her physical characteristics, whereas "socialist" shifts attention to the person's political values, for example.

> **Every description highlights, downplays and hides.**

Ralph and Charles were brothers who ran a mail-order business. When Charles reminded Ralph to do something he'd forgotten or corrected an error he made, Ralph would accuse Charles of "trying to get the upper hand." Whenever Ralph thought about Charles' attempts to get the upper hand, he became angry and refused Charles' requests. Eventually they reached an impasse that threatened their working relationship. When Ralph commiserated with a friend about his problems with Charles, the friend suggested that Charles was only "trying to run a tight ship," and suggested that Ralph think of it that way. Ralph did and much to his surprise Charles' reminders didn't seem to bother him so much after that. When Ralph changed the metaphor he used to think about Charles' behavior, from getting the upper hand over him to running the business as a tight ship, his feelings about Charles changed. Ralph had reframed the situation by changing his metaphors.

Change Meaning with Picture Words

We use metaphors or picture words frequently. In fact, it is difficult to say much without metaphors. In a very subtle way we take the pictures in the words to be reality without realizing it. When you change the kinds of pictures used to describe a situation, you can change the way reality is perceived by other people and by yourself as well. A story about problems and solutions from Lakoff and Johnson's book *Metaphors We Live By* illustrates this powerful phenomenon.

PROBLEMS AND SOLUTIONS

An Iranian student shortly after his arrival in Berkeley took a seminar on metaphor. One of the wondrous things that he found in Berkeley was an expression that he heard over and over and understood as a beautifully sane metaphor. The expression was "the solution of my problems"—which he took to be a large volume of liquid, bubbling and smoking, containing all of your problems, either dissolved or in the form of precipitates, with catalysts consistently dissolving in some problems (for the time being) and precipitating out others. He was terribly disillusioned that the residents of Berkeley had no such chemical metaphor in mind. And well he might be, because the chemical metaphor is both beautiful and insightful. It gives us a view of problems as things that can disappear utterly, and can not be solved once and for all. All of your problems are always present, only they may be dissolved and in solution, or they may be in solid form. The best that you can hope for is to find a catalyst that will make one problem dissolve without making another one precipitate out, and since you do not have complete control over what goes into the solution you are consistently finding old and new problems precipitating out and present problems dissolving, partly because of your efforts and partly despite anything you do.

George Lakoff and
Mark Johnson
Metaphors We Live By

For people raised in the Western tradition viewing problems as puzzles characterizes our current reality. Puzzles have correct solutions; and once solved, they stay solved. A shift to the chemical view, where problems go in and out of solution, would result in a new "reality."

The chemical view of problems works because it fits our experience. We've all had the experience of finding problems that we thought were solved turning up again and again. The chemical metaphor gives us a new approach for solving problems. It says that it is pointless to treat problems as things that can be "solved" once and for all. The reappearance of problems is natural, and not a failure on your part. To live by the chemical metaphor would be to direct your energies to finding out what catalysts will dissolve your more pressing problems for the longest time without precipitating out worse ones.

Escaping from the damned-if-you-do, damned-if-you-don't paradox can be accomplished by introducing a new metaphor that reframes the situation. A community task force, demoralized by reoccurring problems, might be energized by the introduction of the "problems as chemicals" metaphor, for example. As another example, co-workers' discussions about how to accomplish certain objectives inevitably turned into heated arguments that left everyone seething with resentment. They said things like, "He attacked me so I blew him out of the water." "My comments were right on target and he went ballistic!" When listening to their words it became apparent that they looked upon arguments as "war." With the help of their manager, they deliberately changed the metaphors used in their discussions to arguments as "sport." Using the sport metaphor they said things like, "Give me a ballpark figure." "That remark is out of bounds." "You scored that time." "We can set each other up to win." The discussions were more productive with less hard feelings, when using the sports metaphor.

Find a new picture.

There is no right or wrong metaphor to use with any particular situation. As with the woman who joined the group described above, many pictures can be used to describe the same situation. For example, instead of war or sports, arguments can be framed as "a journey." You might say, "I set out to prove it to him and I succeeded!" for example. Or you could say, "What you just said points the way to…" Alternatively, you could use "building a structure" picture words to to describe an argument: "And that supports my argument!" Or, "I laid the ground work and constructed a strong argument."

AN ARGUMENT IS

War	*A Journey*	*Building*
"indefensible claims"	"set out to prove"	"framework for"
"attacked weak points"	"that points the way to"	"supports my argument"
"right on target"	"proceed step by step"	"argument will collapse"
"demolished his point"	"arrived at the conclusion"	"a shaky argument"
"won the argument"	"get to the point"	"argument fell apart"
"strategy to wipe him out"	"points so far"	"I laid the groundwork"
"shot down my argument"	"goal of the argument"	"construct a strong argument"

Many people in large companies find themselves in a damned-if-you-do, damned-if-you-don't bind where they fear that being themselves will result in their being called mavericks, yet if they conform and become "corporate," they feel that they've sold themselves out. Recall the story about the wild ducks. It is an example of how a metaphor can change the meaning of a situation and transform a

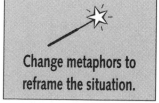

Change metaphors to reframe the situation.

crazymaking dilemma. In Watson's story, wild ducks who were fed stopped flying south for the winter. Instead, they got fat and lazy on the food provided by a well-meaning bird lover. Watson always completed his story with the line, "You can tame a wild duck, but you can't make him wild again!" Then he would point out that IBM needed its wild ducks. With this story Watson created a loophole for people in IBM who were different. The boss could say, "Well, she's just a wild duck." Or the employee could say to the boss, "Can't you cut a little slack for a wild duck?"

EXAMPLES OF METAPHORS

Metaphor	Sample Phrases
Ideas are food	half-baked ideas, warmed-over ideas, it smells fishy, food for thought, meaty ideas, spoon-fed ideas, let ideas percolate, can't swallow it.
Ideas are people	his brainchild, resurrected the idea, breathed life into the idea, fathered the project, ideas live on, ideas are the mother of innovation.
Ideas are plants	come to fruition, budding notion, come to full flower, seeds of the idea, were planted, fertile imagination, it died on the vine.
Time is money	waste time, save time, give time, borrowed time, worth your while, budget time, cost me an hour, invest your time.
Leading is pathfinding	set direction, launch into the unknown, blaze a trail, stay the course, pioneering spirit, reach new summits, go into uncharted territory.

Become aware of the metaphors you use when you think about burnout situations and about bliss situations. How are they different? Identify how your way of describing the situation contributes to your feelings of helplessness and being trapped in it. Challenge yourself to find new ways of describing the situation. Push yourself to use different descriptions and you'll eventually discover how the problem is an opportunity. You'll have transformed your helplessness into a sense of potency. With challenge, opportunity and potency in hand, burnout recedes and bliss becomes possible.

DILEMMA: THE GAME WITHOUT END

The game-without-end paradox is a conflict situation in which one "player"—a person, an organization, even a country—acts and a second "player" responds. The first player then escalates in response to the second player's reaction, which results in an escalation from the second player. This game or dance, as it is sometimes called, goes on without end. The Cold War arms race was a prime example. The Soviets built missiles; so the USA built missiles. The Soviets built more missiles; so the USA built more missiles. Of course, the Soviets probably framed it as "The USA built missiles, so they had to build missiles." When the USA built more missiles, they had to built more missiles. There was no end to missile building. It became a game without end.

The game without end is the proverbial chicken and egg dilemma. It goes on and on and on. Each player punctuates the game with artificial beginnings and endings. This "punctuation" lies at the heart of the game without end. Players each claim that the other one *started* the game, and they are merely *responding* in the only way they 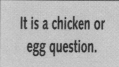 can. Rarely do players see the never ending process. Instead, players each tend to feel like a victim of the other.

It is a chicken or egg question.

The employee sees a demanding boss and resists. The boss sees a resistant employee and demands. From the boss's perspective, the only solution is to demand more. That is, the boss sees the solution *as doing more of the same*—which in this example is making more demands. And from the employee's perspective the only solution is to also do more of the same which is to resist more. If you look at the situation from either one's viewpoint the "solution" seems like a normal and rational response to what the other person has done.

But if you step back and look at the game from a larger perspective, they both look crazy. It is obvious that if the boss demands more, the

Go to the meta-level.

employee will resist more. And if the employee resists more, the boss will demand more. The boss would have to be crazy to demand more, and the employee would have to be crazy to resist more; yet that's exactly what they do, because they're caught in a game without end.

CENTRAL CONTRADICTION IN THE GAME-WITHOUT-END DILEMMA

The central contradiction in the game without end lies in the "attempted solution." In the example the employee's attempted solution is to resist more, and the boss's attempted solution is demanding more. *The problem is the attempted solution.* The boss and the employee each try to solve the problem by doing more of the same. As long as the players continue doing more of the same, the game will go on without end.

TRANSFORMING THE GAME-WITHOUT-END

> *To change the game, you need to do*
> *the opposite of what you've tempted to do.*
> *Instead of rejecting what your opponent says, accept it.*
> William Ury
> *Getting Past No*

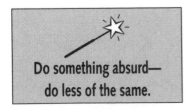

Do something absurd—do less of the same.

The real solution to the game without end is to *do less of the same.* Use the Wand to employ reverse psychology and do the opposite. But doing the opposite looks absurd within the context of the game. In the example, the boss would do the opposite of demanding: be accepting and permissive. Suggesting such a solution sounds absurd to the boss; whereas for the employee the opposite of re-

sisting is cooperating and going the extra mile, which sounds absurd to the employee. Yet if the boss stopped demanding, there would be nothing for the employee to resist. Likewise, if the employee were very cooperative and performed beyond the boss's expectations, there would be little for the boss to demand. The game would end.

Remember Br'er Rabbit? He ordered the fox to do the opposite of what he wanted him to do. "Do anything you want with me, but don't throw me into that there briar patch." The crafty rabbit did something absurd in telling the fox to not do what he wanted him to do. Br'er Rabbit knew that his persecutor would resist whatever he demanded; so he did something absurd, and implored the fox to do what he didn't want to happen. As we all know, the fox promptly threw Br'er Rabbit in to the briar patch where the fox couldn't get to him.

Consider the Chinese Finger Puzzle. You can easily slip your fingers into the open ends of the woven reed tube, but when you attempt to pull them out, the tube tightens so that your fingers are stuck. The harder you pull, the tighter the

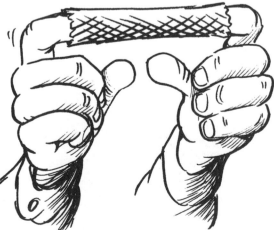

puzzle gets. The "attempted solution" is trying to pull your fingers out. But pulling makes the puzzle tighter. Instead, if you do something absurd and push your fingers into the trap, the tube loosens, and your fingers are freed.

> **Do something absurd—push your fingers in to escape from the trap.**

The game without end is a vicious cycle. If they compete, we compete. If they control, we resist. It is the old knee-jerk, automatic response. Escape from the game without end is accomplished by looking beyond the "attempted solution," which is your usual response, and then doing something absurd, generally the opposite of your usual response.

How to Find the Absurd Solution

Each player in the game without end keeps the conflict or "game" in perpetual motion by doing more of the same. Opposing attorneys, for example, continue locked in battle, with each engaging in legal skirmishes. It's only when one side does something different such as suggesting a settlement conference, that there's a possibility of ending the litigation. It's like a tug of war, with each side pulling, but neither side winning. Even though each side pulls more, they remain stuck in a game without end until one side does less of the same and lets go. The game instantly stops as the side that keeps pulling falls backward.

At first the prospect of doing less of the same seems absurd, until you examine it within the context of what keeps the game going. Finding the absurd solution that releases you from the game without end takes

> **Watch interactions in your Mental Theater.**

observing interactions among the players. A game without end is hard to see when you look at the situation of only one player. The first step is to identify the other player or players involved in the game. Clues about who is involved are hidden in actions and reactions. Look for actions of the other people that cause you to react. Look for actions of yours that cause the other player to react to you. If you observe a repetitiveness in these actions and reactions, you've probably identified a game without end.

Observe the game in action and look for "attempt solutions," which are usually one player's reaction to the other player's reactions. If you can't observe the game directly, use your Vision tool. Go to your Mental Theater, project the game onto your Viewing Screen, and observe actions and reactions. Assume an objective mindset by putting on your White Hat so that you can look

Be objective.

for the facts of the conflict. Without changing or evaluating anything, observe several "rounds" of the game. When you've identified the interaction, describe the game without end. Decide whether the reaction fits the description of doing more of the same. If it does, it is the attempted solution. The next step is to identify the absurd action which is "doing less of the same." Decide what it means in the situation you're observing to do less of the same. This usually involves doing the opposite. Although doing less of the same seems absurd it will release you from the game without end.

Restate your reaction in terms of an attempted solution or doing more of the same. Change to a creative mindset by putting on the Green Hat, and brainstorm actions that would be the opposite of the attempted solution. Include silly and seemingly absurd possibilities. Review your ideas and decide which would involve doing less of the same. These are good candidates for the absurd solution that can release you from the

Brainstorm
opposite actions.

game. Return to your Viewing Screen and replay the game, try out the absurd solutions, and observe what happens. When you find one that stops the game, you'll have discovered your escape from the game-without-end.

ACCEPT OBSTACLES AND TRANSFORM THEM

With the ability to transform obstacles into opportunities, you can feel confident in moving toward your Vision. Certainly you will encounter conflicts and paralyzing dilemmas along the way. But with the transformational techniques afforded by the Wand, you have a variety of powerful strategies for getting around roadblocks to get back on course.

Remember, bliss promoting conditions are challenges matched to your ability, meaningfulness and potency—personal power. With the Wand you transform burnout promoting situations into bliss promoting situations by accepting the situation as a challenge to find opportunities and meaningfulness in solving problems. In the process we empower ourselves where we previously felt powerless. With the Wand, we've transformed burnout to bliss—as we surmount obstacles along the path with a heart—our path to bliss. The final pathfinding tool is the Eye used to oversee and pilot your journey which is the subject of the next chapter.

CHAPTER 14

EYE

PILOTING YOUR JOURNEY

To walk the path of mastery isn't always easy,
but it is the ultimate human adventure.
Destinations will appear in the distance,
will be achieved and left behind,
and still the path will continue.
It will never end.
George Leonard
Mastery

$\mathcal{T}$he way in which you manage yourself in your quest for a path with a heart, your path to bliss, will determine your success. If you use punitive methods to motivate yourself, you are likely to end up in burnout instead. If, on the other hand, you employ positive self-managing techniques, such as setting compelling goals and rewarding yourself for achievements, you will probably experience many moments of bliss.

It is with the Eye
that you pilot your
pathfinding adventure.

The final pathfinding tool is you, the pathfinder, the pilot. The eye in the triangle represents the "I" who sees and decides. The Eye tool is used to manage your adventure by objectively watching and coordinating the process. With the Eye tool you decide what to do when.

TRAVERSING THE COURSE

The pilot is the steersman, the person who steers the ship in and out of the harbor and through difficult waters to get from here to there. The pilot sets direction, manages the crew in traversing the course and takes corrective action as necessary to stay the course. It is with the Eye that you find a path with a heart and lead yourself to your bliss.

SELF-MANAGEMENT

You are the pilot of your pathfinding adventure. As such, you must manage yourself effectively to get where you want to go. As an autonomous being, you're managing yourself all the time.

Where did you learn to manage yourself?

Although your techniques may be more or less effective, every action you take or don't take, every thought you think or don't think, every emotion you feel or don't feel is guided by your personal management. In spite of the importance of self-management, however, few of us have had specific training in how to do it.

> ### THE CYBERPUNK
> Cyber is the Greek word for pilot. The cyberpunk person is one who pilots his/her own life. Cyberpunk describes the resourceful, skillful individual who accesses and steers knowledge-communication technology toward his/her own private goals, for personal pleasure, profit, principle, or growth.
>
> **Timothy Leary**
> *Chaos & Cyber Culture*

The cyberpunk that Timothy Leary describes is a pathfinder. Cyber means pilot and a punk is an individual who questions authority. Pathfinders use the Eye to pilot—to self-direct. Pathfinders don't accept the old paths and the old rules without question. Instead, they think and

question to decide what is best for them as individuals. They ask which choice will lead to a path with a heart, a path to their bliss.

Unfortunately, most of us have not been encouraged to be pathfinders—or cyberpunks—or autotelic, as Csikszentmihalyi called those who lead themselves. Our schools and our teachers, in most cases, did not teach us to be seekers, but avoiders. I remember a beautiful Spring day when I was in a high school study hall looking at a Latin book. Do you suppose I was doing that because I loved learning Latin or because I wanted to avoid getting detention for daydreaming in study hall? Think of college students cramming for exams during "Dead Week." Chances are they are more motivated by the desire to avoid bad grades or the fear of being kicked out of school than by the love of learning.

■ Homework

A teenaged girl struggling with homework complained "I can't do it! I can't do it! I don't want to do it! I don't like this homework."

Her mother lectured back, "Now, the trouble with you, Susie, is that you let it pile up until it is an impossible amount to do at the last minute. If you just did a little bit every day this would never happen."

The girl pleaded again, " Well, Mom, could you help me, please? Please!"

But the mother refused, "No, I can't right now."

The girl demanded, "Well, why not?"

Looking at an enormous stack of unironed clothes that had piled up for over a month, the mother snapped back, "I've got ironing to do!"

Most of us emulate the self-management styles of parents, friends and teachers who are themselves poor self-managers. We've acquired bad habits of procrastination, "guilt tripping," "pulling all-nighters," and other suboptimal methods of getting moving. Self-management is a process of motivating yourself to do certain things. With your Eye you can watch what you respond to and how you respond to it. Sometimes it is easier to understand if you think of yourself, for a moment, as a puppet. The Eye watches what makes the puppet move. When you thoroughly understand the puppet, then you can become the puppeteer and make the puppet do as you please. Before we go further into the use of the Eye tool, it helps to understand a few basic principles of human functioning, beginning with motivation.

> **Study you—the puppet—then become a puppeteer.**

GETTING MOVING AND KEEPING MOVING

Think of motivation as "moving." Being motivated means getting moving and keeping moving. To get moving and to keep moving, there must be a "win" or payoff for doing so. There are two types of wins. The first is where you do something good and something good follows as a result. For example, you have a great idea, write an outstanding report, or make a difficult sale, and as a result you feel good about yourself, or your boss says, "Good report!" or you earn a bonus. Good feelings, acknowledgement from others and extra money are "wins" for most people. Striving for a positive win is "moving toward" or "seeking" motivation.

The second type of win is negative. The joke, "I'm beating my head against the wall because it feels so good when I stop," captures the essence of the negative win. Here a negative situation exists, so you do something to turn it off or to take it away. For example, you have a headache, which is a negative situation, so you take an aspirin and feel better. Absence of pain is a "win," but only because you've taken away a negative. We could say you are motivated or moved to take an aspirin by the desire to turn off or to avoid pain. This is "moving to avoid" or "avoidance" motivation. Unfortunately, this is the predominant motivational style most people learn. Procrastinate, procrastinate, procrastinate, like the girl with too much homework, until you're under tremendous pressure and facing a threat of negative consequence; then work frantically to get the task done which results in removing the threat of being late and accompanying penalties.

Moving to avoid or avoidance is the predominant motivation in our world and most of us learned it in school. We've all experienced it. Have you ever seen anyone "look busy" to avoid getting additional assignments? Avoidance motivation tends to become habitual. The worse thing about avoidance motivation is that there must be a threat before you can get moving to avoid it. No threat, no motivation. This leads to situations where you work hard and long on things you don't like because it

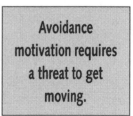

Avoidance motivation requires a threat to get moving.

is part of your "job," but when it comes to doing something you *want to do,* you just can't get started. Why? Because there is no threat to avoid. We've all experienced this phenomenon. The problem is avoidance motivation. You work at the job because of the implicit threats of what would happen if you didn't, but when it comes to doing something you want to do, there is no threat to avoid. Without the threat you can't get moving. If you haven't experienced this trap yourself, you've certainly watched it operate in someone close to you at home or on the job. Clearly, this approach makes work a drudgery and leads to a vicious cycle of getting into negative situations and then struggling to escape them.

■ When the Going Gets Tough The Tough Go Shopping

First woman: I can't stand my job, so I go shopping.

Second woman: I quarrel with my husband, so I go shopping.

Third woman: My daughter stays out all night, so I go shopping.

All three women: Eek! The answer to misery is a sale!

Shopping can temporarily take away the pain of many ills because there is a certain "high" from buying and taking home a new gadget or fancy outfit. Compulsive shoppers, for example, may be motivated by avoiding negative feelings. In another example, a woman hates her job; so she goes shopping, which turns off her frustration. Shopping to turn off emotional distress can become an expensive compulsion.

THE BURNOUT TRAP

Burnout is a malaise of the spirit caused by feeling powerless—being trapped in a situation not to your liking. When it happens at work, working is hell. Since burnout is caused by feelings of powerlessness, the way to beat it is to develop personal power—feelings of potency and the ability to influence situations that impact upon you. *Beating Job Burnout* describes nine paths to personal power. Each path empowers you when you follow it. For example, the fourth path to personal power is to develop social support. When you have supportive friends and colleagues, you'll be more resistant to stress, feel better about yourself even when things don't work out the way you want, and probably accomplish more. When you follow the seventh path, and think more powerfully, you'll focus on what is right about difficult situations and find opportunities in problems. In both cases, you'll have increased your personal power, your ability to influence your situation.

But the process of beating burnout contains an inherent trap: the emphasis on avoidance. This is a trap because it requires that things get bad before they can get better. In other words, you've got to get "a kick in the butt" to get moving. By necessity, beating burnout demands a focus on avoidance. If things aren't so bad, you can easily fall into a state of complacency, in which you don't look for any path to personal power or bother with trying to better yourself until things become unbearable.

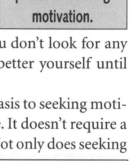

Having a Mission promotes seeking motivation.

The trap can be avoided by transferring emphasis to seeking motivation, where you move toward something positive. It doesn't require a threat or painful situation to get yourself moving. Not only does seeking motivation feel better, but you'll be more productive, too. It takes work and commitment to change your motivational style from avoidance to seeking but it can be done. The results are worth it. You can increase your seeking motivation by establishing a Mission—something you're passionately committed to accomplish. In Chapter

Create a Vision that attracts you like a magnet does.

Five we explored why the key question to ask in clarifying your Mission is: What is the problem I am aiming to solve? Use your Vision tool to conceive of what is possible and create a picture of your problem solved. Recall from Chapter Eight that the trick is to make the picture compelling, so that it draws you toward it like a magnet.

The burnout trap ensnares you in avoidance motivation where you know very well what you want to avoid, but as long as you focus on the negative and avoidance, reaching bliss is unlikely. To strive for bliss you have got to know what it is—for you. If you don't know what your bliss is,

Assess what you need to experience bliss.

then you can't be motivated by it. With your Eye you assess what you need to find a path to your bliss. It is with the Eye that you pilot yourself on your journey along a path with a heart—a path to your bliss.

USE YOUR TARGET TOOL

According to motivational experts there is one vital difference between self-directed people and all others. The difference is not educa-

An effective goal has a compelling positive image, is precise and has a deadline.

tion; it's not money; it's not sex or age. The secret is that self-directed people—pathfinders—have a destination on the horizon to move toward. We know this intuitively, but developing a goal is not so easy. Having a negative goal, without realizing it, is common. For example, a goal to lose 30 pounds in three months sounds positive, but is actually negative, because exer-

cising is hard and resisting fattening food is not fun. Developing a goal takes a lot of consideration and effort. An effective goal provides a compelling positive image—a Target that is precise and has a deadline.

Recall from Chapter Eight, the Target, that it's the compelling positive image that helps stimulate movement toward the goal. You could think of it as being like a magnet that draws you toward it. For

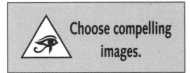

Choose compelling images.

example, an image of resisting a delicious French dinner with rich sauce and eating bland low calorie food instead is negative and undermines your resolve to lose weight.

In contrast, imagining youself looking gorgeous in a bikini and being admired is a positive image that bolsters motivation to slim down.

Use your Eye to evaluate whether or not certain images motivate you. Are they magnetic, attracting you to it, or repellent, pushing you away? Rework repellent images. Use your Target tool to create a compelling image of that time in the future—the goal-state—when you've achieved the goal. For example, when striving to become a better time manager, ask, "What will I be *doing* when I'm a better time manager?" An answer might be, "Having fun on the weekends instead of working in the office." Probing further, you might decide that having fun would be sailing on the bay. If you love sailing, then a picture or Vision of you sailing on the bay on Saturday afternoon would be a strong compelling image that would motivate you to carry out time-management techniques.

OVERCOMING INERTIA

> *People judge a person's greatness by the result of his actions.*
> *If the man who has to act tries to judge himself by the result,*
> *he will never begin.*
> *And even if the result overwhelms the world with joy,*
> *it cannot help the hero; for he has no knowledge of the result*
> *until the whole thing is accomplished,*
> *and it is not in this that he became a hero,*
> *but through the fact that he made a beginning.*
> Søren Kierkegaard
> *Fear and Trembling*

From high school physics you might recall that the definition of inertia is that a body at rest tends to stay at rest and a body in motion tends to stay in motion. When you have decided on the direction and set a specific goal, but have not yet started to move toward it, you are a body at rest. The biggest problem is to overcome the inertia and get into motion.

If you've ever started a car with a dead battery by pushing it and "popping" the clutch into second gear, you'll probably remember that you had to push hardest to get the car moving. Once rolling, it took less effort to keep it rolling. Inertia is the explanation. Overcoming the car's inertia to get it moving takes extra effort.

> **Inertia:**
> **A body at rest tends to stay at rest.**

In the beginning of any project, whether it's on the job, or in a self-improvement activity or a hobby, you are a body at rest. You should expect it to be hard to get moving because you've got to overcome your inertia. The principle of inertia has a corollary that says that once in motion, a body will tend to continue in motion. Have you ever had the experience, near the end of a project, that even when you didn't particularly like what you're doing, you found it easy to keep working? In fact, you might have had trouble pulling yourself away from it. Once again, this was inertia in

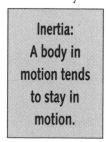

> **Inertia:**
> **A body in motion tends to stay in motion.**

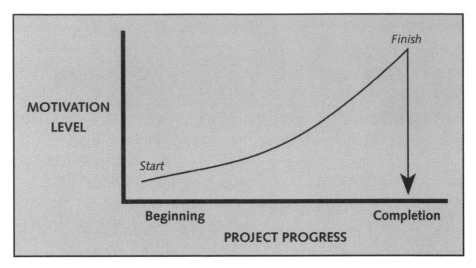

INERTIA

Break inertia with small steps.

action. You were a body in motion, and the tendency was to keep moving until completion.

Think about it. If you can just get yourself into motion, then you can use the inertia of movement to help you stay in motion. This means that breaking the inertia and getting into motion is a key step. If you determine with your Eye that inertia is keeping you from getting going, you can use your Map tool to break the project into small steps and then carry out the easiest step first to get yourself moving. If it is still hard to get going, break the easiest step into even smaller steps until you are able to grab one and get moving.

The man illustrates the "macho approach." He demands of himself a giant step where he must do everything all at once. This is a setup to fail. The woman is a better self-manager because she sets herself up to succeed by breaking the project into small steps and doing a little bit, then a little bit more. As a result she can skip up the steps seemingly effortlessly.

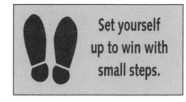

Set yourself up to win with small steps.

PATS ON THE BACK AND OTHER WINS

Getting a payoff or a "win" is essential to sustaining motivation. All animals and humans need a positive reward to keep moving. Imagine working and working with nobody noticing. If you are getting no pats on the back, how are you going to keep moving? Most of us have learned to be dependent on acknowledgment from others, which makes us tremendously vulnerable. It puts us under their control. If they give us a pat on the back, our motivation stays strong; if they ignore us or criticize us, our motivation suffers. Giving yourself wins and acknowledgment can sustain seeking motivation, and it makes you stronger and more independent of others' opinions. Use your Eye to study your motivation and to identify which wins move you.

Getting wins is essential to sustain motivation.

Identify which wins move you.

When you know the wins that move you, you can put together a Want List, which you can use to encourage seeking motivation.

WANT LIST

> *Selfing is knowing what you want —what* you *want, not what you* **should** *want because others say you should want it —and moving toward it.*
> John-Roger and Peter McWilliams
> *Do It!*

It's a funny thing, but a lot of people can describe in great detail what they don't want but don't know what they do want. In my workshops, I ask people to write down what they want on a Want List. It is amazing that some people can't think of anything they want! There is something

wrong with this, and we've all experienced it, at least to some degree. If you don't know what you want, it not too likely that you'll get what you want or recognize it if you do. And worse, you lose a powerful self-motivating tool. Instead, you can become dependent upon what other people think you want and choose to give to you.

Every day we give ourselves treats that can be used as rewards or wins. For example, if reading the paper is something you enjoy doing you

Many people don't know what they want.

can use it as a self-motivator. Here's how: instead of taking a break and reading the paper, you can make reading the paper conditional upon accomplishing a small bit of work. You could say to yourself, "I'll make that cold call *first,* and *then* I'll take a break and read the paper." Taking the break and reading the paper

become a reward or "win" for making the call. And you will enjoy your break more, since you "earned" it, instead of having a nagging feeling that you're goofing off and should be making that call.

A Want List is a list of activities and things you enjoy or want. This includes little things that you already give yourself, such as having a cup

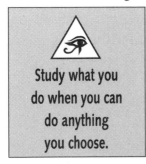

Study what you do when you can do anything you choose.

of coffee, calling a friend, watching a favorite television show, or taking your dog for a walk. List activities you may not do frequently but that you want to do more often. Examples may be going out to the movies, buying yourself a new CD, or going on a weekend excursion. Add bigger things you want, like going on a long trip or buying a new car.

As you think of things you want, add them to your Want List. Be creative with your Want List. Use your Eye tool to identify what you do when you can do anything you want and add them to your list. Use your Heart tool to discover core wants by asking, "What do I love about this?" Continue

Ask: "What do I love doing?"

looking for what you love by asking the question of each thought that comes, until you get to the core. Add these to your Want List. The premise behind the Want List is that you really ought to have everything you want—provided you accomplish certain things first.

SMALL STEPS AND WINS

The Want List is best used in conjunction with the small steps. Complete a small step, then give yourself something you want as a win. Take several steps to reach a milestone, then give yourself something bigger from your list of wants. This is the easiest way to retread your motivational style from avoiding to seeking.

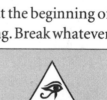

Give yourself lots of wins in the beginning to get going.

Generally, you'll need to get more frequent wins at the beginning of a project when you must overcome inertia to get moving. Break whatever you must do to get started into many small steps, and give yourself frequent wins for doing them. Once you're moving along, frequent wins are less important because of the principle of inertia in which a body in motion will tend to stay in motion. Here you could set milestones to be reached to

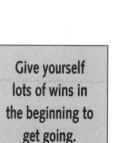

Study which wins work.

obtain bigger wants and stretch out giving yourself smaller wants to encourage stick-to-itness. When you lose momentum or begin to plateau, break steps into smaller ones and increase the frequency of getting wants. Use your Eye tool to study what works and what doesn't work. Use this understanding to improve your seeking motivation. Make working toward something fun, and soon you'll be moving toward bliss.

AVOID PERFECTIONISM

> *Perfectionism is the enemy of mastery.*
> George Leonard

Here's a startling fact that always amuses people in my workshops. Behavioral psychologists now consider perfectionism to be a thought disorder! To illustrate what this means, imagine a hypothetical situation in which identical twins, Bill and Mike, are exactly the same in every way except one. They have the same intelligence and the same training, for example. The difference is that one twin is a perfectionist, the other a realist.

Let's say that the twins have both been invited to submit a paper for publication in a professional journal. Since they have been invited they know it's not a speculative activity because their papers will be published when finished and sent to the editor.

Mike, the perfectionist, sets a standard for acceptability of his paper at 99.9 percent, paying lip service to being human with the .1 percent error margin. By comparison, Bill, the realist, sets his standard at 90 percent. Let's examine the difference in thinking between Bill and Mike as they work. Suppose both twins have gotten their papers to 85 percent of their respective standards. As Mike,

Set a realistic standard.

the perfectionist, reads his paper, he thinks, "Oh, this is just awful. I can't let anybody read this. I'll never get this done. I've got to do a lot more." Mike's thoughts about his work are negative. He exhibits a "glass is half empty" type of mentality. Mike looks at the 14.9 percent that still needs work, not the 85 percent that is good.

Bill's thinking is the opposite, as he focuses on the 85 percent that is good and thinks, "Hm, I'm almost done. This looks pretty good. It needs a bit more shaping here, but it's close." Bill envisions the paper being published and imagines positive responses from colleagues. Unlike Mike, who, attempting to be perfect, sees only flaws, Bill, on the other hand, is a realist who looks at the half-full glass.

Which twin will reach his standard, get the paper done, and get it into the editor first? Obviously, Bill, the realist. Suppose Bill's paper has been submitted to the editor. Which twin is most likely to start on paper number two first? Probably Bill, whereas Mike may still be trying to make his first paper perfect.

The world says different things to the perfectionist and the realist. To the realist, the editor says, "Bill, here's your published paper. It's great that you have another paper. You're really productive." But to the perfectionist, the editor laments, "Mike, where is that paper? You've missed your deadline again! I've got white space to fill." Whereas the world tends to reaffirm and acknowledge the realist, the world criticizes the perfectionist.

You may think to yourself, "Yeah, but I don't want somebody working at only 90 percent." A subjective standard is not a fixed ruler, and not like grades in school. Theoretically, if Bill, the realist, publishes paper two and paper three, through the practice his paper-writing abilities will get better. Bill's work might be rated higher by a team of experts but subjectively Bill would still strive for 90 percent of what he perceived to be perfect. Stated

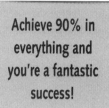

Achieve 90% in everything and you're a fantastic success!

differently, the standard is like a ball floating in water. As the realist gets better and better, there is more water and the ball rises, but it keeps floating at the same 90 percent mark relative to the surface.

Look at it this way. Suppose you must pick between two lawyers, one a perfectionist and one a realist, to review a contract and write a letter summarizing its pros and cons. Which would you hire at $200 an hour? The perfectionist who spends a lot of time struggling to compose perfect sentences with perfect grammar and perfect punctuation? Or the realist who focuses on comparing the contract's pros and cons, even though it may not be stated in perfect syntax? Which lawyer is cost-effective?

PERFECTION OR EXCELLENCE

Perfection means without flaw, whereas excellence refers to superior quality, which means that a task can be completed excellently and not be perfect. Stated differently, something can have a flaw and still be excellent. Similarly, it is possible for something to be perfect: yet of undesirable quality. "That's a perfect example of what not to do!" "He's a perfect idiot."

Many people confuse the two nonetheless, and struggle for perfection, thinking it is excellence. Whereas perfection is a static, flawless state, excellence is relative to the purpose at hand. A BMW is an excellent car, for example, but it would probably perform poorly compared to a Jeep in rural off-road use. Excellence refers to meeting the needs of the situation well. In other words, excellence is the right action at the right time, and this varies from situation to situation. Use your Eye to notice when you are striving for a flawless state. When you catch yourself doing this, stop and ask "What is the excellent act in this situation? What action is optimal—the right action for this situation, at this time?" You might find it helpful to review the "either/or" paradox described in the Wand chapter. The either/or paradox is transformed by finding the excellent action.

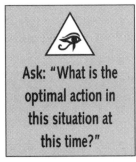

Ask: "What is the optimal action in this situation at this time?"

■ Chopsticks Not Swords

A ronin samurai went to the Bushi Master, who said "You haven't made much progress since I saw you last."

The ronin replied, "What do you mean? I am the fiercest samurai on this island. I have fallen to no man's sword!"

The Bushi Master said, "Yes, but you have fallen to your own sword. The highest skill is not to draw your sword at all."

"Not draw my sword? Without a sword I'll be killed!" the ronin argued.

Later, at the inn, while drinking saki and eating rice the ronin waved away an annoying fly that buzzed around his head as he brooded over the Master's words. Three young punk samurai sitting in the corner, anxious to test their skill, taunted the ronin with jeers and snorts. Feeling his sword and about to attack, the ronin pulled back as he remem-

bered the words of the Master, "The highest skill is not to draw your sword at all."

Wondering how to win without his sword, the ronin suddenly drew his chopsticks and plucked the fly from the air. The three other pests made respectful bows and quickly withdrew.

The ronin defeated the annoying young samurai by showing his unbeatable abaility. While he could have behead the trio with little effort, he followed the advise of the Bushi Master and did not draw his sword. Instead he demonstrated his excellence—the highest skill—by plucking the fly from the air with his chopsticks. It was the right action at the right time.

WAKING SLEEP

Consider this familiar scene. There is a cat and a dog. The cat sees the dog and the dog sees the cat. The cat freezes with its back arched. The dog freezes with one paw up and head extended. They each stand frozen in absolute stillness looking at one another. Then what happens? The cat suddenly makes a dash for the nearest tree. The instant the cat moves, the dog lunges after the cat, yelping hysterically.

■ Jumping on the Donkey

Nasrudin, the Sufi teacher, who often played tricks on his students, was riding out of town on his donkey, and passed one of his students, who asked, "Where are you going, Old Man?"

Nasrudin just grinned as he rode by. So the student thought, "I know he's up to something, and I'm going to find out what it is." The student jumped on his donkey and rode after his teacher.

When Nasrudin looked back over his shoulder and saw his student coming, he kicked his donkey on to a trot. The student thought, "Ah ha! I knew he was up to something." He kicked his donkey and rode after him.

Taking a shortcut through the cemetery, Nasrudin came to a big grave stone, pulled his donkey to a stop, jumped off, and hid behind the gravestone. Right behind him, the student pulled his donkey to a stop, ran over to the gravestone, and looked over expectantly, only to see his teacher crouching behind it. Confused, the student demanded, "Why are you running away?" To which the teacher replied, "Why are you chasing me?"

The mystics say we live our lives in waking sleep and instead of being mindful of the moment, we live reactively. By mindful, the mystics mean

Be mindful— watch and be aware.

using your Eye to watch and be aware. Instead, we go through our lives in "waking sleep." Something happens and we make a knee-jerk response. For example, there you are at work, and the computer crashes. You have just lost five days' work. Do you stop and contemplate, "What is the right action at the right time? What is the excellent response?" Or do you jump on that donkey and just chase right after it? Do you get hysterical, insist that disaster has struck, and yell at everyone around you?

The challenge is to be awake, to stop, and ask, "Wait a minute, what is the optimal action now? What is the right action to get the results that I want?" The tendency is to just jump on that donkey. Good self-management requires conscious, wakeful decision making. At no point can you go on "autopilot" and fall asleep. Becoming awake and using your Eye to be mindful of what you're doing in the moment is a lifelong process.

MANAGING YOUR THOUGHTS

*We are not responsible for every thought that goes wandering through our mind. We **are**, however, responsible for the ones we **hold** there. We're **especially** responsible for the thoughts we put there.*
John-Roger and Peter McWilliams
Do It!

We all know that negative or defeatist think-ing is bad and that positive thinking is good. But most of us don't understand the mechanism whereby thinking affects our mood and our ac-tions.

We carry hassles in our minds.

■ A Muddy Road

Two monks were walking along a muddy road in silence because they were meditating. It was pouring rain and the mud was sticky and deep when they came to a beautiful young woman, who had on dainty slippers and a long, flowing silk outfit. She couldn't get across the muddy road without messing up her shoes and the hem of her dress.

Without saying a word, the first monk picked up the woman, carried her to the other side of the road, and set her down. Then the two monks continued on their way without talking for the rest of the day. At the end of day, when they reached the ashram where they were going and their meditation was complete, the second monk said to the first monk, "You know women are dangerous to us monks. Why did you pick up that woman this morning?" To which the first monk asked in reply, "I left her on the side of the road. Are you still carrying her?"

If you're like most people, you carry your problems and worries around with you, rather than leaving them on the side of the road. This can seriously diminish your quality of life because what you think has a direct impact on how you feel. Even though the event is over your thinking keeps it alive, giving it a kind of virtual reality. It's not here now but your thinking makes it seem to be and your body responds as if you are still in the distressing situation.

THE WAY YOU THINK DETERMINES YOUR MOOD

*Your **past** thinking and personal choices*
*have created your **present** situation;*
*your **present** thinking is now determining your **future**.*
While it is true that you cannot change the past,
you can change the future by changing your present thoughts.
Realizing this is the most powerful, liberating message
you can ever learn. You and only you are in charge!
You are the only thinker in your head.
This is the one area of total freedom!
Accept the power that is yours.
Control your thoughts; control your life.
Alice Potter
The Positive Thinker
Self-Motivating Strategies for Personal Success

In recent years we've been hearing about virtual-reality systems, where you put on a head-mounted display, which is a hood with a

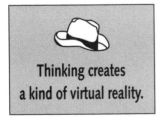

**Thinking creates
a kind of virtual reality.**

computer screen mounted in front of your eyes. The computer screen in the hood is programmed with a variety of simulations something like the ones that jet pilots practice on during training. The sensation of being in the situation feels real; hence the name "virtual reality." The thoughts in your mind function in a similar way to create a kind of virtual reality. The thoughts determine what you see and how you feel. Changing your thoughts is like changing the program in the hood. It creates a completely different picture that feels real.

Unfortunately, most of us are not usually aware of our thinking. We just think. The mystics call it "chatter." It is habitual. We're oblivious to our thoughts most of the time.

Study the words you think.

LOSING A BIG SALE

Situation: You lost a big sale because a mix-up in the warehouse caused the wrong item to be shipped.

Person 1: "Those idiots. They can't do anything right. They're just a bunch of fools."

Person 2: "This always happens to me. I just can't get ahead. I work and work and I still lose. What's the use?"

Person 3: "There must be some reasonable explanation. If I can figure out what went wrong, maybe I can do something to prevent it from happening again."

If you lose a sale and think, "Those idiots! They can't do anything right!" you'll probably feel angry. Once you feel angry, chances are you are going to act on that anger with sarcastic remarks and so forth. On the other hand, if you think, "This always happens to me. I can't win. It isn't fair!" you're likely to feel depressed. If you feel depressed, you'll probably act depressed and mope around.

You could use opportunity thinking instead: "There's a reasonable explanation. Maybe I can show the customer that it won't happen again." This type of thinking leads to feelings of hope and results in different actions.

The way that you talk to yourself is extremely important. In a sense, thoughts are the software that run your biocomputer. If you change the

word-and-image programs, you'll change your attitude and the way you feel. Focusing on the negative, thinking that the glass is half-empty, is obstacle thinking, and it will have a direct affect on the way you feel and act. You don't have to think that way. Instead, you can focus on the positive, the silver lining, the fact that the glass is half-full. That's opportunity thinking.

We all know that you have to make an error to learn. It's the trial-and-error rule. Error is essential to learning. Now there's a new cliche: "Ready, fire, aim." Act—do something and then fix it. If you constantly think about failure: "Oh, this is a failure. Oh, this is wrong," you are likely to become immobilized. But you can think powerfully—in terms of opportunities, learning, challenges and what you can do. Instead of thinking, "I failed" you can think "This is an opportunity to improve. I can make a plan. Next time I will . . ."

MENTAL SOFTWARE

Obstacle Thinking	Opportunity Thinking
Negative focus	*Positive focus*
"He's so messy! I can't stand it."	"He's considerate which makes up for being messy."
Failure	*Learning*
"I blew it. I'm a jerk!"	"I made a mistake and I can learn from my mistakes. Next time I will…"
Problem	*Opportunity*
"This is a very serious problem."	"This is an opportunity to show my ability."
No Can Do attitude	*I Can Do attitude*
"There's nothing I can do."	"I always have options."

Emotions are triggered by the way that you think because your body responds to your thoughts as if they were real at that moment. You can demonstrate this to yourself. If you recall a frightening or depressing situation and dwell on it for only a minute or two, you will notice a distinct change in the way that you feel. You will feel frightened or depressed, depending upon the nature of the recollection. We all know worry-warts who work themselves into a panic by imagining dire circumstances. It is their thoughts of catastrophe that trigger the anxiety and sweating. The disastrous pictures they conjure up are not real but their bodies respond to the fictional images as if they were real.

It is in your control to alter your mental software. Unfortunately, few of us have had training in doing this. If you keep thinking in terms of problem, problem, problem, it will bring you down and you will be headed toward burnout. But you can translate the words into opportunity thinking, and you will see things differently and feel differently as a result. Opportunities are hidden in problems. You can think "No Can Do" and you will end up feeling immobilized. Opportunity thinking leads to an "I Can Do" attitude and seeing the problem

Transform problems into opportunities.

as a challenge. When you transform obstacles into challenges, you've increased your potential for experiencing more blissful moments.

Use your Eye to observe your own thoughts. Watch the things you think. Write down several negative sentences that you hear yourself thinking. Then translate each sentence into a more powerful description of the situation. You might make personal "flash cards" with file cards. On one side of the card, write an obstacle thought. Turn it over and translate it into an opportunity statement.

Study your thinking—notice how you feel.

To reprogram your mental software, read the obstacle thought on the front of one of the files cards, say, "Stop!" and then quickly substitute the opportunity thought. If you can't remember the opportunity statement, turn the flash card over and read it. Repeat this process with each obstacle thought you have written on the file cards.

Finally, go through the cards, reading only the opportunity statements. Add new statements and repeat this exercise often. Be alert to catch yourself thinking the obstacle thought. When you do, say "Stop!" silently and firmly to interrupt the thought, then quickly substitute the opportunity thought you practiced. Keep doing this to reprogram your thinking.

■ We'll See

There was an old farmer who had a horse. Everybody said, "You are so rich because you can ride to town, and you can plow your fields with your horse." The farmer said, "We'll see."

The one day the horse ran away and everybody said, "Oh, isn't it awful that your horse ran away? How will you plow your fields? You'll lose all your wealth and starve." The farmer said, "We'll see."

The farmer sent his son to look for the horse. When the son came back with the farmer's horse and a wild horse everybody said, "You are even richer now that you have two horses." The farmer said, "We'll see."

When the son tried to ride the wild horse, he was thrown off and broke his back. And everybody said, "Oh, how awful that your son can't walk. Who will help you plow your fields?" The farmer said, "We'll see."

Soon a war started, and all the young men had to go to war except the farmer's son, who was still recuperating from his fall. And everybody said, "Oh, you are so lucky that your son isn't going to war." The farmer said, "We'll see."

Whether the farmer met with good fortune or bad, he kept an even temperament because of the way that he thought about his circum-

stances. When he lost his horse and when his son was injured, he didn't panic or despair because he thought powerfully and didn't focus on the obstacles at hand.

Reprogramming your mental software so that you think in terms of opportunities instead of dwelling on obstacles takes lots of practice. But it is worth it because obstacle thinking makes us feel helpless and sets the stage for burnout. Opportunity thinking, on the other hand, transforms obstacles into challenges and encourages bliss.

BE MINDFUL—PAY ATTENTION

Use your Eye to get moving. Set a goal to promote seeking motivation. Then take small steps to break the inertia in order to get moving. As Kierkegaard said, you are a hero because you made a beginning. When you begin, you don't know if you'll succeed.

Help yourself to make a beginning by giving yourself rewards for taking the small steps. Talk to yourself about what you're doing well, "Hey, this is pretty good. This is okay. I'm getting closer," and avoid dwelling on what you're doing wrong.

Remember, your thinking creates a virtual reality. So program your thinking to be positive, to develop an "I Can Do" attitude with a focus on learning and meeting challenges. Remind yourself to stay awake, pay attention, and consider the optimal action for this situation instead of immediately "jumping onto the donkey."

■ Pay Attention

A businessman heard that a Zen master who lived on a mountain top knew the three secrets of life, which were everything anyone needed to know to live a happy, fulfilling life. In spite of financial success, the businessman's life felt empty. So he tried to think what the secrets might be. What could answer all of life's problems and guarantee lasting well-being? Determined to find out, the man sold his business and traveled in

search of the master. After many trials he arrived at the top
of the right mountain, where he found the Zen master.

With great respect the man asked, "Oh, Master, I have
traveled from a long distance to hear the three secrets that
lead to a full and rich life. What are the secrets?"

The master bowed in return and said, " I will tell you.
The first secret is pay attention. The second secret is pay
attention, and the third secret is pay attention."

MAKE THE LEAP

Leap! Make a
beginning and
become a hero—
or heroine.

With your pathfinding tools in hand you are
ready to make the leap. It is time to begin your
pathfinding adventure—at last. Remember what
Kierkegaard said: you become a hero not by what
you achieve, but by making a beginning. Keep the
Zen master's secret in mind, and pay attention.

The Eye is what pays attention. The Eye is the pilot that studies and decides—decides which is the compelling Vision, when to make a beginning, and what size steps to take. It is with the Eye that you become master of your ship, sailing on the flow to your destiny. Be a pathfinder and seek your path with a heart—a path to your bliss—and to fulfilling your purpose—your destiny in life. Perhaps you seek a career path where you can fully express your creativity and capabilities. Perhaps your destiny is providing service others, or perhaps in teaching and inspiring others. Maybe your destiny lies in your contribution to a scientific break-through, or perhaps helping to create a new product. Remember the bricklayers. Ask: to what larger purpose are your efforts contributing? What is your problem to solve? It is with the Eye, the essential "I," that you decide upon your Mission and lead your pathfinding adventure to accomplishing your purpose while following the path with a heart.

■ ■ ■

THE PATHFINDER'S CHECKLIST

The Pathfinder's Checklist is a list of the pathfinding steps, in which each item describes one step and the accompanying tool needed to complete the step. You probably recognize the items as the same as those in the Bliss Potential Inventory on page 12, only this time they are arranged into three pathfinding challenges. First is *setting the course* where you decide where you aim to go and what you seek to achieve. Next is *staying the course* where you develop a method for assessing progress in order to course correct and by-pass obstacles. Last is *traversing the course* where you pilot your pathfinding adventure from here to achieving your purpose—your destiny—while following the path with a heart—the path of many blissful moments.

> INSTRUCTIONS: Read over each of the following items and, using a scale from 1 to 9, rate how characteristic it is of how you approach activities in your daily life—both at work and away from work. When you're done add up your score.

CHALLENGE: SETTING THE COURSE

Setting the course is the initial challenge of personal leadership. Finding a path with a heart involves matching what is really important to you with what must be achieved to define your mission and to develop a vision of what you want to accomplish and where you want to go.

Getting Centered

Finding a path with a heart, your path to bliss, begins with yourself and looking inward to discover what is important to you. This process is commonly called "getting centered." Without a center to begin from, you can easily lose a sense of who you are and where you want to go with your life.

_____ ✐ I check my feelings.
_____ ❤ I clarify what is important to me.
_____ ⚡ I get in touch with my personal power.

Defining Purpose

It is from a sense of purpose that you can draw confidence to act. Without purpose, there is little meaning, so that you can find yourself working aimlessly and wondering why you should bother. Conversely, working with purpose adds "heart" to what you do.

_____   I look for problems to solve.

_____   I articulate a mission.

_____   I appoint myself to act.

Deciding on a Direction

With a purpose and an idea of how to achieve it, you can set a direction for finding a path with a heart. Decide on your direction by imagining a desirable future—your destination—and moving toward it.

_____   I gather information.

_____   I brainstorm what is possible.

_____   I create a mental picture of my mission being accomplished.

Setting Goals

Having a specific target to shoot for focuses your efforts. When you know what you're aiming for, and achieve it, your confidence increases. Accomplishing goals that match your skills and stretch your capabilities promotes bliss.

_____   I match challenges to my ability.

_____   I align my personal goals with my work.

_____   I set specific targets.

CHALLENGE: STAYING THE COURSE

Accomplishing anything important is usually complicated with many steps. It is easy to get off course or to become blocked by obstacles. Staying on the course takes persistence and skill in course correction.

Establishing Milestones

Milestones are markers on the way to your destination. They help you lead yourself along your path in a series of easily achievable steps. By counting the milestones you've reached you can see how far you've traveled.

_____ 🗺 I map out action steps.

_____ 📏 I establish standards of achievement.

_____ 📏 I evaluate progress quantitatively.

Flexible Thinking

Finding a path with a heart involves different kinds of activities. Sometimes you must brainstorm possibilities, at other times you need to evaluate progress. Getting others' cooperation takes a supportive approach, whereas clarifying your values taps your intuition. Optimizing calls on different mindsets for each activity.

_____ 🎩 I look at things from several viewpoints.

_____ 🎩 I adapt my approach to the situation.

_____ ✨ I accept ambiguity.

Course Correcting

You move in a general direction but rarely in a straight line. Getting off course is easy to do, and happens frequently. Expect it. What's important for pathfinding is knowing when you're off course and taking action to correct the course. This is accomplished by checking your progress often.

_____ ⚖ I survey my resources.

_____ ◎ I make contigency plans.

_____ ⚖ I learn from my mistakes.

By-Passing Obstacles

Encountering obstacles is inevitable. Successful pathfinders transform obstacles in their path into opportunities, by challenging assumptions and changing what they do in order to by-pass the roadblock.

_____ ⚖ I view problems as opportunities.

_____ ✶ I question assumptions.

_____ ✶ I do something different.

CHALLENGE: TRAVERSING THE COURSE

Getting from where you are to your destination and accomplishing your mission takes motivation and help from others. You've got to get yourself and others moving, and keep the momentum. You guide the process by focusing on your destination and making many choices.

Getting Cooperation

No one is an island, and neither are you. Other people can help or hinder your progress. Accomplishing anything of consequence involves getting others' cooperation.

_____ 🤝 I create a network of allies.

_____ 🤝 I build team spirit.

_____ 🤝 I set up win-win scenarios.

Motivating Yourself

It is easy to lose momentum. Pathfinders keep motivation high by creating meaningfulness and building enthusiasm for accomplishing their mission. They reward themselves for progress.

_____ ❤ I engage my values.

_____ △ I seek excellence, not perfection.

_____ △ I reward my progress.

Enjoying the Moment

Having many moments of bliss assumes that you have the capacity to become so immersed in what you are doing that you lose yourself and feel at "one" with the activity at hand.

_____ △ I accentuate the positive.

_____ ❤ I find pleasure in small things.

_____ ∅ I get absorbed in my activities.

Piloting

The personal leader guides and manages the process of finding a path with a heart. Like pilots, pathfinders steer themselves, deciding when to take which action, when to move forward, when to hold back, and how to best get around obstacles and stay the course.

_____ ❤ I find meaning in what I do.

_____ △ I focus my attention.

_____ ∅ I go with the flow.

Use the Checklist to remind you of the pathfinding steps, especially when you feel stuck or confused about to what to do next. One approach is to read the items over slowly, while keeping in mind your situation. For each item, ask: "How would I apply this to my situation?" Depending upon the answer, you might want to review the chapter that describes the use of the tool associated with the step in question. You could put on your Green brainstorming Hat to generate numerous possible applications of the tool to your situation—including some that are silly, even absurd, for example.

You can also use the Checklist as a Yardstick to measure your progress in developing and strengthening your pathfinding skills. With this objective, you check that you are regularly carrying out the various steps. Another approach is measuring your effectiveness in each step. You can do this with a rating scale from 1 to 10, for example, where 1 represents "ineffective, or not carrying out" and 10 represents "very effective, or carried out excellently." Of course, only you know your situation and the impact of your actions. When using the Checklist to evaluate yourself, what is important is not a "score," but knowing how to give yourself feedback and remembering to do so. This ability to provide ourselves feedback is important in maximizing bliss in our lives. Csikszentmihalyi's research revealed that people who experienced flow frequently, who have "flow personalities" or a propensity to going into the flow state, even in difficult situations, have an ability to find feedback in any situation. Feedback is empowering because it enables you to create challenge in any situation. When you have feedback, you can set a target, shoot, and then strive to improve your last shot. In doing this you create the conditions for bliss: challenge, a sense of control, and meaningfulness.

MAKING A BEGINNING

You have all the tools before you and a working knowledge of their use. But you won't find a path with a heart, the path of many moments of bliss, until you make a beginning. Making a beginning is not a rash act where you quit your job, give up your life as you've known it to plunge into an unknown future. Your beginning will probably not be visible to anyone else. A beginning can be as simple as dreaming and listening to what your Heart has to say about it. Before we close, here is a story about pathfinding and making a beginning.

DESTINY

"What is my destiny?" the Seeker asked.

"It's what you have always wanted to accomplish," explained the Shaman Woman. "When we are young everything is possible. We are not afraid to dream, and to yearn for what we want to do. But, as time passes we come to believe the world's biggest lie."

"What lie?" the Seeker asked.

"At a certain point in our lives," the Shaman answered, "we begin thinking that it's impossible to realize our destiny. We come to believe that our lives are controlled by circumstances—our jobs, our obligations, our fears. That's the world's greatest lie. We stop dreaming of what could be and forget what we really want to achieve."

"There is one great truth on this planet," the Shaman continued. "Whoever you are, or whatever it is that you do, when you *really* want to accomplish something, that desire originated in the Soul of the Universe. It's your mission on earth. All things are one and to realize one's destiny is a person's only real obligation."

"But how do I find my destiny?" the Seeker wondered.

"You must dream!" the Shaman said emphatically. "*Never* stop dreaming. And listen to your heart for it will tell you which dream you *really* want—which dream is your destiny."

"Is that all?" asked the Seeker.

"That is a great deal!" emphasized the Shaman. "And when you have found your destiny, then you must make a beginning. Pursuing your destiny is a grand lifelong adventure because when you make a beginning you dive into a strong current that will carry you to places you never dreamed of when you began. But you will never achieve your destiny if you don't make a beginning."

Inspired by Paulo Coelho
The Alchemist
A Fable About Following Your Dreams

BIBLIOGRAPHY

Ackerman, Linda, "Flow State Leadership in Action," in Adams, *Transforming Leadership: From Vision to Results*, A Miles River Press, 1986.

Adams, John D. ed., *Transforming Leadership: From Vision to Results*, Miles River Press, 1986.

Adams, John D. ed., *Transforming Work: A Collection of Organizational Transformation Readings*, Miles River Press, 1984.

Aristotle, *Ethics*, Ayers, 1988.

Armstrong, David, *Managing By Storying Around: A New Method of Leadership*, Doubleday: Currency, 1992.

Auletta, Ken, *The Three Blind Mice: How TV Networks Lost Their Way*, Random House, 1991.

Bennett, Hal Zina, and Susan J. Sparrow, *Follow Your Bliss*, Avon Books, 1990.

Bennis, Warren, *On Becoming a Leader*, Addison Wesley, 1989.

Bennis, Warren, *Why Leaders Can't Lead: The Unconsccious Conspiracy Continues*, Jossey-Bass, 1990.

Bennis, Warren, and Burt Nanus, *Leaders: The Strategies For Taking Charge*, Harper and Row, 1985.

Boe, Anne, and Bettie B. Youngs, *Is Your "Net" Working? A Complete Guide To Building Contacts and Career Visibility*, John Wiley, 1989.

Braham, Barbara, *Finding Your Purpose: Learning How to Follow Your Heart*, Crisp Publications, 1991.

Brown, Edward Espe, *The Tassajara Recipe Book: Favorites of the Guest Season*, Shambala, 1985.

Buzan, Tony, *Use Both Sides of Your Brain*, Dutton, 1976.

Castaneda, Carlos, *The Teachings of Don Juan*, Pocket Books, 1968.

Catford, Lorna, and Michael Ray, *The Path of the Everyday Hero: Drawing on the Power of Myth to Meet Life's Most Important Challenges*, Tarcher, 1991.

Chopra, Deepak, *Creating Affluence*, New American Library, 1993.

Coelho, Paulo, *The Alchemist: A Fable About Following Your Dream*, Harper San Francisco, 1993.

Cohen, William A., *The Art of The Leader*, Prentice Hall, 1990.

Coulter, N. Arthur, *Synergetics: An Adventure in Human Development*, Prentice-Hall, 1976.

Csikszentmihalyi, Mihaly, *The Evolving Self: A Psychology for the Third Millennium*, Harper Collins, 1993.

Csikszentmihalyi, Mihaly, *Flow: The Psychology of Optimal Experience,* Harper and Row, 1990.

Deal, Terrence E., and Allen A. Kennedy, *Corporate Cultures: The Rites and Rituals of Corporate Life,* Addison Wesley, 1982.

DeBono, Edward, *Lateral Thinking: Creativity Step by Step,* Harper Colophon Books, 1970.

DeBono, Edward, *The Six Thinking Hats,* Little, Brown, 1985.

DePree, Max, *Leadership is an Art,* Doubleday/Currency, 1989.

de Saint-Exupèry, Antoine, *The Little Prince,* Enrique Sainz Editores, 1986.

Fezler, William, *Creative Imagery: How to Visualize in All Five Senses.*

Gallwey, Tim, and Bob Kriegel, *Inner Skiing,* Random House, 1977.

Garfield, Charles, *Peak Performers: The New Heroes of American Business,* Avon, 1986.

Gawain, Shakti, *Creative Visualization: Use the Power of Your Imagination to Create What You Want in Your Life,* New World Library, 1978.

Glouberman, Dina, *Life Choices and Life Changes through Imagework.*

Harrison, Roger, "Leadership and Strategy for a New Age," in Adams, *Transforming Work: A Collection of Organizational Transformation Readings,* Miles River Press, 1984.

Hawkins, Paul, *Growing a Business,* Simon and Schuster, 1987.

Heider, John, *The Tao of Leadership: Leadership Strategies For a New Age,* Bantam, 1986.

Heller, Trudy, "Authority: Changing Patterns, Changing Times," in Adams, *Transforming Work: A Collection of Organizational Transformation Readings,* Miles River Press, 1984.

Heller, Joseph, *Catch-22,* Dell, 1961.

Houch, Tony, and Cynthia Foust, *That's a Great Idea: The New Product Handbook: How to Get, Evaluate, Protect, Develop, and Sell New Product Ideas,* Gravity Publishing, 1986. (Subsequently republished by Ten Speed Press.)

Iacocca, Lee, *Iacocca,* Bantam, 1984.

Jaffe, Dennis, and Cynthia Scott, *From Burnout to Balance: A Workbook for Peak Performance and Self-Renewal,* McGraw-Hill, 1984.

Jaffe, Dennis, and Cynthia Scott, *Take This Job and Love It: How to Change Your Work Without Changing Your Job,* Simon & Schuster, 1988.

Kawasaki, Guy, *Selling the Dream: How To Promote Your Product, Company, or Ideas and Make a Difference Using Everyday Evangelism,* Harper Collins, 1991.

Keyes, Ken, *Handbook to Higher Consciousness: The Science of Happiness,* The Living Love Center, 1975.

Kierkegaard, Søren, *Fear and Trembling ,* Princeton University Press, 1983.

Kierkegaard, Søren, *Either/Or,* Princeton University Press, 1987.

Koestenbaum, Peter, *Leadership: The Inner Side of Greatness,* Jossey-Bass, 1991.

Kotter, John P., *The Leadership Factor,* Free Press, 1988.

Kotter, John P., *Power And Influence: Beyond Formal Authority,* Free Press, 1985.

Kouzes, James M., and Barry Z. Posner, *The Leadership Challenge: How to Get Extraordinary Things Done in Organizations,* Jossey-Bass, 1989.

Lakoff, George, and Mark Johnson, *Metaphors We Live By,* The University of Chicago Press, 1980.

Leary, Timothy, *Chaos and Cyber Culture,* Ronin Publishing, 1995.

Leavitt, Harold, *Corporate Pathfinding,* Dow Jones Irwin, 1986.

Leonard, George, *Mastery: The Keys to Success and Long-Term Fulfillment,* Penguin/Plume, 1991.

Lynch, Dudley, and Paul L. Kordis, *Strategy of the Dolphin: Scoring a Win in a Chaotic World,* William Morrow, 1988.

Marks, Linda, *Living with Vision: Reclaiming the Power of the Heart,* Knowledge Systems, 1989.

McWilliams, John-Roger and Peter, *Do It! Let's Get Off Our Butts,* Prelude Press, 1991.

Miller, William, *The Creative Edge: Fostering Innovation Where You Work,* Addison Wesley, 1987.

Musashi, Miyamoto, *Book of Five Rings:The Real Art of Japanese Management,* Bantam, 1982.

Musashi, Miyamoto, *Book of Five Rings,* Shambhala, 1993.

Nair, Keshavan, *Beyond Winning: The Handbook for the Leadership Revolution,* Paradox Press, 1990.

Naisbitt, John, *Megatrends: Ten New Directions Transforming Our Lives,* AMACOM, 1985.

Naisbitt, John, and Particia Aburdine, *Megatrends 2000: Ten New Directions for the 1990s,* William Morrow, 1990.

Ohmae, Kenichi, *The Borderless World: Power and Strategy in the Interlinked Economy,* Harper Business, 1990.

Owen, Harrison, *Spirit: Transformation and Development in Organizations,* Abbott Publishing, 1987.

Pascale, Richard Tanner, and Anthony G. Athos, *The Art of Japanese Management: Applications for American Executives,* Simon and Schuster, 1981.

Peters, Tom, *Liberation Management: Necessary Disorganization for the Nanosecond Nineties,* Alfred A. Knopf, 1992.

Pinchot, III, Gifford, *Intrapreneuring,* Harper and Row, 1985.

Pirsig, Robert, *Zen and the Art of Motorcycle Maintenance: An Inquiry into Values,* Bantam, 1975.

Posner, Bruce, and Bo Burlingham, "The Hottest Entrepreneur In America," *INC Magazine,* Jan. 1988, pp. 44-58.

Potter, Alice, *The Positive Thinker: Self-Motivating Strategies for Personal Success,* Berkeley Books, 1994.

Potter, Beverly A. *Beating Job Burnout: How to Transform Work Pressure into Productivity,* Ronin Publishing, 2nd ed., 1993.

Potter, Beverly A., *The Way of the Ronin: Riding: The Waves of Change at Work,* Ronin Publishing, 1988.

Ray, Michael, and Rochelle Myers, *Creativity in Business,* Doubleday, Garden City, 1986.

Ray, Michael, and Alan Rinzler, *New Paradigms in Business: Emerging Strategies for Leadership and Organizational Business,*

Reisman, David, *The Lonely Crowd: A Study of the Changing American Character,* Yale University Press, 1961.

Robbins, Tom, *Even Cowgirls Get the Blues,* Houghton Mifflin, 1976.

Scheele, Adele, *Skills for Success: A Guide to the Top,* William Morrow, 1979.

Sinetar, Marsha, *Do What You Love The Money Will Follow: Discovering Your Right Livelihood,* Paulist Press, Mahwah, 1987.

Sher, Barbara, *Wishcraft: How To Get What You Really Want,* Ballantine, 1979.

Stevens, Jose, and Lena S. Stevens, *Secrets of Shamanism: Tapping the Spirit Power Within You,* Avon, 1988.

Tzu, Lao, *The Way of Life,* Editions Poetry, 1946.

Tzu, Sun, *The Art of War,* Delacorte Press, 1983.

Ury, William, *Getting Past No,* Bantam, 1991.

Waterman, Robert H., Jr., *Adhocracy: The Power to Change,* Whittle Direct Books, 1990.

Watts, Alan, *The Book: On the Taboo Against Knowing Who You Are,* Collier Books, 1966.

Watzlawick, Paul, *The Language of Change: Elements of Therapeutic Communication,* Basic Books, 1978.

Watzlawick, Paul, Janet H. Beavin, and Don D. Jackson, *Pragmatics of Human Communication: A Study of Interactional Patterns, Pathologies, and Paradoxes,* Norton, 1967.

Wilson, Larry, *Changing the Game: The New Way to Sell,* Simon and Schuster, 1987.

Zaleznik, Abraham, Manfred Kets de Vries, and John Howard, "Stress Reactions in Organizations, Causes and Consequences", *Behaviorial Science,* vol. 22, 1977, p. 161.

INDEX

A

a-count-ability 201, 207

absurd, do something: to escape from game without end 304

accelerated-learning xiii - xviii

accelerated-learning principles:
  engage your senses xvi;
  holistic presentation xv;
  learning through associations xiv;
  metaphors and stories xviii;
  nonlinear learning xvi;
  repetition xvi

acceptance: and Be Spontaneous! paradox 274

accountability: and staying the course 252; standard of achievement 207

Ackerman, Linda 237

acknowledgment: and seeking motivation 317

acquaintance links 134

act: how to authorize yourself 90

actions 166; definition 165

activity: versus result 204

alignment 263; values and company mission 75

allies: how to identify 150

analytic thinking: definition 253

Anderson, Ole 119

Apple Computers 67

arguing: why avoid 227

Aristotle 29, 169;
  and golden mean to transform either/or dilemma 282

associations: and accelerated-learning xii

assumptions, reframing 288; let it percolate 293; look through others' eyes 292; turn it upside down 293

AT&T 78

Athos, Anthony 270, 295

attachment: definition 274

attempted solution: and game without end 302

attention, paying: and Eye 332

attitude 32

attunement: and values 54; Heart tool and 51

Auletta, Ken 135

authorize yourself 89

autonomous-directed 25

autotelic self 26, 29, 311; conditions to facilitate 30

B

baby-boomers 24

balance 16; either/or dilemma 284

balance point: changing 284; definition 283

Banta, George 68

Banta printing plant 68

Barbarella 79

baseline: comparing 44; definition 38; establishing standard of achievement 203, 212; Hat 40; how to establish 38; Yardstick 38, 43;

Bateson, Gregory 272

Be Spontaneous! paradox: central contradiction 273; letting go of attachments 274; transforming 273

beginning: making a, See Kierkegaard, Søren; making a and pathfinding 338; making a with small steps 331

behaviors: nonverbal 227

Bennett, Hal Zina 11, 37

Bennis, Warren 112

Bill of Rights 9

blank-page panic 189

bliss: conditions that promote 14, 16; definition 10; follow yours 11; how Map helps 179; and meaningfulness 51, 73, 126; and measuring progress 208; need for flexible thinking 254;

opportunities 29; path to 71; point on
Compass 36; positive goals 173; potential for
11; purpose 86; striving towards goal 199;
studying how it feels 42; the experience 44;
using Eye to assess what you need for 313;
and work 21, 271;

Bliss Potential Inventory 12

Boe, Anne 133, 134, 153

boredom and burnout 16

Boyer, Herb 239-241

Braham, Barbara 90

brainstorming: discovering absurd action 305;
using mind maps 184

Br'rer Rabbit: and doing something absurd 303

Brown, Edward Espe 139

Burlingham, Bo 121

burnout 36; beating it 34; and Black Hat 268;
causes 33, 42; definition 2, 3; and either/or
traps 284; and Eye 48; and having no Map
179; and helplessness 33; how to steps 49;
inoculation 48; and "just doing my job"
attitude 80; and lack of progress toward goals
199; and letting go of dreams 158; negative
Targets 173; no one is immune 2; opposite of
bliss 22; overcoming with personal power 4;
and paradoxes 269, 271; as self-management
challenge 20; self-perpetuating process 249;
sensitivity to early signs 44; studying how it
feels 39; symptoms 3; as a trap 3, 6, 312-
313; when values not attuned 54

Burns, Robert 190

Bush, President George 73

Bushi Master 322

business: starting one 90, 92

but: why avoid 228

Buzan, Tony: and mind maps 184

buzzwords: and corporate culture 63; and
Corporate Cutlure Audit 64; examples 65;

C

Campbell, Joseph 1

career paths: project teams as 143

careers: changing 90, 92

Castaneda, Carlos 30, 51, 277

Catch-22: how viewpoint traps you in 289

centered, getting 334

challenge: and flow channel 14; chart of 15; of
new millennium 35; and Pathfinder's Checklist
333;

change: constant 35; and nature of work 252;
as opportunity 26; resisting it 7; and ronin
27; spontaneous 202; unavoidable 6

changing hats 250

charts and graphs: using and motivation 218

chatter 327

check-out question asking technique 232

chicken and egg dilemma: See game without an
end 301

Chinese Finger Puzzle: and game without end
303

Chopra, Deepak 202

Cisco Systems 143

closed question: definition 229; when to use
232

Coelho, Paulo front section, 339

Columbus 82, 246

communication networks: and corporate culture
64

company stories, identifying 68

Compass 162; and assessing job fit 62, 70;
calibrating for bliss 42; calibrating for burnout
39; and challenge 16; used to course correct
195; and creating powerful goals 174; and
defining your mission 93; definition 30, 35,
36, 38; using to develop the Heart 71;
developing 37; and discovering doing level of
goal 173; and identifying resistance 152; and
identifying values 53, 55, 57; and making
decisions 47; and motivation 45-46; and
testing your Mission 92; and using Red and
White Hats 262;

compelling image: creating 169; and motivation
169; and observing doing of goal-state 175;
positive 314; uncovering 170; using Heart to
discover 171

compelling targets 162

complaints: as seeds of opportunity 126

conclusions, jumping to: how a problem 229,
231

confidence: and having a plan 195

conflict: cause of being fired 61

conformists 25

conformity modes 53

consultant network: developing yours 153-154

contradictory communication: and feeling crazy 272

control: feelings of 4; and personal power 17; and preventing burnout 33;

cooperation: and definition of Team tool 32; getting 236, 242, 247; getting and Pathfinder's Checklist 336; identifying 60-65; including people and 150; need for 222; and the Team 61

corporate culture: and fitting in 135; how to study 62; introduction to 61; questions to reveal 64; and the Survey 62;

Corporate Culture Audit 62, quick 65

corporate ladder 143

corporate philosophy: and company mission 78

corporate tribes 61

coruse correction: and stress inoculation 196

cost and income 209

Coulter, N. Arthur 125

counting devices: and feedback 214

course correction 191, 192; brainstorming 195; using Compass to 195;; how to create a plan 195; and using Pathfinder's Checklist 336; strategy to avoid the detour 193; restructure your activities. 193; substitution 193; using Yardstick 208

craft: metaphor 28

crazymaking paradoxes 272

crisis: source of unassigned problems 146

Csikszentmihalyi, Mihaly 14, 15, 18, 21, 26, 29, 30, 43, 55, 56, 311, 338; and description of flow 15

cultural diversity 26

culture 135, See company culture

culture shock 62

customs: and corporate culture 64

cyberpunk 310

cyberspace xvii

D

damned-if-you-do, damned-if-you-don't paradox: escaping with new metaphor 298; central contradiction 287; and powerlessness 286; transforming: reframe 287-288

daydream: and reframing 293

de Vries, Manfred Kets 269

deadline: and standard of achievement 210; unrealistic 163

Deal, Terrence 61, 66, 68, 245

death by overwork 33

DeBono, Edward 249, 289; and thinking hats 254-268

decision making: and Compass 46; and corporate culture 64; and strategic positions 145; and Vision 50

decisions: when poor 53; and powerful goals 177;

decisiveness: showing 235

DePree, Max 285

de Saint-Exupèry, Antoine 52

destiny, story 340

detached concern: as path to personal power 6

detours 190: and course correction 196; and using Eye to identify 191; how to identify patterns with Eye 192; how you get 190

dichotomy, false 281

direction: deciding upon and Pathfinder's Checklist 334; see setting the course

dog metaphor 67

doing less of the same 305

doing level: defination 164; example 164; see goals 164

Don Juan 30, 52, 71, 276

double bind 286, See damned-if-you-do, damned-if-you-don't paradox

downsizing 143

Dragnet 255

dreamer and doer: being both 279

duty, sense of 24

E

80/20 Rule: defintion 161

either/or paradox: central contradiction in 281;

deciding and acting 280; definition 277; envisioning versus regulating 281; how to finding balance 283-284; Jobs vs Scully as example of 281; pathfinding as 278; transforming 282;

either/or paradox, kinds: act or decide 280; act or dream 279; critique or create 281; envision or correct 281; facilitate or control 280; get participation or exert control 280; individual contributor or a teamplayer 279; lead or control 281; lead or manage 280; set the course or stay the course 281; set the course or traverse the course 279; traverse the course or stay the course 280

Ellis, Albert 274

emotions: reading with the Heart 53; triggered by thoughts 329

engaging senses: and accelerated-learning xvi

enjoying the moment: and Pathfinder's Checklist 337

enjoyment: and flow state 15

errors: essential to learn 328

Evelyn Wood Reading Dynamics: and mind maps 184

excellence: and setting realistic standards 320; definition of 321; as different from perfection 321; question to determine 322; using Wand to find 322

Eye tool 191; and choosing compelling images 314; and creating powerful goals 174; definition of 32; and establishing baseline 39, 40; and identifying detours 191; and identifying values 57, 58; and mindfulness 324; and paying attention 332; and studying bliss feelings 43; and studying words you think 327; evaluating nature of motivation 314; changing thoughts 329; and identifing wins 317, 319; and using White and Blue Hats 267

F

fast track 278

feedback: delayed: and motivational decline 213; and empowerment 338; and motivation 200; and peak performance 200; and using the Eye 202; definition 200; immediate 213; tools to create 213

feelings 166

Fezler, William 104

feudal social order 24, 27

file cards: and feedback 214

fit, job: good: and leveraging power base 135; poor 138; as reason for being fired 61

flow: flow channel 14; graph 15; flow state 10, 21, 86; and the Heart tool 17; how it feels 43; increasing potential 15; and meaningfulness 51; scientific study of 14; at work 11

flow map: creating 181; example of 183; questions to develop 181

flow personalities: definition 338

foes: identifying potential ones 150

Follow Your Bliss: quote 37

Founders Research Center: See Genentech 240

Foust, Cynthia 293

frame of reference xiii; and metaphors 245; context and accelerated-learning xiii

frequency 209

FUD: definition 7

G

Gallwey, Tom 10

game without end: absurd action: accept obstacles 305; and punctuation 301

Game-Without-End: central contradiction 302; transforming 302

gap, bridging 159

Garfield, Charles 190, 193

Genentech: and telling the story 239; statue of meeting Swanson and Boyer's first meeting 241

generalizations 166

glass: half full 216

glass ceiling 143

Glouberman, Dina 180

goal: definition 160; guidelines for setting 163; using to promoted seeking motivation 314

goal-state: and using Vision to see 174; definition 164, 175; observing the doing-level of 175

goal-statement: writing 171

goals: aligned 86; and action steps 179; and decision making 177; and definition of Target

31; and detours, setbacks and roadblocks 190; and motivation 199; and Pathfinder's Checklist 335; and using Compass 163; and using the Eye 174; characteristics of powerful goals 167; compelling image 169; powerful: guidelines 171; using mental theater 174; profile of people using 160; purpose 169; See Target 157; setting powerful 160; vague 167

golden mean: and Either/Or dilemma 282; definition 282

Grateful Dead 247

Grossman, Larry 136

GTE Strategic Systems 69, 247

H

H & R Block 239

happiness: story about, creating 21; See front section

Harrison,Roger 86

Hat 266; and accelerated-learning xii; and carrying problems 325; and virtual reality 326; basic question: Black Hat - what's wrong? 259; Blue Hat - next step? 260; Green Hat - what if? 259; Red Hat - feelings? 258; White Hat - facts? 257; Yellow Hat - what's right? 258; Black: definiiton 256; Black Hat and Heart tool 263; Black Hat and Survey tool 264; Black Hat and Target tool 265; Black Hat and Yardstick tool 266; Blue: definition 256; Blue Hat and Eye tool 268; Blue Hat and Hat tool 267; Blue Hat and Wand tool 267; definition 32, 249; establishing baseline 40; Green: definition 256; Green Hat and Mission 263; Green Hat and Target 265; Green Hat and Vision 264; Green Hat and Wand 267; how to practice changing 257; need for flexible thinking 254; One-Hat Thinking 250; Red: definition 255; Red and Compass 262; Red Hat and Heart 263; Red Hat and Mission 263; Red Hat and Team 266; right Hat with the right tool 261; switching: and reframing 292; White: definition 255; using to escape game without end 305; White and Compass 262; White Hat and Eye 268; White Hat and Map 265; White Hat and Survey 264; Yellow: definition 255; Yellow and Blue Hats 267; Yellow Hat and Hat tool 267; Yellow Hat and Map 265; Yellow Hat and Mission 264; Yellow Hat and Team 266; Yellow Hat and Yardstick 266

Hat tool: pathfinding use of 257

Hats: changing 250, 257; how to practice changing 261

Hawkins, Paul 199, 291, 294

head-mounted display 326

Heart: and assessing job fit 62, 70; and creating Want List 319; and defining your mission 93; and flow 17; and identifying resistance 152; and identifying values 57; and Mission 85; and Team 242; and the Compass 71; definition 30, 51; evaluating suitable of projects 128; goals: and using Heart 163; like a tuning fork 51; Red and Black Hats 263; testing attunement with culture 135

heart: good 16, 51; when path contrary to values 52

Heller, Trudy 59

helplessness: cause of burnout 17

Hemingway, Ernest 3

Herman Miller 285

heroes: and Corporate Culture Audit 63

heroism 8

Hewlett Packard 65

Hill, Napoleon 112

hippies 53

holistic presentation: and accelerated-learning xv

homing device: points to bliss 37

Houch, Tony 293

Howard, John 269

I

I Can Do attitude 329; definition of 4; and learning 331; and personal power 34; and success 19; personal power and bliss 17

Iacocca, Lee 222

IBM 68, 245, 246, 300

IRS 65

icon, how used xiv

ideas: capturing 187; organizing with mind maps 188

illusion of an alternative: damned-if-you-do, damned-if-you-don't 287

images and sensory impressions: and acelerated-learning xiv

implementing: *See* traversing the course 251

impossible demand: and Be Spontaneous! 273; let go 274

industrialism: to information age 252

inertia: definition 192, 315; example at work 315; overcoming 315

inertia of movement: and staying motivated 316

inertial: example at work 315

information: and power 133; exposure to as strategic position 144

information age 252

informed, keeping people: and cooperation 225

inner skiing 10

inner-directed 24

inoculation: against burnout 49

input: *See* feedback 200

insignificance: the myth of 131

Internal Revenue Service 65

International Labor Organizations 33

interrogation: avoid 229

interview: pathfinder's: example 137; objective 136

Interview Technique: Probe 230; Repeat 230; Review 232; Silence 231

intrapreneuring 89

intuitive thinking: definition 253

involve others: and cooperation 225

J

Jaffe, Dennis 6, 23

Jefferson, Thomas 9

job: changing 5; hired to solve a problem 80; how to revitalize 80; tailor the 5

job fit: and the Compass 62, 69; and the Heart 62, 69; assessing 69; good 58; and values 59; poor 59; and burnout 60

Jobs, Steve 66

John Scully 281

Johnson, Mark 296, 297-301

K

karoshi: and overwork 33

Kawasaki, Guy 215

Kennedy 245

Kennedy, Allen A. 61, 66, 68, 245

Kennedy, President John F. 14

Kennedy, Robert 97

key factors for success: and leverage 162

Keyes, Ken 274

Kierkegaard, Søren 8, 277, 315, 331

killer experiment: getting to heart of feasibility 260

King, Jr., Martin Luther 97

knowledge: and power 133

Koestenbaum, Peter 158, 169

Kotter, John 131, 132, 141

Kouzes, James 35, 115, 120, 221

Kriegel, Bob 10

Krishnamurti 274

L

Lakoff, George 296, 297-301

leader: personal: definition 337

leadership: how to monitor personal leadership skills 219; how to show 234, 235

leadership, personal xiii

leading yourself: and pathfinding 19

leap: to achieve bliss 332

leap into the unknown: and bliss 9

learning: need for error 328

Leary, Timothy 308

Leavitt, Harold 119, 250, 254, 278-281

left brain: analytic thinking 101, 253

Leonard, George 307, 320

leverage 161; key factors for success 162

lifestyle: and how we're directed 24

LIND Institute x

log book: and feedback 213; and identifying values 55; as compass 199; to establish baseline 42

logbook: and identifying values 58

M

macho approach to motivation 316

Macintosh computer 66

management functions: chart 278; implementing 250; leading 250; regulating 250 managing thoughts 325

Map: and breaking inertia 316; definition 31, 179; mind maps 184; outlines 184; paradox of developing 180; using Vision to see steps 183; using Yardstick to pinpoint location 200; White and Yellow Hats 265; working backwards 159

McWilliams, Peter and John-Roger 317, 325

mean and lean 143

meaning: creating 241; leading by creating 242

meaningful activities: and bliss 73

meaningfulness: and flow 51; feelings of 16

meaninglessness: and burnout 242

measurement: and accountabiity 208; and Yardstick 208; key factors for success 215; kinds 209; wrong variables 215

mechanistic systems 270

megatrends 26

mental rehearsal: and decision making 49

Mental Research Institute 272

mental software: and emotions 328; reprogramming exercise 329

mental theater xvii; and developing flow map 183; and identifying values 56; and powerful goals 174; and testing your fit with company 70; brainstorming ways to course correct 195; to identify detours 191; use to see others' view 243; used to reframe 292; using to find absurd solution 305; using to identify opportunity vehicles 126; using to overcome resistance 235, 237; using to understand resistance 151

meta-level 302

metaphor: birds flying in a flock 75; chemical metaphor 298; craft 27; definition 295; dog 67; for argument 299; hat metaphor 254; how it works 245; impact of 244; military 69; mirror 275; pathfinding 28, 246; pirate. *See* Jobs, Steve; ronin 27; samurai 246; tools xiv; wild ducks. *See* Watson, Jr, Thomas

metaphors. *See* stories; and accelerated-learning xvii; and corporate culture: examples 65; change reality 295; examples 300; finding 247; pathfinding xviii

Middle Ages: and tradition-directed 24

milestone 212; definition 203; *See* small steps 319

milestones: and feedback 203; definition 335; establishing and Pathfinder's Checklist 335

millennium, new: and challenges 35

Miller, William 75

mind map: as brain dump 189; converting to outline 188; example of 185; tool for brainstorming 184; uses of 189; writers use of 189

mindfulness: and paying attention 331; and using Eye 324; definition 324

mindset: creative: and Green Hat 256; detached: and Blue Hat 256; intuitive: and Red Hat 255; judgmental: and Black Hat 256; objective: and White Hat 255; optimistic: and Yellow Hat 255

mindsets 279

Mission: aligning personal values with company mission 86; and confidence to act 90; and creating meaning 73; and empowerment 82; and engaging values 85; and meaning 80; and promoting seeking motivation] 313; and resonating with the Heart 93; and the Survey tool 146; and the Vision tool 83; and the Wand 84; and using the Vision tool to try on 93; authorizing yourself 89; choosing yours 93; definition 31, 73, 74; getting company resources to accomplish 87; Green and Red Hats 263; how to identify 79, 82; identifying way to engage values 152; mission statement: definition 90; provides direction 76; question to identify 82; SUIT-Analysis 128; using the Heart tool to discover 85

mission: how helps in organizations 76; how it benefits 77; organization's: questions to uncover 77; versus tasks 79; when unclear 76

mommy track 278

monitor progress: using Yardstick to 212

mood: determined by thoughts 326

mores: and corporate culture 64

Mother Teresa: and nonattachment 276

motivation: and Compass 45; avoidance 310; and need for threat 311; example 91; how it is a problem 311; how it's a problem 92; predominant motivation 311; avoidance motivation: definition 45; effects of burnout and bliss on 45; getting moving 309; kinds 45; moving away from burnout 45; moving

toward bliss 45; seeking 310; and
acknowledgement 317; and Mission 313; and
using Target 314; and Vision 313; to avoid
burnout 313; seeking motivation: definition
45

moving to avoid: negtive wins 310

moving toward: positive wins 310

Murphy's Law 190

Musashi 27

myths: and corporate culture 63

N

Nair, Keshavan 226

Naisbitt, John 26

Nanos, Burt 112

Nasrudin 323

NBC News 136

negativity: getting trapped in 249

networking: definition 134

new product ideas 293

Nihon Electric Company 224

Nine-Dot Puzzle: example of damned-if-you-do,
damned-if-you-don't 288

No Can Do 329

non-linear presentation: and accelerated-learning
xvi

nonattachment: like sportsmanship 276

O

obstacles: and definition of Wand 32; by-passing
and Pathfinder's Checklist 336; transforming
with Wand 269; ways around 87

obstacles as teachers 293

off course: frequency 193; how to avoid 190;
using Yardstick to course correct 208

office politics 131

Ohmae, Kenichi 160

on course: plan to get back 193

opinions and advice: ask for 226

opportunities: which are suitable 127

opportunity: Chinese symbol for it 128

Opportunity List 126, 129

optimal action 282; definition 322

organizational structure 251

organizations: and using resources 87; evolving
78; identifying mission 78; threatened by
individuals 270

Organization's Literature: and identifying mission
78

other-directed 53

outcome: See result 204

outline 185; from mind map 188

outlines: as maps 184

output: See feedback 200

Owen, Harrison 243

P

Pacific Bell 78

paradox: between organizations and individuals
271; See dilemma 271

paradox, power: overcoming 282

paradoxes: Be Spontaneous! 273; Damned-If-
You-Do, Damned-If-You-Don't 286; The
Either/Or Choice 277; The Game Without End
301

paradoxes: between organizations and individuals
270; defintion 269

partner: act like a 223; be one with company 86

Pascale, Richard 270, 295

path to personal power 5

Pathfinder's Checklist: as a Yardstick 338; how to
use 219, 338; use to evaluate pathfinding skills
333

Pathfinder's Mission 74

Pathfinder's Slogan 86

pathfinding: as a craft 6, 28; as a skill 33; as
self-leadership challenge 20

pathfinding adventure: piloting with the Eye 307

pathfinding story: Initiation 239; Partners Get
Things Done 224

pathfinding tools xiii; definition 30

pats on the back: and wins 317

peak performance: and feedback 200

perfectionism: and excellence 321; as enemy of
mastery 320; as thought disorder 320;
definition 321

perfectionist's standard 209

personal leader: becoming one 27

personal leadership 32; lack of training in 23
personal leadership skills 218
personal power 4; and Wand 17; definition 4, 17, 34; paths to 5, 312
persuasion: and building team 233
Peters, Tom 142
picture words: See metaphors xvii, 66, 248, 296
pilot: definition 308; See Eye 307
piloting: and definition of Eye 32; and Pathfinder's Checklist 337; definition 337
Pinchot III, Gifford 89, 138
Pirsig, Robert 290
plan backward and implement forward 180
plateauing 143
police 149
position: strategic value of 141
Posner, Barry 35, 115, 120, 221
Posner, Bruce 35, 115, 120, 221
postwar era: and other-directed 24
potency, feelings of: and personal power 4, 17
Potter, Alice 326
power: definition 130; positions 141; sources 133; influence skills 140; interpersonal skills 138; knowledge 133; networking skills 134; relationships 134; strategic ability 138; technical skills 140; track record 140
power base: difficulty in transfering 132; how to develop 132; how to survey 130; when not developed 131
power dynamics: working them 131
power structures: and corporate culture 64
power-development strategies 141
powerlessness: cause of burnout 33; feelings of 3
power sources: fitting in 135
priorities 53
problem: versus solution 84; versus tasks to complete 85
problems: carrying 325; carrying them with you 326; to opportunities 329
process: versus result 204
project management: as stragetic position 141
project teams: as career pathways 143

projects: as opportunity vehicles 125
puppet: you as 309
purpose: and definition of Mission 31; and self-esteem 85; articulating yours 84; benefits of identifying 94; defining and Pathfinder's Checklist 334; finding yours 73, 81; identifying yours in the company 82; of the enterprise 75; using Vision tool to identify 83

Q

quality 209
quantity 209
question asking: guidelines: avoid leading questions 228; avoid yes/no questions 229; don't argue 227; don't jump to conclusions 229; don't talk too much 228; establish rapport 227; technique: probe 230; repeat 230; silence 231; techniques: review 232
question, leading: how a problem 228
questions: asking good 226

R

Raab, Kirk 241
rapport: how to 227
reality: changing with metaphors 295
reciprocity: and cooperation 224
reframe: to excape damned-if-you-do, damned-you-don't 289
reframing: challenge each assumption 290; change your viewpoint 291; how to use metaphors 296; identify assumptions 290; looking through others' eyes 292; rephrase assumptions 291; use metaphors 295
regulating: See staying the course 252
relationships: and power 134
relevant parties: how to survey 148
Renaissance: and inner-directed 24
resources: how to identify 152
reprogram thinking 330
resistance: causes of 235; overcoming 236; preventing 236; reasons for 151; when it's you 152; who will 150
resources: ability to access as strategic position 145
result: how it helps 205; standard of achievement: definition 204

reverse psychology: and game without end 302

review and sum up: how to 232

rewards: and small steps 331; *See* wins 318

Riesman, David 24, 25, 53

right brain: 101, and picturing compelling goals 176; visionary thinking 253

rituals: and corporate culture 63

road blocks 190

Robbins, Tom 8

role models: and corporate culture 63

ronin xvii; and excellence 322; and how we're directed 24; as metaphor 246; metaphor 27; way of 28

rugged individualism: and inner-directed 24

rulers: and feedback 215

S

samurai: ronin 27

Sawyer, Tom: and reframing 292

scales: and feedback 215

Schmid, Charles and accelerated-learning xiii

Scott, Cynthia 6, 23

Scully, John 67

self: loss of 10; sense of 25

self-assignment 127

self-directing mechanism 25

self-leadership. *See* personal leadership; essential for pathfinding 20

self-leading: and ronin 246

self-management: and mindfulness 324; definition 309; examples of poor 309; path to personal power 5; *See* Eye 308

self-manager 316

self-monitoring: and leading yourself 201

self-motivation: and Pathfinder's Checklist 337; essential to beat burnout 19

self-motivator: and self-motivation 318

senses, engaging xvi

seppuku 27

Sergeant Friday 255

setbacks, 190

setting the course 278; and direction: definition 251; and upper management 250; definition 333

Sher, Barbara 157, 160, 171, 179; and flow map 181

skills: influence: and power 140; interpersonal: and power 138; networking: and power 134; people 140; technical: and power 140

small steps: and setting yourself up for success 316; and wins 319; to avoid detouring 192

social support: how to get 221; path to personal power 5

Sparrow, Susan J. 11, 37

specialization 250

spirit, malaise of 312

sportsmanship, good: as nonattachment 276

standard of achievement: and attainability 209; and deadline 210; and setting like a yogi 210; components of 204; definition 202; examples 211; how to set 203; measurable 207; result versus activity 204; what versus how 205

Stanford University 65

staying the course 278; and middle management 250; and Pathfinder's Checklist 335; and regulating: definition 252

steps, giant: and detouring 192

steps, learning in xv; small: and breaking inertia 192

stories: *See* metaphors and Stories; and accelerated-learning xiii; and communicating values 67; and corporate culture 64; identifying 69; share the Vision with 243; what to look for 239

Stories: Apollo Was Mostly Off Course 190; Catch 22 286; Chopsticks Not Swords 322; Destiny 339; Either Millwright or Poet 285; A Good Business Has Interesting Problems 294; Homework 309; Is That So? 275; Jumping on the Donkey 323; A Muddy Road 325; One Person's Bliss Is Another's Burnout 18; Pay Attention 331; Problems and Solutions 297; Real Men Watch TV at Dinner Parties 136; Steamrolling Consultants 148; Three Bricklayers 81; Tie Your Shoeslaces Impeccably 277; Two Monks Who Smoked 139; We'll See 330; When the Going Gets Tough The Tough Go Shopping 312

story, telling the 66, 68; creating a database of

241; telling the: example 239; why tell the 238

storytellers 66

strategic ability: and power 138

strategic alliances 145

strategic partners 141

strategic position: kinds of, Exposure to Information 144; Exposure to Unassigned Problems 145; Get Visibility 146; Supporting Upwardly Mobile People 146

strategic position: access to resources 145; analyzing 143; project management 141; project team membership 143; proximity to decisionmaking 145

stress: and bvrnout 33

stress inoculation 196

stress management: path to personal power 5

substitution strategy 193

success: and team support 221; setting yourself up for 316

success syndrome: establishing 131

Sufi 323

SUIT-Analysis: definition 127; how to do it 127

support: giving 224

Survey: and identifying corporate culture 62; and identifying your Team 153; definition 31, 123; discovering obstacles 123; using Vision to determine suitable projects 127; White and Black Hats 264; why do it 124

Suzuki, Yoshitaka 224

Swanson, Bob 239-241

T

Target: and using the Compass 173; and avoiding burnout trap 314; and starting too soon 180; compelling: articulating 176; definition 31, 158, 162; guidelines 162; exercise to get picture of 171; from vision to action 157; getting to heart of 171; Green and Black Hats 265; identifying steps backward 182; positive is magnetic 162; which is right one 160

target: and Map 159

Targets: aiming at negative ones 173

Tassajara 138

Team: and power base 134; and the Survey 138; and using the Heart 242; and values 61; definition 32; Yellow and Red Hats 266

team spirit: check out 232; building 237, 248; definition 237

think strategically: and Blue Hat 261

thinking: and mood 326; defeatist 325; flexible and Pathfinder's Checklist 335; managing it 5; obstacle 328; opportunity 327; and I Can Do attitude 329

thinking style: dominant 253, See Hat 253

thoughts: changing 327; like virtual reality 326; managing 325

time 209

timers: and feedback 214

touchstone 171

track record: and building power 140

tradition-directed 24

traversing the course: and implementing: definition 251; and lower-level management 250; and Pathfinder's Checklist 336

traversing the course, 278

trial and error 200, 328

trust: building 225; building and freedom at work 140

try: why avoid 233

tying your shoe laces impeccably 277

Tzu, Lao 273

Tzu, Sun 123

U

unassigned problems: access to as strategic position 145; defintion 127

upwardly mobile people: access to and strategic positions 146

Ury, William 282, 302

V

values: aligned with company 75; and coopera-tion 61; and emotions 53; and path with heart 51; and the Compass 55, 57, 71; and the Eye 57; and the Vision tool 70; articulating 58; clarifying 56; clues to identifying 57; patterns and surprises 58; definition 52; engaging yours and purpose 85; identifying 55; provide guidance 54; suitable assignments 128;

unclear 54; weighing compatible and incompatible 70

vehicles, opportunity: definition 126; how to identify 125; make an opportunity list 126

vicious cycle 61. See burnout trap and game without end 304

viewing screen 56, 174

virtual reality 326, 331

visibility, getting: as strategic position 146

Vision: and action 158; and bridging the gap 159; and decision making 50; and identifying Mission 83; and identifying values 55, 70; and promoting seeking motivation 313; and seeing goal-state 174; and seeing Map action steps 183; and Target 157; creating 236; definition 31, 157; example 7; Green and Yellow Hats 263; how to tie compay values to 242; resources and moving towards 145; share by telling the story 243; sharing: uding metaphors to 244; testing reaction to it with the Survey 124

vision: sharing with stories 243

Vision tool: using to escape game without end 305

visionary thinking: definition 253

W

waking sleep 323

Wand: definition 32, 269; and excellence 322; and Eye 302; and Hat 305; and personal power 17; and the Mission 84, 87; reframing a question 130; and Vision 304; Green and Blue Hats 267

Want List: and seeking motivation 317; use with small steps 319; using Eye to develop 319; using Heart to create 319

warriors: at work 27

Watson, Jr, Thomas 68; and wild duck metaphor 245, 246, 299

Watts, Alan 289; Be Spontaneous!: using the mirror 275

Watzlawick, Paul 272, 287

wave man: ronin 27

Welch, Jack 136

why: why avoid 231

Why bother? attitude: and burnout 3; and

unattainable standard 209; can't sustain when have a purpose 73; when values not attuned 52

wild ducks: IBM metaphor 245, 246, 299; IBM story 68

wild ducks story: See Watson Jr. 299

Wilson, Colin 131

Wilson, Larry 224

win-win strategy: and cooperation 243

windows xvi

wins: and motivating self 318; frequency and breaking inertia 319; negative: moving to avoid 310; positive: moving toward 310

work world: changing and pathfinding opportunities 22

working smarter 161

World Labor Report of the United Nations: stress study 33

writer's block 189

Y

Yardstick: and critical thinking 249; and determining excellence 320; and monitoring progress 212; and Pathfinder's Checklist 338; and using Vision 205; benefits of using 202; Black and Yellow Hats 265; definition 32, 199; giving feedback on progress toward Target 200; guidelines: focus on the positive 216; make feedback visual 218; measure key facotrs for success 215; portable and easy 213; sooner is better 212; how it works 201; how to develop 202; seeing progress and rewards 218; standard of achievement 202; to establish baseline 39; two essentials 202

yes, but: why avoid 228

yes/no questions: See closing 229

Youngs, Bettie B. 133, 134, 153

yuppies 25, 53

Z

Zaleznik: Abraham 269

Zen master 331

ABOUT THE ARTIST BEHIND THE ART

Phil Frank understands the art of communicating with humor. He is the creator of the exclusive *San Francisco Chronicle* comic strip *Farley.* His cartoons have been featured in local and national shows and in numerous award-winning publications.

Now Phil Frank's cartooning talent is available to desktop publishers in the MEGATOONS clip art collections. These signature illustrations are delivered on disks or CD ROM. For additional information contact Creative Media Services, PO Box 5955, Berkeley, CA 94705 or 800-358-2278.

NEW DIMENSIONS RADIO ®

Justine Toms & Michael Toms
co-founders of New Dimensions Radio
photo credit: Stan Ulkowski

New Dimensions is an independent producer of radio dialogues and other quality programming that supports a diversity of views from many traditions and cultures, and strives to empower listeners with practical knowledge and perennial wisdom. New Dimensions fosters the goals of living a more healthy life of body, mind and spirit while deepening connections to self, family, community, environment and planet.

New Dimensions Radio provides a new model for exploring ideas in a spirit of open dialogue. Programs are produced to include the listener as an active participant, while respecting the listener's intelligence and capacity for thoughtful choice. The programs are alive with dynamic spontaneity. "New Dimensions" programs celebrate life and the human spirit while challenging the mind to open to fresh possibilities. We invite your participation with us in the ultimate human adventure—the quest for wisdom and the inexpressible.

For a free *New Dimensions Journal,* including a list of radio stations currently broadcasting the "New Dimensions" radio series, or an audiotape catalog, please write:
New Dimensions Radio
Dept. ZM
P.O. Box 410510
San Francisco, CA 94141-0510
or you may telephone (415) 563-8899.

BOOK COVER DESIGNER

BRIAN GROPPE lives in Memphis, Tennessee with his wife & two daughters. He has been creative director for Towery Publishing since 1986. His work focuses on book and poster design. He is principal art director for Towery's *Urban Tapestry Series*, a collection of casebound photojournals showcasing American cities. A 1979 graduate of the California College of Arts and Crafts, he gained publications experience at Leisure Press, a subsidiary of Charles Scribner's Sons. Recent awards include ADDY awards in 1994 for *Chicago: Second to None* & the *Memphis in May International Festival Fine Art Poster*, a 1992 Silver Award from *Photo Design* magazine for poster design, and work in *Print* magazine's regional design annual.

BRIAN GROPPE
co/ TOWERY PUBLISHING, INC.
1835 Union Ave, Memphis, TN 38104
PHONE 901 725 2400
FAX 901 725 2401

BOOK DESIGN

JUDY JULY

Judy July co-founded Generic Type in Emeryville, California with partner Norman Mayell in 1982. While coming from a traditional typography and graphic background, they interfaced easily into the computer world, merging tradition with technology. Generic Type is a production house and state-of-the-art service bureau where Judy designs and produces catalogs, books, ads, brochures, and newsmagazines. Other publications designed for Ronin Publishing include: *Beating Job Burnout: How to Transform Work Pressure into Productivity, Brain Booosters: Foods and Drugs that Make You Smarter,* and Timothy Leary's *Chaos & Cyber Culture.*

Generic Type
5925 Doyle St., Suite U
Emeryville, CA 94608
510/428-9200

Ms. July—born in September—has a 7-year-old son, Max, and a 23-year-old stepson, Tobin, who is also employed at Generic Type. As a working mother in a family business, she is seeking to find the balance and boundaries between business, home, and pleasure—while actively carving out her path to bliss.

The intention was to create a book as pleasing to look at as it is insightful in finding your own path with a heart.

BEATING JOB BURNOUT
How To Transform Work Pressure Into Productivity
Second Edition

Dr. Beverly Potter

Beating Job Burnout tells how to renew enthusiasm for work by developing personal power.

This upbeat guide shows how to recognize job burnout and overcome it through a progression of positive changes, including setting goals, managing stress, building a strong social support system, modifying the job, developing needed skills, changing jobs, modifying powerless thinking and developing detached concern.

Tens of millions of workers in the United States suffer from feelings of powerlessness in the workplace which can destroy motivation and enthusiasm for work. Burnout is especially prevalent in this era of restructuring and job displacement.

Beating Job Burnout provides important information that managers, counselors, and individuals can utilize daily to eliminate feelings of powerlessness on the job.

This new edition is a complete rewrite and update of the 1980 classic. Includes the "Burnout Potential Inventory."

Career/Self-help
256 pp
Illustrations
Appendix
Questionnaire
$12.95
ISBN 0-914171-69-0

"If it's possible to cure burnout with a book, this one could do it."
— Savvy Magazine

"A valued contribution."
—Midwest Book Review

"Dr. Potter's sure-fire burnout remedy."
—Berkeley Voice

Career/Self-help

252 pp

Illustrations

Appendix

$9.95

0-914171-26-7

THE WAY OF THE RONIN
Riding The Waves Of Change At Work
Dr. Beverly Potter

The Way of the Ronin offers an inspiring strategy for handling change while performing excellently in today's workplace.

Ronin or "wave-men" were masterless samurai. To survive they became their own masters and had to live by their swords. When feudalism collapsed it was the ronin who led the way to industrialize Japan. *The Way of the Ronin* tells how to be excellent and self-mastering like a warrior and how to deal with "corporate feudalism"—a rigid system that resists change and that tries to squelch your spirit.

First published by The American Management Association, *The Way of the Ronin* draws upon the wisdom of philosophers, the findings of trend watchers, the latest research of management experts and the technology of behavior psychology to show how to:

- **Thrive on change**
- **Tell excellence from perfectionism**
- **Turn enemies into allies**
- **Become a workplace warrior**
- **Manage self-starters**
- **Develop maverick career strategies**

"Intelligent and inspiring book."
— **ALA Booklist**

"One of the best business books of the year."
— **Library Journal**

"A mix of zen and behavior modification, case histories, thought-control exercises, and goal-setting tips."
— **The Argus**